MORTALITY AND MORALITY

Northwestern University
Studies in Phenomenology
and
Existential Philosophy

Edited and
with an Introduction by

Lawrence Vogel

MORTALITY AND MORALITY

A Search for the Good after Auschwitz

Hans Jonas

Northwestern University Press
Evanston, Illinois

Northwestern University Press
625 Colfax
Evanston, Illinois 60208-4210

Second paperback printing 1999

ISBN 0-8101-1286-8

Library of Congress Cataloging-in-Publication Data

Jonas, Hans, 1903–
        Mortality and morality : a search for the good after Auschwitz / Hans Jonas.
            p.   cm. — (Northwestern University studies in phenomenology & existential
        philosophy)
        A collection of essays edited by Lawrence Vogel.
        Includes bibliographical references and index.
        ISBN 0-8101-1285-X (alk. paper). — ISBN 0-8101-1286-8 (pbk. : alk. paper)
            1. Ethics. 2. Metaphysics. 3. Existentialism. 4. Phenomenology.
        5. Holocaust (Jewish theology). 6. Heidegger, Martin, 1889–1976. I. Vogel, Lawrence.
        II. Title. III. Series
        BJ1031.J66   1996
        170–dc20   96-12063
                                                                                    CIP

Contents

CONTENTS

Acknowledgments

My deepest debt of gratitude goes to Mrs. Lore Jonas, who nurtured this project at every stage. When we first discussed it, I had in mind a much shorter book consisting of three essays: "The Burden and Blessing of Mortality," "Immortality and the Modern Temper," and "The Concept of God After Auschwitz" (chapters 3, 5, and 6 herein). I still believe that these can be profitably read as a trilogy marking Hans Jonas's place within post-Holocaust Jewish theology. But Mrs. Jonas persuaded me that this collection of her husband's writings—his last testament, so to speak—should reflect the full range of his philosophical concerns. We are lucky that in the final decade of his life Hans Jonas wrote essays summarizing the entire spectrum of his thought. So this volume has expanded threefold, and now consists of ten essays, five of which are freshly translated from German into English. I hope that this collection leads to Jonas's being as widely read and discussed in English-speaking circles as he is on the continent.

At several conferences in honor of Jonas's work I was fortunate to meet individuals who have facilitated this project: first and foremost, Hans and Lore Jonas at the Hebrew University, Jerusalem, in January 1992. The Jerusalem conference also introduced me to Strachan Donnelley of the Hastings Center, who has provided encouragement ever since. A symposium in honor of Jonas's ninetieth birthday in June 1993, sponsored by the Evangelische Akademie Hofgeismar and Philipps-Universität Marburg, was a bittersweet event, as Hans Jonas died in February 1993. But the gathering was a celebration of his life, and allowed me a second chance to meet Lore Jonas and first encounters with Sybille Tönnies, Haiko Dahle, and Erhard Gerstenberger, all of whom heightened for me the meaning of Jonas's work. Finally, a November 1993 memorial conference at the New School for Social Research in New York introduced me to Leon Kass of the Committee on Social Thought at the University of Chicago, who has offered help at crucial junctures along the way, and to the Jonas children—Gabrielle, Jonathan, and Ayallah—who cherished their father as a whole human being.

On the more local front, I owe a long debt of thanks to Louis Goldring, a friend and former colleague at Vassar College, who first insisted that I read *The Phenomenon of Life* in the early 1980s. Mitchell Miller of Vassar and Dermot Moran of University College, Dublin, responded with the right mixture of enthusiasm and criticism to my early attempts to write about Jonas. My current colleague at Connecticut College, Mel Woody, goaded me to submit a paper to the Jerusalem conference, an act that has opened up unforeseen possibilities. Students in a Spring 1993 seminar on bioethics at Connecticut College forced me to clarify my thoughts on Jonas. Conversations with friends at Trinity College—Frank Kirkpatrick and Helen Lang—assisted me with aspects of my introduction to this volume. Doug Nygren helped me in intangible ways to keep my eye on the ball throughout. Incomparable thanks go to my wife, Carol Freedman who, while teaching in the Philosophy Department at Williams College, and carrying our first child, Max, has helped me through every phase of this project and whose appreciation of our mortality reminds me every day of the Psalmist's passage so dear to Hans Jonas: "Teach us to number our days, that we may get a heart of wisdom."

I am enormously grateful to the staff at the Northwestern University Press, especially John McCumber, Professor of Philosophy at Northwestern and Editor of this series, for accepting this project and shepherding it along through many changes. Thanks, too, to Nick Weir-Williams, Heather Kenny, and Susan Harris for all their support.

I consider it manna from heaven that Mrs. Jonas picked Hildegarde and Hunter Hannum to be principal translators: responsible for the prologue and chapters 1, 2, and 4. Collaborating with them has been a joy and has deepened my feeling for the art of translation. Thanks also go to Paul Schuchman, translator of the first draft of daunting chapter 8.

For converting many different manuscripts into a common software program, my appreciation goes to Diane Monte, Humanities secretary at Connecticut College.

This volume would not have been possible without permission to publish material from a number of sources. Special thanks go to Insel Verlag Frankfurt am Main und Leipzig for the rights to translate and publish all of the essays that were previously available only in German. The prologue, "Philosophy at the End of the Century: Retrospect and Prospect," is translated from *Philosophie: Rückschau und Vorschau am Ende des Jahrhunderts* (Frankfurt: Suhrkamp, 1993). Chapters 1, 2, 4, and 8 herein are translations of chapters 1, 2, 6, and 10 respectively in *Philosophische Untersuchungen und metaphysische Vermutungen* (Frankfurt: Suhrkamp, 1992). "The Burden and Blessing of Mortality," chapter 3 herein, is reprinted with permission from *Hastings Center Report*, where it originally appeared in vol. 22, no. 1 (1992), 34–40. "Immortality and the Modern Temper," chapter 5 herein, appears with permission from Harper and Row, the original publisher of *The Phenomenon of Life* (New York: Harper and Row, 1963), where this piece appeared as the eleventh essay. "The Concept of God after Auschwitz: A Jewish Voice" is published with permission of *The Journal of Religion*, where it appeared in Spring 1987, 1–13. Finally, "Is Faith Still Possible?: Memories of Rudolf Bultmann and Reflections on the Philosophical Aspects of His Work" is reprinted with permission of the *Harvard Theological Review*, where it appeared in vol. 75, no. 1 (1982), 1–23.

My introduction contains passages from two articles I have written on the work of Jonas: (1) "Hans Jonas's Diagnosis of Nihilism: The Case of Heidegger," *International Journal of Philosophical Studies* 3, no. 1 (1995), 55–71; and (2) "Does Environmental Ethics Need a Metaphysical Grounding?" *Hastings Center Report* (December, 1995). Thanks to these journals for permission to reprint relevant material.

Editor's Introduction
Hans Jonas's Exodus:
From German Existentialism
to Post-Holocaust Theology

Along with Karl Löwith, Herbert Marcuse, Hannah Arendt, and Emmanuel Levinas, Hans Jonas was among Martin Heidegger's foremost Jewish students. Jonas received his doctorate under Heidegger at Marburg in 1930, and was eventually invited to join the Graduate Faculty at New York's New School for Social Research in 1955, where he served as the Alvin Johnson Professor of Philosophy until his death in 1993 at the age of 89. What happened between his student years in Germany and the period of his scholarly maturity in New York, however, reveals a man for whom the life of the mind was rooted, in practice as well as theory, in the life of the body and the body politic: a man who was actively engaged in among the most traumatic events of the twentieth century.

Upon discovering in 1933 that the German Association for the Blind had expelled its Jewish members, Jonas bore witness to the Nazis' "betrayal of the solidarity of a common fate" by abandoning the homeland where he had hoped to pursue an academic career.[1] After a detour through England, Jonas arrived in the British protectorate of Palestine in 1935 with two books to his credit—one a revision of his dissertation on Gnosticism, the other on the Pauline problem of freedom—but little money and no job. Unable to secure a scarce university position, he kept his academic aspirations alive with part-time work in publishing. But when war broke out in Europe in 1939, Jonas, certain that Hitler needed to be conquered by force, volunteered for the Jewish Brigade of the British 8th Army. And he refused to accept a post in Intelligence; he wanted to fight.

The life-and-death battle, especially on the Italian front, hardened Jonas's resolve to move beyond the historical inquiries of his student years and develop his own philosophy. Appropriately enough, his musings came to focus on the corporeal, metabolic basis of all life and the struggle of all organisms to maintain their lives in the face of the ever-present threat of not-being or death. His bride-to-be, Elinore, sent Hans the latest publications in biology, and Hans replied with two sorts of letters: *Liebebriefen* and *Lehrebriefen*, love-letters and teaching-letters. In the latter he sketched ideas that would form the heart of *The Phenomenon of Life*, to be published over twenty years later.

After marrying Elinore while on leave in 1943, Jonas did not see her again until he returned to Palestine in November 1945, and only then received the devastating news of his mother's murder at Auschwitz. And war would shortly take its toll again. The Balfour Declaration and U.N. resolution of November 1947 granted independence to Palestine, partitioning the territory between Arabs and Jews, but fighting soon erupted between them. Jonas saw combat once more, this time in the Israeli army. By the end of the Israeli War of Independence, he was convinced that the Arabs would never be satisfied with a Jewish state and he would never be able to pursue his philosophical investigations in peace.

With the encouragement of his wife, Jonas accepted a fellowship at Montreal's McGill University in 1949, and his family made the transatlantic journey to Canada, again to take on a new language and culture. Only in 1951, at the age of forty-eight, did Jonas finally receive his first full-time appointment as an Assistant Professor of Philosophy: at Carleton University in Ottawa. After completing the second volume of his work on Gnosticism, and with the departure of Karl Löwith for Heidelberg, he was invited to join the Graduate Faculty at the New School for Social Research in 1955. His academic career interrupted for some two decades by exile and combat, Jonas found a home at last, and he drew on all of his experience to transcend historical research and work out a mature, creative philosophy addressing the nihilistic temper of his time.

Jonas's work displays extraordinary breadth and continuity. *The Gnostic Religion*, begun in the late 1920s but only completed in the mid-1950s after the cataclysm of two wars, is still a classic today.[2] It traces the roots of metaphysical dualism at the beginning of the first millennium A.D. His second major book, *The Phenomenon of Life* (1963), discovers a Gnostic pattern of thinking at the core of modern philosophy, including Heidegger's "existentialism." Jonas argues that metaphysical dualism is responsible for the difficulty that we moderns have thinking of nature, even human nature, as more than an object for technological manipulation. As a cure for modern "nihilism" Jonas provides an account of nature that is more in the spirit of Aristotle than Descartes, while still keeping in step with modern science.

Jonas's final major work, *The Imperative of Responsibility: In Search of an Ethics for the Technological Age* (1979), connects his speculation about nature to the domain of ethics. He thinks that unless we can think of nature as being a source of value, and not a mere resource upon which we project our interests, we will be unable to believe in the importance of limits to our technological remaking of nature. Such limits are especially urgent given our increasing power to destroy our habitat and to alter "the human image" by exerting control over behavior, the process of dying, and even the genetic makeup of life. *The Imperative of Responsibility* had a significant impact on the Green movement in Germany, has sold close to 200,000 copies in German, and won both the 1987 Peace Prize of the German Booksellers' Association and the 1992 Premio Nonino in Italy for the best book translated into Italian that year. In addition, Jonas has become famous for his many essays and radio interviews on topics in medical and environmental ethics.

Less well-known, especially to an Anglo-American audience, is Jonas's effort to develop a Jewish theology for our time: one that takes seriously both modern natural science and the reality of evil. Until now, this line of thought has been scattered in journals, and "Matter, Spirit and Creation," published shortly before his death, was available only in German. One of the purposes of the present book is to let the voice of Hans Jonas be heard as one of the most significant Jewish theologians of the post-Holocaust period: a voice as systematic and relevant as that of any contemporary Jewish thinker.

But Jonas wanted to be known first and foremost as a philosopher, not a Jewish philosopher, because he believed that ethics—an account of responsibility most sorely needed in our time—must be grounded without recourse to theological categories. In an increasingly secular world, an ethics based upon a particular theology must seem parochial and dogmatic. Consequently, Jonas seeks to derive an imperative of responsibility from nature—more specifically, from the phenomenon of life—on its own terms. Such an imperative satisfies "the need of reason" to account for the dignity of human life and to ground our obligation to future generations. In a Kantian vein, Jonas considers theological speculation to be "a luxury of reason": the raising of questions about the origins and ultimate ends of nature that the mind cannot help but ask, even though our answers can only be conjectures. The best we can hope for is that theological claims about the transcendent remain consistent with what we know more firmly from the immanent testimony of nature.

Accordingly, the structure of this volume parallels the two lines of Jonas's thought: naturalistic and theological. The four essays comprising part 1, all written during the last decade of Jonas's life and three freshly translated from their German originals, summarize and extend the main arguments in *The Phenomenon of Life* and *The Imperative of Responsibility*.

These essays aim at meeting reason's "need" for an ethics founded neither on divine authority nor even in the autonomy of the self or the
needs of the community, but rather in "a principle discoverable in the
nature of things" (*PL*, 284).[3] The four essays of part 2 enjoy reason's
"luxury" to speculate about theological matters, particularly in light of
this century's gravest challenge to Jewish, if not all, faith: the Holocaust.
Jonas tackles the central question: What, if any, concept of God is credible
after Auschwitz?

In this introduction I shall trace Hans Jonas's exodus from German
existentialism to post-Holocaust theology. I aim to provide an overview
of Jonas's philosophy as a whole, explaining how his naturalism and
theology alike provide antidotes to what he takes to be the nihilistic
character of modern thought. Because he sees this nihilism crystallized in
Being and Time—the master work of his *Doktorvater*, Martin Heidegger—
Jonas's fundamental project can be seen as no less than an overcoming
of his intellectual father-figure, whose behavior during the Third Reich
Jonas diagnoses as a symptom of the ethical weakness of Heidegger's
nihilistic ideas. Jonas presents a survey of his own educational itinerary
in the prologue, "Philosophy at the End of the Century: Retrospect and
Prospect," a lecture delivered shortly before his death.

Besides interpreting Jonas's project as a reply to Heidegger, I also
aim to situate his philosophy of nature on the map of contemporary
environmental ethics, and locate his theology on the landscape of post-
Holocaust Jewish thought. In accounting for Jonas's naturalism, I shall
place the essays in part 1 in the wider context of *The Phenomenon of Life* and
The Imperative of Responsibility. An explanation of Jonas's theology must rely
on the essays presented in part 2 here, for they offer his most definitive
statement on the subject. An issue that must loom in the background is
whether his naturalism and theology are independent yet compatible, as
he insists, *or* whether his attempt at a naturalistic grounding of ethics
depends upon theological premises after all. In any case, Jonas's philosophy offers one of the most systematic and challenging rejoinders to
the legacy of Heidegger in particular, and to the spirit of the twentieth
century as a whole.

The Need of Reason: Grounding an Imperative of Responsibility in the Phenomenon of Life

For the past several decades until his recent death, Hans Jonas alerted
us to an "ethical vacuum" at the core of our culture: a vacuum caused by

both traditional ethics and modern natural science (*IR*, 22). Technology today has altered the very nature of human action by allowing us to affect nature, both outside ourselves and within, in ways that are long-range, cumulative, irreversible, and planetary in scale. But traditional ethics has presumed that the effects of our actions are quite limited. With the exception of medicine, *techne* was believed to be ethically neutral. Ethical significance belonged to relations between humans, not between us and nature. Humanity was a constant, not an object of reshaping *techne*. And while the moral good or evil of our actions lay close at hand, the long run was left to chance, fate, or providence. But all of this has changed with the advent of modern technology, and traditional ethics leaves us ill-equipped to account for our responsibilities when the very future of humanity is at stake.

But this vacuum is intensified by the dominant scientific view of nature in the modern period: reductionistic materialism. On this view, nature is a machine; it harbors no values and expresses no purposiveness. The idea that there are ends in nature is rejected as an anthropomorphic conceit. Extrahuman nature is indifferent to itself and also to human beings, who are cast adrift in it. We may matter to ourselves, but there is no larger scheme of mattering to which we belong. Though human beings may be subjects who posit ends and act in light of purposes, nonhuman organisms are mere objects: matter in motion. And eventually humans, as part of nature, become objects of their own fabrications to be shaped according to the designs of biotechnology. If nature presents us with no ethical norms, then no effort to change our own nature in the name of perfection, convenience, or experimentation could count as a transgression of essential limits or a violation of a natural standard of goodness.

Herein lies the deepest root of our cultural crisis: nihilism. Lacking grounds for judging nature to be good and deprived of any stable "image of humanity" to which we owe reverence, we are unable to answer the fundamental ethical challenge posed by our novel powers: Why should we care about the distant future of mankind and the planet? Unable to justify why the presence of humankind on the Earth is a categorical imperative, we are unprepared for the attitude of stewardship that we must cultivate if we are not to squander the future in the interests of a profligate present.

If nihilism is at the root of our cultural crisis, then the only sufficient response would be a philosophical critique of nihilism. This is precisely the task that Hans Jonas sets for himself, and not only in his later writings, but from the very beginning. I shall show how his project unfolds in three stages: existential, metaphysical, and theological. Each stage is a response to the crisis that Jonas diagnoses in his early essay, "Gnosticism and Modern Nihilism."[4] First, in *The Phenomenon of Life,* Jonas offers "an existential interpretation of the biological facts," arguing that purposive existence is not a special attribute of human beings, but is present throughout living nature. Second, in *The Imperative of Responsibility,* he provides a metaphysical grounding of our ethical obligations to nature and to ourselves as special products of its evolutionary labors. These first two stages of Jonas's path are aspects of his naturalistic project. But finally, in the third stage, Jonas presents a theology of divine creation that he takes to be consistent with, though not necessitated by, his naturalistic existentialism and metaphysics.

While many environmentalists presume that nonanthropocentrism must be a defining feature of any ecological ethics, Jonas does not believe that overcoming nihilism requires a renunciation of anthropocentrism in favor of biocentrism or ecocentrism. Instead, I shall contend, he tries to undercut the very distinction between anthropocentrism and its supposed alternatives. Furthermore, I shall argue that Jonas does not take theology to be necessary for an overcoming of nihilism. Rational metaphysics must be able to ground an imperative of responsibility without recourse to faith. Finally, I shall raise some critical questions about Jonas's project. In particular, I worry that a pluralistic culture cannot bear the burden of such a substantive metaphysics. If our future depends on citizens agreeing with Jonas's speculations, then I fear we are not up to the task. But first let us explore the three stages along Jonas's way beyond nihilism.

The Phenomenon of Life: An Existential Interpretation of the Biological Facts

Jonas completes the first stage of his journey in *The Phenomenon of Life* through an attack on his mentor, Heidegger, whose existentialism Jonas takes to be the most powerful expression of nihilism in our time. Like so many of his generation, Jonas was drawn to the existential depth of Heidegger's departure from the Cartesian path of Husserl's phenomenology and to the description of humanity's way of Being as "Care"—but was soon appalled by Heidegger's political commitments. Heidegger's "treacherous" and "shameful" rectoral address of 1933 forced Jonas, a Jew, to look for the "hidden" meaning of the philosophy his teacher had professed so spellbindingly in seminars during the 1920s.[5] And, with the benefit of hindsight, Jonas found symptoms of his mentor's moral weakness in Heidegger's early work of genius, *Being and Time.*[6]

While acknowledging *Being and Time* as "the most profound and important manifesto of existentialism" (*PL*, 229), Jonas traces Heidegger's susceptibility to Nazism to an ethical vacuum at the heart of fundamental ontology. In his 1952 essay, "Gnosticism and Modern Nihilism," Jonas recounts the irony of how he discovered this ethical vacuum by way of his early work on Gnosticism under the tutelage of Heidegger and Rudolf Bultmann. Existential interpretation helped Jonas to understand Gnosticism: a variety of religious teachings in the Hellenized Near East of the first three centuries A.D., which shared a radically dualistic cast of mind. According to Gnostic theology, God utterly transcends the material world, which is under the sway of an evil demiurge. A person's task is to attain *gnosis* or knowledge, allowing his soul after death to be freed of all worldly substance and to reunite with God. The *pneumaticos*, or spiritual person, liberates himself, through sacramental and magical preparations, from mundane norms—both natural and moral—for laws are rules of the demiurge's game. Jonas labels this dualistic attitude "anthropological acosmism," and sees in it the roots of nihilism.

> As the totally other, alien, and unknown, the Gnostic God has more of the *nihil* than of the *ens* in his concept. For all the purposes of man's relation to the reality that surrounds him, this hidden God is a negative term; no law emanates from him—none for nature, and thus none for human action as part of the natural order. His only relation to the world is the negative one of saving from the world. Antinomianism follows naturally, even if not inevitably, from these premises.[7]

While existential interpretation allows Jonas to enter the Gnostic world, his study of Gnosticism in turn provides a clue to the nihilistic pattern of thinking at the heart of contemporary "existentialism," for these two philosophical movements, so distant in time, share two fundamental premises: (1) the denial that the cosmos is ordered for the good, and (2) a belief in the transcendence of the acosmic self. Like the Gnostic *pneumaticos*, "the authentic individual" of existentialism stands above any moral law or *nomos*. Without belief in a transcendent God, however, the authentic individual is free to create values from his own perspective "beyond good and evil"—with an eye toward the open future, but no orientation toward an eternal measure to stabilize the present.

In *The Imperative of Responsibility* and an interview on Swiss radio in 1987, Jonas develops the same critique, associating the resoluteness of Heidegger's authentic individual with the antinomian freedom of the Gnostic *pneumaticos*. *Pneuma* is to *psyche* as authentic is to inauthentic *Dasein*. Jonas traces Heidegger's "leap" into Nazism to the "absolute formalism of his philosophy of decision" in which "not *for what* or *against what* one resolves oneself, but *that* one resolves oneself becomes the *authentic* signature of *authentic* Dasein."[8]

Jonas seeks to overcome nihilism not by rejecting Heidegger's approach altogether, but rather by extending his teacher's categories to yield "an existential interpretation of the biological facts." From Heidegger's perspective, however, the very idea of "an existential interpretation of the biological facts" must sound like an oxymoron. It would be inappropriate to interpret nonhuman organisms existentially, because only humans "exist." We are the only beings whose Being is an issue for us: that is, whose behavior and expression manifest a stance toward the sort of being we resolve to be within the constraints of our "thrownness." Whatever significance the rest of nature has, then, it possesses through the lens of our care.

Jonas charges that Heidegger's fundamental ontology does not fulfill its promise to delineate *transhistorical* structures of human existence. Instead, it bears testimony to the particular, historically fated situation of modern humanity: a situation defined by "the spiritual denudation of [the concept of nature] at the hands of physical science" since the Copernican revolution (*PL*, 232). In Heidegger's analysis of existence, there is no room for nature as possessing intrinsic value, for nature is assumed to be a realm of "un-meaning" (*sinnlos*), only taking on significance in relation to our workaday world. As Karl Löwith puts it,

> The world which is concretely analyzed by contemporary existentialism . . .
> is only our historical world of selfhood and interhuman relations. . . .
> Nature, says Heidegger, cannot elucidate the ontological character of
> world and of our being because it is only a kind of being *within* our world,
> and we encounter it therefore *within* the analysis of man's being-there.[9]

Heidegger's supposedly ontological account of temporality presupposes the modern, materialistic understanding of nature in which there is no eternity, only the flux of time. This flux lacks a genuine present, according to Jonas, because authentic *Dasein*, at the moment of decision, stands unguided by any eternal measure; and this because *Dasein* is not seen as being part of "an objective order of essences in the totality of nature," but only as a "transessential, freely projecting existence," who must create values on the basis of nothing but the shifting soil of history. The loss of eternity, Jonas contends,

> accounts for the loss of a genuine present. . . . If values are not beheld in
> vision *as being* (like the Good and the Beautiful of Plato), but are *posited*

by the will as projects, then indeed existence is committed to constant futurity with death as its goal; and a merely formal resolution to be, without a *nomos* for that resolution, becomes a project from nothingness to nothingness. . . . Will replaces vision; temporality of the act ousts the eternity of the "good in itself." (*PL*, 215)

Heidegger's existentialism, on Jonas's reading, uncritically accepts the metaphysical background of the nihilistic situation: the dualism between humanity and nature. The idea that nature has no ends and is indifferent to human purposes throws us back on ourselves in our quest for meaning. No longer able to find our place in a sacred order of creation or an objective order of essences comprising the totality of nature, we have lost not only the grounds for cosmic piety, but also a stable image of our own nature, even the conviction that we have a nature. Jonas writes,

That nature does not care, one way or another, is the true abyss. That only man cares, in his finitude facing nothing but death, alone with his contingency and the objective meaninglessness of his projecting meanings, is a truly unprecedented situation. . . . As the product of the indifferent, his being, too, must be indifferent. Then, the facing of his mortality would simply warrant the reaction: "Let us eat and drink. For tomorrow we must die." There is no point in caring for what has no sanction behind it in any creative intention. (*PL*, 233)

In other words, Heidegger's existentialism gives us no good reason to care about future generations or the long-term fate of planet Earth.

But existentialism, as we have seen, is not an idiosyncrasy of modern thought; it is rather the most complete expression of "the ethical vacuum" caused by the two key assumptions of the modern credo: (1) that the idea of obligation is a human invention, not a discovery based on the objective being of the good-in-itself; and (2) that the rest of Being is indifferent to our experience of obligation (*PL*, 283). Jonas's whole philosophy aims at providing a reasonable account, consistent with modern science, of why it does make an objective difference how we relate to nature because living nature, from which our own caring selves emerge and on which we depend, is essentially good, is worth being cared for, and even cares that we care for her so that we, her most magnificent creation, can continue to be.

What is so subversive about the first stage of Jonas's reply to nihilism is that he uses *Heidegger's* own existential categories as a point of departure for undermining the modern credo that human being is the source of all value in nature. By attributing "existence" to all organisms, not only humans, Jonas challenges the metaphysical prejudice of materialism and begins to ground a heteronomy that supersedes all authenticity. Though only we humans can take stock of our lives as a whole, reflect on the ontological structure of existence and be thematically aware of death, all organisms show concern for their own being and reach out to the world in order to fend off not-being. The materialist, of course, claims to remain metaphysically neutral and accuses those who impute purposes to nature of being all-too-metaphysical. But Jonas insists that one cannot offer a phenomenological description of an organism's way of being without finding purposes in "the things themselves."

Even the most primitive organisms are not mere destructible chunks of matter, but possess an inward relation to their own being. Their being is their own doing. Metabolism is the most basic expression of an organism's struggle for life. Each organism exhibits what Jonas calls "needful freedom." It is free with respect to its own substance: a dynamic unity, not identical with any simultaneous totality of its parts. Yet it remains forever needful: dependent on exchange with an environment which it must use to avoid dying. By clinging to itself, Jonas remarks, life says "Yes" to itself (*IR*, 81). Only in confrontation with the ever-present potentiality of not-being can Being come to feel itself, affirm itself, make itself its own purpose. Through negated not-being, "to be" turns into "existence": a constant choosing of itself. Because all life is relation, and relation implies transcendence, polarities that we find in ourselves—being/not-being, self/world, form/matter, and freedom/necessity—have traces in even the most primitive forms of life. Existential categories—concern, transcendence, freedom, possibility, world, not-being—are necessary to describe powers of mind (*psyche*) that are "objectively discernible" in all life. Some measure of "mind" (or "subjective inwardness") and "freedom" are present at all levels of the lifeworld.

In this volume, Jonas sketches his phenomenology of plant and animal existence in chapter 1, "Evolution and Freedom: On the Continuity among Life-Forms," and proceeds to consider what is distinctive about human life in chapter 2, "Tool, Image, and Grave: On What Is beyond the Animal in Man," and chapter 3, "The Burden and Blessing of Mortality."

Each new level of mind—metabolism, moving and desiring, sensing and perceiving, imagining and thinking—brings with it a new dimension of freedom and peril alike. Though all organisms share the vegetative functions of nutrition and reproduction, the evolution of sensitive capacities in animals marks a major advance in the quality of freedom in the lifeworld. Whereas plants, moved by need but not desire, are immediately immersed in their surroundings and are at the mercy of adjacent matter and impinging forces, animals have a mediated relationship to their environment, in virtue of their perceptual awareness of discrete things at a distance from them and their ability to move toward or away from these things in response to their passions. The "secret of animal life" is the gap they are able maintain between their immediate desires and mediate satisfactions. They participate in existential space and time because, as Jonas puts it, "motility guided by perception and driven by desire turns 'there' into 'here' and 'not yet' into 'now' " (*PL,* 101). Among animals an inner dimension blooms forth and externalizes itself in behavior and communication, yet at the same time there emerges a new liability: the capacity to suffer pain, fear, and even abandonment.

Only with humans, and the interposition of an *eidos* between subject and object, does mediacy become reflective: an explicit relation between a self-conscious subject and objects identified and classified as such. In our imaginations, we can make present what is materially absent. By comparing past and present perceptions we can discern between truth and falsehood. Furthermore, we can reflect upon essences or "thought-objects" in their own right. The eidetic capacity present in our power to recognize and create images as representations of objects is the root of our ability to live in light of an image of who we are and ought to be. And we are fundamentally metaphysical organisms, for we can, and even must, try to comprehend our place in the whole of which we are a part. Though the twofoldness of self-reflection is the condition of having a "self" and of possessing the special kind of freedom that Heidegger delineates when he calls us the only beings "whose Being is an issue for us," this split within the self is the source of perils peculiar to human existence: the threat of anxiety when we are deeply uncertain about what our standards should be, and the sting of unhappiness, guilt, and even despair when we judge ourselves unfavorably from the distance of our wishes, aspirations, and approvals (*PL,* 186).

Once we recognize mechanistic materialism for what it is—a metaphysical prejudice, not a neutral description of the physical world—we are free to interpret the biological facts existentially and to appreciate the reality of value independent of us, for all organisms are "ends-in-themselves" who value whatever contributes to their existence and welfare. This is not the case simply from our point of view, for we have no reason to doubt that they flourish or suffer in their own right. A crucial step in Jonas's reply to nihilism has been achieved, and one might think that there is little, if anything, more to be done. Once we see that humanity is not the sole locus, much less the creator, of all value in nature, we would seem to be in a position to accept our duty as guardians of living nature. But if our technological incursions into nature are destined to disrupt the ecosystem and destroy whole species at an unprecedented rate, why would we not be doing nature a favor by taking ourselves out of the picture? Even if there are centers of purpose in nature outside of us that command our respect, it has not been shown that there is an overarching purposiveness in the evolutionary process as a whole in which we play a crucial role and by virtue of which we have an obligation to ensure that human beings remain among the Earth's citizens.

Darwin's theory of evolution does not seem to be of much help in this regard, for it explains natural history as a wholly mechanistic process in which higher and more complex species result from utterly contingent alterations in lower elements. The official Darwinian view is resolutely antiteleological in holding that life first came into being through spontaneous generation from inorganic matter and evolved by chance through the joint processes of random genetic variation and natural selection. But Darwin's materialist explanation of evolution, according to Jonas, "contains the germ of its own overcoming" (*PL*, 53) for, against the spirit of mind/matter dualism, evolution displays a continuity between nonhuman and human organisms. Rather than interpreting mind as an utterly novel and sudden emergence coinciding with humans, Darwin makes room for the idea that the whole lifeworld is a chain of psychophysical organisms whose minds and bodies co-evolve so as to allow for greater freedom and individuality. Being has achieved in us a being who can reflect her back to herself in thought. We can interpret ourselves as the outcome of a teleological process whose immanent purposes are self-knowledge and freedom: an evolution in which mind ultimately answers to the qualities that nature shows forth and individuality, rooted in each organism's concern for its own being, reaches its maximal intensiveness in the capacity of each person to speak for himself and forge his own unique story.

Against the reductionistic tendency of modern thought, which boils the complex down to its simplest parts, Jonas, in a synthesis of Aristotle, Hegel, and Darwin, finds the germ of what is higher in the lower forms from which it evolves. "Reality, or nature, is one and testifies to itself in what it *allows* to come forth from it" (*IR*, 69). The extension of mind to the entire organic world enables Jonas, in *The Phenomenon of Life*, to make several speculative, metaphysical claims that cannot be proven, but are consistent with the biological facts, existentially interpreted: (1) that matter's feat of organizing itself for life attests to latent organic tendencies in the depths of Being; and (2) that the emergence of the human mind does not mark a great divide within nature, but elaborates what is prefigured in all organic existence (*PL*, 4). These two points allow for a third speculation with dramatic ethical consequences: insofar as we see ourselves, with our capacity for reflecting Being in knowledge, as "a 'coming to itself' of original substance," we should understand ourselves as being called by nature, our own source, to be her guardian (*PL*, 284). By extending the category of existence to all organisms, Jonas makes possible a radical conversion of modern thought: "a principle of ethics which is ultimately grounded neither in the authority of the self nor the needs of the community, but in an objective assignment by the nature of things" (*PL*, 283).

The Imperative of Responsibility: Living Nature as a Good-in-Itself

But *The Phenomenon of Life* is only preliminary to the ethical task of *The Imperative of Responsibility*, because the disclosure of value in nature is not yet sufficient to ground a principle of responsibility for the future. It is still possible, Jonas suggests, for a "nihilist" to acknowledge the presence of subjective value in Being, of organisms willing their own existence, while doubting "whether the whole toilsome and terrible drama is worth the trouble" (*IR*, 49). Jonas worries that "our showing up to now that Nature harbors values because it harbors ends and is thus anything but value-free, has not yet answered the question of whether we are at pleasure or duty-bound to join in her 'value-decisions' (*IR*, 78). Yet Jonas admits that once the immanence of purpose in nature has been shown "the decisive battle for ethical theory has already been won" (*IR*, 78).

What must be established in the second stage of Jonas's reply to nihilism is the *objective* reality of value—a *good-in-itself*—because only from it can a binding responsibility to guard Being be derived. Jonas summarizes the central argument of *The Imperative of Responsibility* in chapter 4 of this volume, "Toward an Ontological Grounding of an Ethics for the Future." He seeks to establish that the good is not relative to already existing subjective purposes, but rather that it is good that there is purposiveness in nature in the first place: that "the very capacity to have any purposes at all is a good-in-itself" (*IR*, 80). Jonas admits that, empirically speaking, the quantity of suffering in life may well outweigh the sum of enjoyment. But, nonetheless, suffering rarely destroys the sentient self's will to live. "The very record of suffering mankind teaches us that the partisanship of inwardness for itself invincibly withstands the balancing of pains and pleasures and rebuffs our judging it by this standard" ("The Burden and Blessing of Mortality"). The metaphysical judgment of life's essential goodness cannot be made on hedonistic grounds.

On the basis of the "intuitive certainty" that purposiveness is abso-lutely and infinitely superior to purposelessness in Being, Jonas derives the "ontological axiom" that "purpose as such is its own accreditation within Being" (*IR*, 80). Being is "for itself"; and the facts bear testimony to the idea that Being favors the maximization and intensification of purposiveness, ultimately the freedom and peril that comes with the human ability to think about, and deeply affect, nature as a whole. From these ontological premises, filled as they are with axiological significance, he draws the ethical conclusion that purposive nature, being good-in-itself, addresses an "ought" whenever it comes under the custody of a will. Though such a will must be infused with a feeling of responsibility in order to be moved by the object that obligates it, it must experience itself as responding to a transcendent summons in order for the moral sentiment "to be in its own eyes more than a mere impulse" (*IR*, 86).

Just as Jonas grounds the ontological goodness of *Being as such* prior to the ontic goods that are relative to the purposes of particular living beings, so he grounds the ontological goodness of *human being* prior to the goods that are relative to existing human individuals and to the rights that belong to them. Though from an ontic point of view our first commitment is to members of the present generation, especially our kin (and nature guarantees it), this proves inadequate to the task of demonstrating a *principle* of responsibility for future mankind. For if the not-yet-existent have no rights, on what basis can there be a duty to ensure the possibility of their existence and the quality of their lives? Jonas argues that our first duty is ontological: future human individuals matter because the *idea of humanity* matters.

> Since in [man] the principle of purposiveness has reached its highest and most dangerous peak through the freedom to set himself ends and the power to carry them out, he himself becomes, in the name of that principle, the first object of his obligation, which we expressed in our "first imperative": not to ruin (as he well can do) what nature has achieved in him by the way of his using it. (*IR*, 130)

Essential to the idea of humanity is the capacity for responsibility. The duty to ensure the future existence of mankind includes the duty to preserve his essence by not undermining the conditions in which man can show himself to be "the executor of a trust which only he can see, but did not create" (*PL*, 283). Here we are reminded of a Heideggerian theme: a command of Being arouses our *conscience* and calls us to take responsibility. But instead of Heidegger's silent call of conscience commanding us to own up to our ownmost possibilities in a moment of resolve in the face of nothingness, Jonas's call has moral substance because it emanates from the *plenitude of Being*. The expansion of existential interpretation to include the biological facts allows Jonas "to ground an ethics in the depths of Being": to find value in nature and so to conceive of our freedom as subject to a heteronomous source of authority. The goodness of Being, reality, or nature opens up a "*genuine present*" because it gives us a future worth caring for. This is the meaning of Jonas's pointedly anti-Heideggerian motto: "Responsibility is the moral complement to the ontological constitution of our temporality" (*IR*, 107).

The present, according to Jonas, is governed by an imperative to preserve the human essence forever, and this because our essence is the outcome of a natural process that is good. Our fundamental responsibility is to that which allowed us to come into being, nature herself, but this responsibility is exercised first of all in our relationships to other human beings. The archetype of responsibility is the care of parent for child, where the goal of parenting is the perpetuation of the capacity for responsibility itself.

> [The] highest fulfillment [of parenting], which it must be able to dare, is its abdication before the right of the never-anticipated which emerges as the outcome of its care. Its highest duty, therefore, is to see that responsibility itself is not stifled, whether from its source within or from constraints without. (*IR*, 107)

The ultimate ground of our duty to our children, however, is not our ontic relationship to them in particular, but our duty to humankind as such: to the idea of humanity which is part of the idea of purposive nature.

Has Jonas provided the glimpse of eternity that he claims is necessary to overcome the loss of a genuine present in Heidegger's nihilism? Jonas remains a modern in that he cannot rely on the vertical orientation of Platonic ontology, which found the eternal beyond the transient: pure Being apart from becoming. Today, Jonas reminds us, it must be becoming rather than abiding nature that holds out the promise of a reunion between ontology and ethics. But nature evolves and can be irreversibly altered by our behavior. If all becoming is simply change *within* nature, and not the destruction of nature, then how can our spoiling of the environment or even collective suicide be a violation *of* nature? "We must seek the essential in transience itself. It is in this context that responsibility can become dominant in morality. . . . Only for the changeable and perishable can one be responsible, for what is threatened by corruption" (*IR*, 125). The good-in-itself is living nature, including humanity as the highest expression of nature's purposiveness. Unlike the permanent and indestructible Good of Platonic ontology, Jonas's good—our privileged, but delicate place within the totality of nature—is at the mercy of our actions. Insofar as our coming-to-be was "of cosmic importance," an "event *for* Being itself," it matters *to* Being that we preserve our existence and essence (*PL*, 284).

Jonas hopes to have disclosed an ontological foundation for a principle of responsibility for the future. His *ontological axioms*—(1) that the very presence of purposiveness in Being implies that being is better than not-being; and (2) that the idea of humanity matters to Being itself as the maximal actualization of its potentiality for purposiveness—ground his *ethical axiom*: that "never must the existence or essence of man as a whole be made a stake in the hazards of action." And given scientists' uncertain ability to predict the long-term effects of our technological incursions into nature, Jonas's ethical axiom yields a "*pragmatic rule*": that we be cautious and only pursue modest goals, paying heed to prophets of doom before being seduced by prophets of bliss. Jonas chides utopians for being, in a sense, more pessimistic than prophets of doom, because the promise to perfect humanity presupposes that our nature is not essentially good enough already. For the sake of the perfect they would risk the good. The rhetoric of hope animating their "starry-eyed ethics of perfection," conceals contempt for the essential condition nature grants us. Against this, Jonas advocates the "sterner" ethic of responsibility—a meliorism that aims at modest improvements in our lot—born of a veneration for "the image of man" and fear for what we might lose in the name of progress. The link between nihilism and utopianism is the absence of veneration for the image of humanity, and so the loss of a "genuine present" oriented by the "plain truth" that "genuine man is always already there and was there throughout known history: in his heights and in his depths, his greatness and wretchedness, his bliss and torment, his justice and guilt—in short all the ambiguity that is inseparable from his humanity" (*IR*, 200).

Beginning from an existential interpretation of the biological facts, Jonas accomplishes precisely the *turn toward Being* that Heidegger hoped to initiate by way of fundamental ontology, but could not accomplish so long as existential categories were confined to the human way of being. Having so restricted his existential analysis, Heidegger could only see nature as a mode of being *within* our world, and so could not appreciate its intrinsic value or our continuity with it. For Heidegger the turn toward Being spells "the *end of metaphysics*" because it reminds us that Being hides itself and that our approach to any supposed unconditioned ground is a conceit that necessarily bears the trace of our finitude. For Jonas, on the other hand, existential analysis provides the thread by which we can find our way beyond ourselves to what is good-in-itself. His expansion of "the ontological locus of purpose from what is apparent at the subjective peak to what is hidden in the breadth of being" (*IR*, 71) permits him to make the *metaphysical* claim, though on admittedly speculative grounds, that Being reveals itself to contemplation *if* thought gives itself the right to abandon materialist assumptions about nature and instead to see the human essence as part of a unified, continuous, intelligible order: what in older times was called a "great chain of Being." Existentialism, far from presaging the end of metaphysics, proves to be the beginning of a metaphysics that is compatible with the modern idea that Being is dynamic and unfolds in time.

Has Jonas's turn toward Being provided a foundation for a *non*anthropocentric attitude that many environmentalists take to be the sine qua non of any ethic up to the task of saving our habitat? We often hear that, by according moral worth only to persons, traditional ethics is anthropocentric, and so cannot do justice to our duties to extrahuman nature. If nature has no moral worth for its own sake, then our environment has value only insofar as it is a means to satisfying our human ends. Environmentalists often decry this instrumental attitude as the philosophical core of our ecological crisis. Two alternatives to anthropocentrism are usually proposed. Some thinkers follow Albert Schweitzer down the path of biotic egalitarianism, claiming that all living beings have equal moral worth. Others—like the American preservationist, John Muir, and more recently deep ecologists like Arne Naess—pursue the way of ecocentric holism, asserting that the environment as a whole has intrinsic moral worth independent of its relationship to us.[10] From both perspectives, Jonas is open to the accusation that his philosophy is too anthropocentric, for he accords us a privileged place in evolution and insists that our primary obligation is to protect the existence and essence of human life.

I believe, however, that Jonas's metaphysics undercuts the very distinction between anthropocentrism and nonanthropocentrism. He thinks we can, and indeed must, have it *both* ways. While living nature is a good-in-itself commanding our reverence, and while all organisms participating in this goodness are vulnerable ends-in-themselves who exhibit concern for their own being, humans have special dignity as moral agents, for our will is responsive to ends beyond our own vital ones. "Only human freedom," Jonas writes, "permits the setting and choosing of ends and thereby the willing inclusion of the ends of others in one's immediate own, to the point of fully and devotedly making them one's own" (*IR*, 235). Our first duty is to preserve the noble presence of moral responsibility in nature: of a being who is able to recognize the good-in-itself as such.

This does not mean, however, that we must adopt an instrumental stance toward the rest of nature, viewing it as a mere means or resource to be mastered for our sake. We must come instead to respect ourselves not in virtue of our utter difference from nature, but for "what nature has achieved in us" (*IR*, 129). Our difference in kind is rooted in our continuity with the rest of the biotic community: with others who share in life's goodness, regardless of whether they serve our vital needs. So our self-respect requires "cosmic piety": reverence for the whole of which we are a part. Our obligation to the future of humanity is not based simply on our natural prejudice toward ourselves, but on an objective "assignment" by Being to take care of the delicate web of life that has allowed us to come forth from it. According to Jonas, "the threatened plenitude of the living world" issues a "silent plea for sparing its integrity" (*IR*, 8). This claim upon us is "not a mere sentiment which we may indulge as far as we wish or can afford to," but a categorical imperative emanating from Being when it is "disclosed to a sight not blocked by selfishness or dimmed by dullness" (*IR*, 90). So there need be no important divide between anthropocentrism and nonanthropocentrism: between self-respect for our unique title as nature's stewards and reverence for "mother nature" who gave birth to us as her guardian.

Jonas is not a biotic egalitarian because the amount of moral regard organisms deserve as individuals depends upon the quality of their individuality in the psychophysical hierarchy. There is a natural distinction between nutritive and sensitive souls, and among sensitive souls between animals who experience primitive pleasure/pain responses and those who suffer the passions of desire and fear. Finally, there are humans: metaphysical and moral beings who can take the interests of others to heart beyond our own vital needs. It is no anthropocentric conceit that our first obligation is toward ourselves, for we are the necessary condition of there being obligation in the world at all. Though we should feel awed by the diverse web of species that let us evolve and sustain us, we are often justified in letting our nonvital interests—like desires for cultural institutions—override even the vital needs of other organisms. There should be no guilt attached to swatting a mosquito. And we do not owe mammals in the wild the sort of protection from suffering that they merit when we have domesticated them. Our primary focus should not be on each and every individual organism, but, in the words of Aldo Leopold, the American advocate of "land ethics," on protecting "the integrity, stability and beauty" of our environment as a whole.[11]

Having rejected biotic egalitarianism, however, Jonas would not join the camp of radical ecocentric holists either, for they contend that nature has moral worth regardless of whether human beings are on the scene. Although Jonas believes that nature carries value independent of us because Being is "for itself" from the inception of life, the *moral* worth of life only comes into being with the phenomenon of obligation, and obligation requires the evolution of a being capable of moral responsibility. We are "an event for Being" precisely because our arrival marks the transition from vital goodness to moral rightness: from desire to responsibility. It might seem that we would do the greatest justice to the ecosystem as a whole by removing ourselves from it in an act of supreme impartiality so that other species might flourish. But collective suicide would annihilate the phenomena of justice and injustice alike, and so deprive Being of the metaphysical and moral dimensions it took so long to produce. We not only must, but should—out of respect for what nature has achieved in us—appreciate the ecosystem from the perspective of its suitability for our well-being.

Why Theology is Not Necessary for Overcoming Nihilism

We have now passed through the first two stages of Jonas's reply to the nihilist who asks, "Why should I care about the distant future of humankind and the planet?" The first, or existential, stage establishes the presence of "subjective inwardness"—mind, freedom, value, and purpose—throughout the entire organic realm. We are not aliens caught up in a lifeless machine, but citizens of a biotic community teeming with life. But the nihilist may still ask how we know that the presence of subjective value throughout the earthly environment is objectively good, and so really worth protecting: not simply "a tale told by an idiot, full of sound and fury, signifying nothing" (*IR*, 50). The second, or metaphysical, stage offers a grounding of the objective goodness of life and of our ethical obligation to safeguard the existence and essence of evolution's most sublime outcome: humanity itself. If Jonas has succeeded, what more could the nihilist want?

There is one last condition that the nihilist may believe is necessary to ensure that human life is worth caring for: namely, that we are creatures of a benevolent God. For if God does not exist, the nihilist may cry out, then we are but a flicker in the darkness and our prayers ultimately go unanswered in the silence of the universe. Jonas invites this worry when he asserts that "there is no point in caring for what has no sanction behind it in any creative intention" (*PL*, 234). One might assume, therefore, that theology comprises a necessary third stage for the overcoming of nihilism. Although Jonas does provide us with a theology that is compatible with his existentialism and metaphysics, he calls theology "a luxury of reason," not a necessity, and explicitly denies that nature needs to have been created by God in order to ground an imperative of responsibility. Our duty to be "executors of an estate that only we can see but did not create" is founded on a judgment concerning the value of life "that can be separated from any thesis concerning [the world's] authorship" (*IR*, 48). If rational metaphysics proves insufficient on its own, then no appeal to a Creator will satisfy the nihilist. For if life can be shown to be worthwhile without reference to God, then whether God exists is superfluous to ethics. But if life cannot be shown to be worthwhile without reference to God, then appealing to a benevolent Creator will only provide hollow consolation for our experience of life's worthlessness.

In a reaction against theological voluntarism, a reaction whose conceptual formulation dates back to Plato's *Euthyphro*, Jonas insists that the cause of life's coming-to-be is irrelevant to the question of whether it ought to be, for if the world was created by a God worthy of our reverence, then the intrinsic goodness of the world must have been a prior and independent reason for His creating it. The presupposition of a Creator offers us no reason for judging the world to be good if the world does not justify our perception of its value in its own right. Theological voluntarism runs the risk of lapsing into Gnostic dualism, wherein faith is owed to a divine will that is wholly absent from the perceptible testimony of His creation. Yet because theological rationalism posits the priority of the good-in-itself over God's will, it renders the question of life's authorship irrelevant to the issue of its goodness, and so cedes to metaphysics the task of providing a foundation for ethics (*IR*, 47).

If the nihilist is to be defeated, reason must be able to replace revelation in the office of guiding our ultimate choices. But reason, triumphant through modern natural science, is precisely the root of nihilism. It undermines the cosmic piety that is supported by the Old Testament tradition, a tradition that Jonas identifies with four key propositions: (1) God created heaven and earth, (2) God saw that His creation was good, (3) God created man in His own image, and (4) God makes known to man what is good because His word is inscribed in our hearts (*PE*, 169).[12] It may seem, then, that theology provides the only alternative to the nihilism of modern reason. But I think that Jonas's metaphysics should be read as an attempt to preserve the meaning of the latter three Biblical propositions on rational grounds, without relying upon theology at all. Once the metaphysical prejudice of modern reason—materialism—has been challenged by Jonas's "existential interpretation of the biological facts," he can defend the three latter propositions without recourse to the premise at the heart of the Biblical tradition: that God created heaven and earth.

In each case, we must be able to translate a theological proposition into a naturalistic one. First, that "God saw that His creation was good" gets reinterpreted in Jonas's metaphysics as the good-in-itself of living nature whose very being imposes an "ought-to-be" whenever a responsible agent is there to appreciate it. Second, that "God created man in His own image" gets recast as the notion that the idea of humanity is an event of cosmic importance because our unprecedented power to reflect Being in knowledge and to recreate nature in our own image is constrained by the good-in-itself: the uncreated ethical measure of our cognitive and technical powers. Finally, that "God makes known to man what is good because His word is written in our hearts" gets translated as the idea that the objective imperative of responsibility is answered by our subjective capacity to feel responsible for the totality, continuity, and futurity of the object that commands our respect: namely, ourselves as, in Hegelian language, the "coming to itself" of original substance.

Jonas's metaphysics provides a wholly naturalistic interpretation of these Judaic ideas based on an internal teleology: the view that nature is purposive even if there is no purposer, that it makes sense to speak of a creative intention in nature without reference to a Creator, and that life is a gift to be received with gratitude even if there is no giver. Though external teleology—the view that nature is God's creation—may be grafted onto an internal teleology, there is no need to ground metaphysics in theology. Rational metaphysics must stand on its own. If it fails, Jonas contends, theology cannot rescue it from the nihilist's protests. It may be gratifying to those of a religious temper that faith complements Jonas's post-Kantian *Grundlegung*, but theocentric commitments are not necessary to address nihilism and so to meet the emergency of ecological ethics today.

Still, reason is not satisfied simply by meeting its needs, for there are questions like "How did the universe begin?" and "Is there any mind outside of us who cares about our plight?" that we as thinkers are moved to ask even if answers to them are speculative and not required in order for us to have scientific and ethical knowledge. Even if the existence of God is not necessary to complete a philosophy of nature corresponding to "what theology used to call the *ordo creationis*" (*PL*, 283), God may in fact happen to exist. Not everything that is true needs to be true in order to preserve the world's intelligibility. The issue then would be how to imagine God so as to leave the integrity of naturalism intact. I want to say that this is just what Jonas's theology does. But this must raise the question: What *difference* does it make whether we can conceive of a God worthy of our faith if the self-testimony of life is sufficient unto the day? Shouldn't we use Ockham's razor, and excise unnecessary metaphysical hypotheses? What does faith *add* to what reason already supplies? Before we explore this issue, we should see what motivates Jonas to supplement his naturalistic ontology with a theology in the first place.

A Luxury of Reason: Theological
Speculations after Auschwitz

In "Immortality and the Modern Temper" (chapter 5 in this volume), Jonas introduces his own theological speculations indirectly: as a way of providing an account of immortality consistent with premises acceptable to modern thought. He points out that two credos of modernity make us uncongenial to the idea of immortality: (1) the belief that mind depends on body and so death brings an end to both; and (2) the related view, canonized by Darwin's theory of evolution, that there is no realm of timeless Being transcending the temporal order of becoming. Jonas suggests, however, that "our idea of eternity is a cryptic signal of the self-surpassing quality of temporality in man," and he asks whether the prospect of immortality, given the impossibility of either proof or disproof, can at least be meaningful for us today.

Having rejected the traditional picture, based on dualism, of souls residing in a hereafter, Jonas proposes a way of linking eternity with modernity's realism about temporality and our finitude: a realism most evident in Heidegger's existentialist account of human existence as being-unto-death. Jonas suggests that what connects mortals to immortality may not be what is most enduring in us but instead what is most transitory: the moment of decision. For when our whole being is involved in what we are doing we may feel that we are acting "under the eyes of eternity." But how are we to make sense of the idea that our deeds are immortalized without referring to the immortality of individual persons who perform them?

Here Jonas draws on two symbols from his own Jewish tradition: "the Book of Life" and "the transcendent image of God." Hebrew prayer speaks of our names being inscribed in the Book of Life according to our individual deserts. What we add to this record, on Jonas's interpretation, bears not on any future destiny of ours as individuals but on the welfare of God who keeps a unified memory of the world-process. Our experience of the call of conscience in the moment of decision may attest to our holding the fate of "the becoming deity" in our hands, insofar as our acts form His image. By the way we exercise our moral responsibility in our daily behavior, we determine the plight of the caring, suffering, and becoming God, for His welfare depends on our fulfilling the promise of goodness that His gift of life offers us.

But, Jonas asks: Into what metaphysics would these symbols fit? He offers a "tentative" myth according to which God withdraws from His own creation in order that the world might be "for itself," fraught with possibilities. Jonas imagines that God pronounces creation to be good only with the long awaited but accidental emergence of life: of creatures who value their own existence against the threat of death. Prior to the advent of knowledge God's cause cannot go wrong because life retains its innocence. Eventually, with the evolution of humanity, life arrives at the highest intensification of its own value, for our capacities for knowledge and freedom represent "transcendence awakened to itself." But there is a price to be paid for our capacities, for with knowledge and freedom come the power to will and do evil, and this power becomes absolute in a technological age with our ability to destroy ourselves.

Still, moral responsibility is the mark of our being made "for" God's image, though not "in" it. Among earthly creatures only we can acknowledge the transcendent importance of our deeds: that we are "mortal trustees of an immortal cause." To God's self-limitation we owe thanks, for this gives us room to help Him by bearing responsibility for our own vulnerable affairs. Even "the burnt children of Auschwitz," who had little chance to be inscribed in the Book of Life, are mourned for all eternity and may be redeemed insofar as we succeed in healing the wounded God by "lift[ing] the shadow cast by our inhumanity." Jonas's myth does not offer the consolations of the traditional concept of personal immortality, for his interpretation of the Book of Life and the transcendent image have nothing to do with rewarding the virtuous and punishing the vicious. The immortality of deeds is for God's sake, not our own. One must care about the divine in its own right in order for it to bear upon how we spend our time. But one only has reason to care about God's destiny if one experiences His goodness reflected in the immanent goodness of creation itself.

We should notice that Jonas, by focusing on the moment of decision as the clue to immortality, has drawn once again on a key aspect of the existentialism of his mentor, Martin Heidegger, only to use it for purposes antithetical to Heidegger's own. For, on Heidegger's account, authenticity at the moment of decision demands that one choose one's direction in life without reference to any transcendent, eternal authority. Conscience calls, but its voice is silent, for it imposes no moral requirements, only the demand that one take personal responsibility for deciding upon one's own possibilities. Jonas speculates, by contrast, that the call of conscience at the moment of decision attests to the eternal presence of God. Consequently, Jonas exploits the dramatic center of Heidegger's existentialism for the purpose of articulating a metaphysics capable of sustaining the faith of the Jewish people: a purpose that runs counter to Heidegger's intention, to say the least!

Jonas turns to his Jewish roots in the first instance as a way of showing that the idea of immortality can be meaningful for us today. The immortality of deeds, not souls, is consistent with the modern credo that individual lives are temporal and finite through and through. But this must lead us to wonder why we should be attracted to any image of immortality whatsoever if, as Jonas suggests in "The Burden and Blessing of Mortality," finitude is the condition of life's preciousness and of the demand that we "number our days and make them count." If the way life is meaningful to us depends on our mortality, then it would seem unnecessary to believe in the immortality of deeds, much less of souls, to ensure that it "really matters" that we live in a morally responsible manner: promoting the good and thwarting evil. And as the presence of meaning in life does not depend on the prospect of immortality, so a grounding of ethics does not depend on faith in God. As we have already seen, Jonas insists that the ethical question "Why ought we to care about the distant future of humankind and the planet?" can be answered on the basis of a comprehensive ontology without recourse to theology. Even if there is no Creator, and instead the world has always been or came into being mindlessly, and even if there is no God to ensure the immortality of our deeds, Being remains a good-in-itself—and so solicits our responsibility— in virtue of the presence of purposiveness within it. If Jonas's theology, and the idea of immortality it supports, do not answer a need of reason, then what does faith add to the ethics available on the basis of reason alone? Any exploration of Jonas's theological writings should remain haunted by this question, and we shall reserve a reply to it for our conclusion.

A more immediate worry, however, is that Jonas has fashioned an idea of immortality palatable to "the modern temper" only by drawing on a concept deeply at odds with this very same temper: namely, the concept of a personal God who created the physical universe. Modernity would seem to be just as inhospitable to theology as it is to the prospect of immortality. If so, then shouldn't the appeal to both immortality and the transcendent God be rejected in favor of a wholehearted affirmation of our mortality and the immanence of nature? It is no accident, then, that the rest of the theological essays presented in this book attempt to show that the concept of God implicit in Jonas's myth is compatible with the modern temper after all.

Following Plato, Jonas contends that recourse to myth is consistent with a commitment to reason insofar as a myth symbolizes what can never be an object of knowledge for us but can only be imagined "through a glass darkly." And Jonas follows Kant's idea that the aim of metaphysics is not to reject as meaningless what lies beyond the realm of our knowledge, but rather to show the limits of knowledge in order to make room for faith. Each of Jonas's theological essays explores an obstacle posed to faith by what moderns take to be a matter of knowledge. And each suggests a way in which one can be true to what is best in modernity and still retain one's faith in the God of the Old Testament. Though God's existence cannot be proven beyond a reasonable doubt it cannot be disproven either. So the most theology can hope for is to develop a concept of God that is rational in the sense that the meaning of the concept does not contradict what falls within the scope of our knowledge. Theology becomes irrational only when it insists that we sacrifice what we know in order to have faith in the unknowable.

Jonas's rational theology offers a concept of God that accommodates three dimensions of modern knowledge. First, in "The Concept of God after Auschwitz: A Jewish Voice" (chapter 6 herein), he articulates an image of God that does not explain away the brute reality of evil in our experience, especially given the shadow cast by the Holocaust. Second, in "Is Faith Still Possible?: Memories of Rudolf Bultmann and Reflections on the Philosophical Aspects of His Work" (chapter 7), Jonas defends a faith, rooted in revelation, that embraces modern science's exclusion of divine intervention from the explanation of nature. And finally, in "Matter, Mind, and Creation: Cosmological Evidence and Cosmogonic Speculation" (chapter 8), Jonas argues for the compatibility between faith in the divine origin of the world and modern cosmological evidence supporting the belief that the universe began with "the big bang" and that life is a late, rare, and precarious product of nature's labors. Jonas's goal throughout is to show that Jewish faith in the goodness of a God who created the world and revealed Himself to uniquely elected individuals is a living and meaningful option today for thoughtful people who refuse to turn their backs on the knowledge that reason commends to them.

In "The Concept of God after Auschwitz," Jonas wrestles with the traditional problem of evil, dramatized in the story of Job. But he addresses this problem in the modern context of the Holocaust, symbolized by Auschwitz, where his mother was murdered. Millions died neither for the sake of their faith—like the martyrs of the Maccabean age—nor even because of their faith, but rather on account of "the fiction of race." Survivors cannot avoid a question that poses the deepest challenge to Jews' faith in "the Lord of History": What God could let it happen?

In the tentative myth he initially proposed to account for "the immortality of deeds" Jonas finds theological implications that enable him to respond to the problem of evil. He contends that the suffering, becoming, and caring God represented in his myth is familiar to the Old Testament tradition, but that these qualities require a denial of a central article of Jewish theology: divine omnipotence. For if the Lord really responds to worldly events "with a mighty hand and an outstretched arm," then why the Holocaust? Jonas refuses to accept standard ways of rationalizing monstrous evils as the inscrutable outcome of God's omniscience, omnipotence, and benevolence. If God had been all-powerful, Jonas protests, He would not have stood aside while the butchery was taking place.

Forced to choose between divine benevolence and omnipotence, we must conclude that God is wise and good, but limited in power. And this is precisely what Jonas's myth implies for, in it, God divested Himself after the moment of creation of the power to intervene in the physical course of things. Jonas goes so far as to speculate, in a manner that admittedly "strays far from the oldest Judaic teaching," that God was silent not because He *chose* not to intervene but because He *could* not intervene. But this limitation was self-imposed for the sake of cosmic autonomy. God's withdrawal permits nature to unfold according to its own possibilities and ultimately allows humanity the freedom to make God's cause our own. God remains impotent in the physical realm but He addresses us through the manifest goodness of creation itself with "the mutely insistent appeal of his unfulfilled goal."

Jonas finds precedent for his self-limiting God in teachings of the Lurianic Kabbalah regarding *tzimtzum,* or divine self-contraction. But Jonas goes even further than the Kabbalah, holding that God's contraction is total so far as physical power is concerned. He feels confirmed by the discovery that his speculations were anticipated by Etty Hillesum, a Dutch Jewess who volunteered for the Westerbork concentration camp in order "to help in the hospital and share in the fate of her people." Her diaries, published in 1984, some forty years after her murder at Auschwitz, reveal that the basis of her martyrdom lay in the conviction that God has no more to give to creation and it is our turn to give in return. "You cannot help us," she writes, "but we must help You and defend your dwelling-place in us to the last." Like Jonas, Hillesum answers Job's question by invoking the chosen voidance, not the plenitude, of God's power. But this radical version of *tzimtzum* is a song of praise, not despair, for God suffers with the victims of injustice as He hands responsibility over to us that we may complete His work.

Though Jonas offers one way of coping with the problem of evil, it would appear that his God is so self-effacing that we are left with the functional equivalent of a naturalistic view. God's role in history is restricted to the creation of the primordial stuff out of which life gradually evolved and to the spiritual presence in creation that commands our conscience. But Jonas admits that, even if God does not exist, a comprehensive ontology of nature is sufficient to ground an ethics for the future. Again, we are moved to wonder whether we lose very much by not taking the leap of faith at all. Jonas insists that we lose the most, however, by retaining a faith in the traditional "Lord of History," for then God must bear responsibility for letting Auschwitz happen.

Nonetheless, in "Is Faith Still Possible?," Jonas allows in principle for the possibility of divine intervention in the course of history, for God's acting would not necessarily break the chain of causality to which modern natural science is committed. Jonas takes issue with his beloved teacher, Bultmann, who, in order to protect modern belief from an untenable commitment to miracles and myths, holds that God's actions must be nonworldly, transcendent *noumena* on a wholly different level than the *phenomena*. Bultmann's project of "demythologization" betrays his adherence to Kantian dualism and stems from what Jonas calls "an exaggerated conception of the tightness of worldly causality." This leads Bultmann to "concede more to the scientific worldview than science itself demands." Though Bultmann fails to make room for revelation in his theory, he needs to appeal to God's ingression into the world of appearances for the sake of Christian practice.

According to Jonas, divine agency, of which revealed religion must speak, need not be represented in the form of visible, spectacular miracles that violate nature's laws. Instead, it can involve the direct inspiration of uniquely elected individuals. If we can accept the compatibility between causality and freedom in the case of human action, then we can permit a similar compatibility in the case of divine action. As the laws of nature do not preclude freedom in our acting upon the external world, so the principles of psychology do not block entry to a transcendent initiative into our inner life. In this respect Jews have an advantage over Christians, Jonas contends, for while the counternatural miracles of Jesus's birth, resurrection, and ascension touch upon the core of Christian faith, "nothing much hangs on [such] miracles in the Old Testament."

Jonas concurs with his teacher's view that God abstains from physically intervening in the course of nature, but they arrive at this conclusion on different grounds. According to Jonas, the main reason for limiting our reference to divine intervention is not the alleged incompatibility between divine agency and worldly causality, but rather two other considerations. First, as we saw in Jonas's discussion of the problem of evil, one risks ascribing the world's horrors to divine intention by granting God too much worldly power. Second, it is safer to stay within the bounds of scientific explanation: not, Jonas points out, because faith in revelation must conflict with science, but on account of the arrogance and dogmatism invited by claims that one possesses "the one true religion." So the cause of faith remains difficult, Jonas reminds us, even though divine action need not contravene our scientific knowledge.

Finally, in "Matter, Mind, and Creation," Jonas turns from revelation to creation itself, asking whether the evidence of modern cosmology is consistent with, or even supports, the hypothesis that the world has a divine origin. We know that in Jonas's cosmogonic myth God had nothing left to give after the creation and let nature run its course. But does anything in the testimony of nature bear witness to this speculation? Jonas notices that the cosmological evidence can be read as a physically improbable, anti-entropic story of development from chaos to order: from simpler, commonplace concatenations of matter to rarer, more complex, increasingly inward forms of life. All organisms possess subjectivity, the "will" to live embodied in metabolism, though this power seems only to have arisen in a minuscule region of the universe. Rarer still are animals with their capacities for feeling and perceiving. Rarest of all is the human mind—at once the most inward and self-transcending product of life. Jonas wonders whether our own evolution lends credibility to the idea that the cause of the universe was not merely random.

He asks, first, how the fact of subjectivity, characteristic of all life, contributes to the cosmological evidence. He finds it most reasonable to infer the presence of a predisposing tendency in matter toward life, for otherwise one assumes that subjectivity is utterly alien to the matter that gives rise to it. Jonas associates this tendency with the classical concept of *eros*: as if matter possesses a yearning that is causally active in seizing upon a chance opportunity for the emergence of mind. While the conditions necessary for life are enormously improbable, matter's readiness for life indicates that more than a neutral accident is at work: that matter harbors latent subjectivity from the very beginning. Though the vital evidence warrants the teleological speculation that subjectivity is the actualization of a potentiality in matter, the hypothesis of an immanent cosmogonic *eros* need not make reference to a divine, transcendent will executing a conscious plan.

The transition from animal subjectivity to the human mind raises the stakes, however, for "a horizon of transcendence unfolds when human thought is added to the vital evidence." This horizon manifests itself in three freedoms of thought: (1) the freedom to choose an object to reflect upon; (2) the freedom to invent imaginary objects; and (3) the freedom to transcend the dimension of sensation altogether and ponder the infinite, eternal, and absolute. These three imply a fourth: the freedom of practical reason to impose goals for behavior upon itself. And practical reason takes on a moral dimension when freedom acknowledges that it is transcended by objects that command one's responsibility. Finally, there is the freedom of self-reflection: the ability to make oneself an object of thought. Jonas calls this "the eminent mode of immanent transcendence," for this freedom enables the value-oriented self to make itself an object of evaluation, subject to the judgment of conscience.

But does the fact of mind or "immanent transcendence," and most eminently the human capacity for responsibility itself, tell us anything at all about the distant "In the beginning . . ."? Does it justify Jonas's moving from an internal to an external teleology: from his hypothesis of cosmogonic *eros* as a brute fact of nature to a theological stance which interprets this *eros* as the materialization of a transcendent will? After criticizing different ways in which philosophers from antiquity on have inferred the existence of God from the faculties and experiences of human thinking, Jonas finds a kernel of truth in the traditional proofs of God's existence, leading him to make a cosmogonic conjecture that, he confesses, "is in all probability mistaken." The first cause of mind, Jonas proposes, must have been nothing less than mind itself.

Yet if mind can emerge from mindless matter in both the growth of the individual human being and the evolution of the human species, if the origins of development point away from mind in both instances, then what supports the conjecture that primal matter had its origin in mind? Contending that mind must attribute its own arisal to what is latent in universal matter, Jonas offers the metaphor that "matter from the very beginning is mind asleep," and derives the "intuitive thesis" that "the really first cause, the creative cause, of mind asleep can only be mind awake." When thought turns to the beginning of all things, Jonas reminds us, "we can at most be reasonable without compelling assent." But once his "intuitive thesis" is accepted, clear and definite questions can be discussed in the light of rational argument. Most centrally, one may ask: How did the Creator entrust the business of mind to originally mindless matter?

Whereas Descartes's dualism cannot account for the evolution of mind from matter and Spinoza's psychophysical parallelism fails to acknowledge the rarity of mind in the universe, Hegel's dialectic prefigures Jonas's notion that the beginning of the universe lies in the self-alienation of primal mind and that mind regains itself in the course of natural history. But Jonas parts company with Hegel's account of becoming for it offers "a self-guaranteed success story" in which the divine act of creation leaves God with no doubt that His purpose will be realized in time. Jonas believes that his own myth of the self-limiting God does more justice to the evidence of both natural and human history than does any metaphysics of predetermined success. For his myth leaves room for the gamble that God wagered with creation: the risky element in the adventure of the universe. If God renounced His power for the sake of cosmic autonomy and its chances, then the self-alienation of creative mind runs far deeper than Hegel thought. Ultimately, the fate of the divine adventure lies in our hands, for the very evolution of responsible life in the universe imposes upon us a cosmic responsibility to come to the aid of the caring, suffering, and becoming God by ensuring that there be future generations who can act on behalf of God's image.

Jonas's Place in Contemporary Jewish Theology

The place of any view, Jonas's included, in the spectrum of contemporary Jewish theologies can be defined in relation to Richard Rubenstein's simple argument rejecting the plausibility of faith "after Auschwitz."[13] Rubenstein invokes two premises that he takes to be incontrovertible: (1) that "the Lord of History"—as He is conceived in the Jewish tradition—could not have allowed the Holocaust to happen; and (2) that the Holocaust did happen. These premises compel Rubenstein to conclude that the God of the Jewish tradition does not exist.

Objections to Rubenstein's second premise, introduced by so-called "Holocaust revisionists," do not deserve the dignity of serious debate. So it would appear that the only avenue for believers is to take issue with the first premise. On the one hand, one may insist that the Lord of History, being both all-powerful and good, must have had reasons to let the Holocaust happen. On the other hand, one may contend that the Jewish tradition makes room for other concepts of God besides the Lord of History: in particular, for a God who is good but limited in power. On this view, the Holocaust happened, but not because God let it happen.

There are a number of ways of rationalizing the first option: that the Lord of History, being almighty, allowed the Holocaust to occur.[14] First, one may take a retributive view: holding that God imposes the Holocaust as punishment for the sins of the Jewish people, either individually or collectively. But such a Draconian judgment, applied even to children, must raise serious doubts about God's benevolence. Second, one may, in the vein of Ignaz Maybaum, see the people of Israel as a servant chosen by God to suffer vicariously for other peoples' sins.[15] But unless one believes that humanity is perfectible, one must worry that the plight of Jews throughout history is destined to be miserable, and this makes it difficult to be grateful to God for the gift of creation.

One may also offer nonretributive explanations of why an omnipotent and benevolent God would allow the Holocaust to occur. First, one may interpret the Holocaust as a test of Jewish faith: a sequel to the story of Job and the Akedah. But only a demonic God would use the gas chambers of Auschwitz as a test. Second, one may imagine that the Holocaust, when viewed by God *sub specie aeternitatis*, is a brief, but necessary chapter in a much larger story of historical progress. But the thought that God adopts a stance so detached from the suffering of individuals who live in the historical present undermines the faith that God cares about the dignity of each individual. Third, one may claim that the purposes of an infinite God must remain an inscrutable mystery to finite intellects. But to drive such a wedge between God's purposes and our experience of His ways in the world makes it incomprehensible for us to attribute goodness to Him. Fourth, one may refer to "the eclipse of God": times when He is inexplicably absent from history or turns His face away. But this simply begs the question of why a God with the power to intervene in history would withdraw at such a crucial moment.

Among those theologians who trust that God was present at Auschwitz as "the Lord of History," Emil Fackenheim is perhaps the most influential.[16] Where, during the Shoah, was the saving God of Exodus? Fackenheim asserts that although we cannot fathom why God did not intervene, faith requires us to affirm His almighty presence. The greatest tragedy of all would occur if Jews allowed their despair over the Holocaust to justify the abandonment of their faith. Fackenheim bids Jews to receive a divine commandment, nothing less than a revelation, emanating from the mass graves at Auschwitz: "Jews must survive!" For Jews to conclude that their God does not exist because of the abomination of the Nazi genocide would be for Hitler to attain a posthumous victory. The solidarity of the people of Israel offers the promise of hope and redemption. Still, Fackenheim insists, this is not to say that the Nazis' victims were used as God's instruments to bring about the Jewish homeland.

Yet if the message at Sinai and the legacy of Abraham, Isaac, and Jeremiah are genuine, Jews do not need Auschwitz to learn that Hitler should not win. Fackenheim's interpretation implies that God must be demonic that we might be just. And this paradox displays the heart of the problem with all attempts to make God's omnipotence compatible with "the slaughterbench of history." For to credit God with being the all-powerful Lord of History logically requires seeing Him as the agent behind the Holocaust. And if God worked His will through the destruction of European Jewry, then we must draw the perverse conclusion that Hitler was doing God's bidding as a means of bringing about the Lord's good purposes in the long run.

The problem of evil drives many theologians, including Jonas, to criticize Rubenstein's first premise by denying that the Jewish tradition commits Jews to believe in the almighty Lord of History. If it is acceptable for Jews to believe instead that God's power is limited, then the case can be made that He bears no responsibility for Auschwitz. The assumption that omnipotence is an essential attribute of God's nature derives less from sacred Hebrew writings than from the Aristotelian, and hence Greek, premises of medieval theology. The dogma that God equals pure substance and that pure substance needs nothing but itself in order to exist leads to the conclusion that God contains everything, is complete and immutable. But if Being, goodness, and power are complete in God, then the world and humanity add nothing to what really is. God is the same with or without creation.

According to one of Jonas's students, Rabbi Jack Bemporad, the Aristotelian dogma of pure substance is the root of two confusions that bedevil traditional Jewish theology: the problem of freedom and the problem of evil.[17] First, if God is omnipotent, then there is no power other than God's, and so no human freedom. Creation simply reenacts a pattern already present in the divine mind. Second, if God is all-powerful, then He must have the power to prevent any evil. Assuming that God is good and that everything occurring in the world expresses His almighty will, we must conclude that evil is illusory or a part of God's plan to bring about more good than would otherwise be possible. Consequently, human freedom and responsibility, and so the possibility of real evil, require that God's power is limited. Only then do God's creatures make a real difference in actualizing His will. But there are a number of ways of imagining the nature of a God whose power is limited: a God who makes room for the human struggle to fulfill His purpose on Earth.

Henry Slonimsky presents a most unorthodox defense of this position, contending that God stands at the end of history, not at the beginning or in the middle.[18] Slonimsky's God is not the Creator of the universe, but rather an Ideal whose realization would bring unity to the world. "On that day the Lord shall be One and His name shall be One!" God is the *telos* of history, and we are responsible for helping Him emerge into actuality. The paradox of Jewish faith is that those who, by way of the Torah, bear witness to God's word in the world also assume more than their fair share of the world's burdens and sorrows. The key problem with Slonimsky's view, however, is that he immunizes God from responsibility for evil by rejecting a central article of Jewish faith: belief in the divine Creator.

But one need not go as far as Slonimsky if one conceives of creation not as an act of divine omnipotence, but rather as an expression of divine self-limitation. The most familiar defense of this position is provided by Eliezer Berkovits's free-will theodicy.[19] Berkovits contends that God's presence in history consists precisely in His absence, for by removing Himself from the flow of historical events, God creates the reality of human freedom that is necessary for moral responsibility. Humanity would be impossible if God managed human affairs in accordance with perfect justice. If God's love extends beyond the requirements of strict justice, then there must be human evil and suffering. Like a good parent, God reveals his spiritual power by curbing His physical might so that His children can become more powerful in their own right. And the continued existence of Israel, according to Berkovits, bears witness to the paradox of God's presence by way of His self-limitation. Berkovits does not go so far as to say that God could not get involved in preventing evil: only that He chooses not to act out of respect for the human capacity to respond autonomously to His noncoercive love. One may reply to Berkovits, however, that in emergencies a good parent may have to intervene in order to keep his children from destroying each other. By analogy, even if God's abstention for the sake of human freedom is a good thing in general, mightn't there be crises—and the Holocaust is surely one of them—when God would forego His usual policy of nonintervention? If God's power is limited not by His nature but by His own choice, then can He not make exceptions under extenuating circumstances? And if He can, we must ask why He does not.

To meet this challenge, Hans Jonas, whose position resembles Berkovits's free-will theodicy, goes even further: conjecturing that God *could not* intervene because He spent all of His physical power on the act of creation. Having chosen at the beginning of time to sacrifice His physical might for the sake of the autonomy of His uncertain and vulnerable creation, God divested Himself of all power to direct or correct the adventure of nature. For surely if God could have intervened to prevent the Holocaust, Jonas insists, He would have. As we have seen, Jonas radicalizes the Kabbalic notion of *tzimtzum*—the self-contraction of God—and sympathizes with the voice of Etty Hillesum, who apparently kept her faith, even as she was herded off to Auschwitz, out of the conviction that it is no longer up to God to help us, but only up to us to help God. Whereas Henry Slonimsky attributes God's impotence in history to the fact that He lacks creative power altogether, Jonas accepts the traditional notion of God as Creator. And whereas Eliezer Berkovits claims that God the Creator chooses not to intervene in order to allow for human freedom and responsibility, Jonas speculates that God, having chosen to risk the wager of creation, is powerless to prevent evil from occurring.

Hans Jonas's theology bears some similarities to theodicies, like Hegel's, that interpret history as the progressive realization of God's goodness. On the basis of the cosmological evidence, he concludes that matter possesses a predisposition to form life and that, with the emergence of life, nature offers immanent testimony of its own goodness.

Furthermore, the evolutionary evidence supports the conjecture that life harbors the tendency to form ever more sophisticated powers of subjectivity, culminating in a mind that can appreciate its place in the whole scheme of things and take responsibility for preserving the conditions of its own existence. Finally, the anthropological evidence warrants the speculation that the first cause of "mind asleep" was "mind awake": that a mind transcending nature created the universal matter that eventually gave rise to mind within nature. But the historical evidence makes a mockery of Hegel's effort to see creation as the necessary actualization of God's goodness. The uncertainty of nature's course and the ineluctable reality of cruel suffering and evil testify to the limits of God's power.

Using Richard Rubenstein's argument for atheism "after Auschwitz" as a point of reference, I have situated Jonas's position on the spectrum of post-Holocaust theologies and have indicated how the weaknesses of other theistic positions on this spectrum lead Jonas toward his own distinctive reply to the crisis of Jewish faith. He joins other advocates of a "finite theism" in taking issue with the traditional premise of God's omnipotence. But he occupies a unique place within the camp of finite theists by virtue of his rigorous effort to frame a concept of God that does justice to evidence provided by the cosmological, evolutionary, and historical records. Still, Jonas's theology invites several objections.

A first worry is that his view verges on pantheism. For if God risks His very being in spending His power on creation, then it would seem that God's very existence depends on humanity's execution of its cosmic responsibility, for we can annihilate Him by destroying ourselves. But one must distinguish between God's existence and His self-realization through us. Jonas holds that God does not control the actualization of His own purpose, for it is up to us to safeguard the presence of responsibility in creation. But God's existence transcends the world to which He ceded His physical energies. Through the goodness of life and our corresponding feeling of responsibility toward it, God reveals His will. He is affected by the extent to which the world-process fulfills His hopes, but He continues to exist even if humanity lets Him down.

The most familiar and fundamental objection to Jonas's helpless deity is registered by Louis Jacobs, who complains that the God of *tzimtzum* is too weak and pathetic to supply life with meaning.[20] A Lord who cannot respond to the cries of the people of Israel "with a mighty hand and outstretched arms" is not the living God to whom Jews prayed at Auschwitz, Jacobs protests, but merely a philosopher's abstraction. Jonas has forged such a wide divide between the Creator and His creation that he inadvertently presents a version of the very Gnostic dualism he so vehemently opposes. God, the source of all goodness, remains isolated from our appeals for His help, and so creation seems to have been delivered over to the forces of darkness.

Jonas would justifiably take issue with Jacobs's objection. The example of Etty Hillesum indicates that there were those who found meaning at Auschwitz in a God who was powerless to help. But why would such a God infuse life with meaning rather than leaving us feeling abandoned and desperate? Jonas contends that the only deity worthy of our devotion, given the magnitude of evil in the world, is a caring, suffering, and becoming God who is helpless to prevent evil. Though this is not the God of traditional theodicy, neither is He the Gnostic *deus absconditus* who remains so hidden from the perceptible testimony of His creation that faith amounts to refuge from a diabolical world. On Jonas's view, creation does reveal itself to be good enough in its own right that life on Earth deserves our allegiance and commands our responsibility.

In what does God's perceptible goodness consist if we can neither count on Him to come to our aid nor take solace in the thought that everything is destined to work out for the best in the long run? First, we should be grateful for the gift of life, for with the emergence from universal matter of organisms who struggle to remain alive in the face of death, Being says "Yes" to itself. Second, we should appreciate the special goodness of human life in the chain of Being, for the experience of conscience attests to the idea that God created humanity for His own image and makes known to us what is good because His word is inscribed in our hearts. In ontological terms, this means that the objective imperative of responsibility, rooted in living nature as a good-in-itself, is answered by our subjective capacity to feel responsible for preserving this goodness. Our trust in God consists in gratitude for His having bequeathed to us a good enough world out of His love: a dynamic and precarious world that is better than any "guaranteed success story" because the limits of God's power free us to return to Him and help Him on our own.

Faith in God may strengthen our confidence in the value of life and the cosmic importance of our responsibility even when overwhelming natural and human evils seem to provide evidence favoring an attitude of nihilistic despair. On Jonas's view, however, trust in God is only as strong as the confidence that is already warranted by the value that shines forth in the phenomenon of life itself, once life is interpreted existentially and understood metaphysically. For the belief that Being is a good-in-itself can no more be falsified by the empirical data than can faith that Being is God's creation. Though the judgment that Being says "Yes" to itself is based on the empirical evidence provided by the phenomenon of life, this judgment is ultimately metaphysical, because it is impervious to any hedonistic calculus showing the predominance of pain over pleasure in life. Jonas embraces the "intuitive thesis" that deems the adventure of life to be worthwhile even if suffering does outweigh satisfaction. And if this ontological thesis is metaphysical because it can be neither verified nor falsified by the empirical data, then the theological hypothesis that life's goodness traces back to the creative act of God raises the metaphysical stakes to an even higher level, for it commits our thought to a dimension beyond the immanence of nature.

Ultimately we are faced with the question that has haunted us throughout our survey of Jonas's theological writings. If the categorical imperative at the heart of Jonas's ethics for the future—that we ought to safeguard and nourish the presence of human responsibility on Earth—can be grounded on the basis of reason alone, independent of any thesis concerning the divine authorship of the world and without recourse to divine commandments, then what is the need for faith? Even if Jonas has shown that a myth referring to divine acts of creation and revelation does not contradict what science teaches us, and even if faith is consistent with the reality of evil in the world, does faith add anything to the ethical sensibility that is already available to a secular culture? Again we are reminded of Jonas's point that theology is not a need, but a luxury, of reason. The world is not left any less intelligible, either from a scientific or an ethical viewpoint, if one cannot appeal to a transcendent ground of the immanent world-process. But intelligibility—the need of reason—is not the only longing of the human spirit.

Jonas might say that faith answers two spiritual longings which are not "needs" of reason, strictly speaking. First, we may wish that the unavoidable question "How did it all begin?" finds an answer in a personal ground: a loving presence who created and sustains the world. For if God is ever-present, then we may feel that we are never utterly alone, cast adrift in the immense universe, but are always loved. Second, we may wish that nothing good be lost and forgotten: that there be an eternal memory even of those innocent children whose lives have been cut short throughout history by "pestilence, war, and famine." No immanent ontology of nature or internal teleology can satisfy these longings. Yet they are just what the Jewish God answers, symbolized as He is by "the Book of Life" and "the transcendent image."

Concluding Critical Reflections

I have traced Jonas's reply to nihilism through three stages—existential, metaphysical, and theological—and have argued that his answer to the question "Why should we care about the distant future of humankind and the planet?" does not require recourse to either radical nonanthropocentrism or theology. At the same time, his answer is far more metaphysically substantial than that of simple anthropocentrists who appeal only to our fear for ourselves or disgust at handing a degraded habitat down to our children. The need to move beyond pragmatism to metaphysics arose because a "heuristics of fear" and prudence for our children's sake proved inadequate to the task of grounding a principle of responsibility on behalf of the not-yet-existent who have, Jonas contends, no individual rights. But if Ockham's razor permits us to answer the nihilist without theological commitments, might we also, in this allegedly postmetaphysical time, meet the emergency of our ecological plight without relying on a metaphysics that is the functional equivalent of theology?

I am persuaded by Jonas's extension of existential interpretation to the biological lifeworld; it helps us to acknowledge the continuity and kinship among life-forms and to appreciate what we lose when we cut ourselves off from them and replace nature with artifice. Even without the metaphysical leap to the idea of nature as a good-in-itself, Jonas's critique of dualism lets us "see" differently, and in such a way that we may be moved to act less violently and instrumentally. This monistic revisioning of life opens up new existential choices for us.

Even so, Leon Kass has pointed out a striking omission in Jonas's description of the phenomenon of life.[21] Whereas he pays the closest attention to metabolism as a process inherent in all organisms, Jonas makes virtually no mention of reproduction and its psychic correlates: animal lust and human *eros*. While metabolism permits the individual organism to persist in the face of the ever-present threat of death, the special desire rooted in sexual differentiation aims at generativity and places the animal firmly in a social world. How can Jonas have overlooked a phenomenon so central to life?

A simple explanation is that reproduction and sociality are not essential to an organism's vitality; after all, a solitary and sterile creature is still alive. But animals and humans cannot come into being or develop their specific potentialities outside of a social environment. A better explanation for Jonas's oversight is that he remains too committed to Heideggerian premises. He still focuses on solitary individuals pitted against death, even if, contra Heidegger, he includes nonhuman individuals in his analysis. So Jonas's way of interpreting the biological facts ends up sustaining Heidegger's oblivion to the depths of our social being.

Though this is a telling criticism of the comprehensiveness of Jonas's description of life, I believe that he could accommodate reproduction and sociality within his basic framework. And he does already make room for these phenomena in *The Imperative of Responsibility* in his discussion of the parent-child relationship as the archetype of responsibility. One can imagine an account of human *eros* drawing on this dimension of generativity. So one can see Kass's comments not as a fundamental criticism of Jonas's project, but as a call to expand and supplement his categories.

A potentially more subversive worry concerns the metaphysical level of Jonas's reply to nihilism. I wonder whether we need to turn the purposiveness embedded in nature into an *imperative* in order to establish limits. Correlatively, I wonder whether we need such a weighty *metaphysics*—one which turns the presence of value throughout nature into a *command* proceeding from Being itself to us—in order to ground our responsibility toward future generations.

This worry takes several forms: pedagogical, speculative, and ethical. First, the pedagogical. If a nihilist is not moved to appreciate nature by an existential interpretation of the biological facts combined with his own experience of the world around him, I doubt that there is any hope of convincing him by way of the metaphysical claim that we are the self-realization of nature's purposiveness and are called upon to be her guardian—any more than an atheist can really be converted by the ontological proof of God's existence or an immoralist might be shown the errors of his ways by an argument that persons are, after all, ends-in-themselves. It is not clear to me how or whether the metaphysical arguments that Jonas thinks *need* to be added to his existential interpretations improve the possibilities of moral *education*. I worry that insisting on metaphysical support as being necessary to ground a principle of responsibility may have the negative effect of deflecting attention from the concrete appreciation of nature to abstract argumentation that may be understood only by a few.

The response to this point may well be that metaphysical argument is not meant primarily to convert the unconverted but, like Kant's *Grundlegung*, to articulate the background assumptions that are necessary to support a feeling of responsibility that many feel prereflectively, but run counter to the presuppositions of the official philosophical culture. This leads to my second, speculative point. Jonas claims that an ethics rooted in metaphysics does not *require* theology, though his metaphysics remains *compatible* with the theology laid out in the essays comprising part 2 of this volume. But it remains unclear to me what it can mean to speak of human life as "an event for Being" or "an event of cosmic importance" or as being the outcome of "a creative intention" sanctioning our care *without* there being a conscious perspective outside our own *for* whom our destiny matters. If human life were somehow to be extinguished, would this be a disaster for nature herself? One can hold that it would be a tragedy for *us*, and that we ought to do everything we can to avoid it, without assuming that it would be a subversion of nature's final cause or purpose. The death of our star will eventually occur by nature. In the meantime, the biosphere itself might be better off without us; certainly many species would. Can we concur with Jonas that "purpose is in general indigenous to nature" (*IR*, 74) *without* concluding that *our* way of being purposive is special from a larger perspective than our own?

This raises a third, psychological point. One might wonder, along with all advocates of "the hermeneutics of suspicion," whether the insistence that we be subject to an imperative coming from beyond us lest "things fall apart" is not driven by a psychological need to be at the center, linked to eternity, in order to avoid the bitter truth of our contingency. There is no hint of the terror of nature in Jonas's writing. Though he rejects Hegelian dialectic as a way of understanding human history, he finds a kind of reason at work in cosmic history. It is one thing to say that teleology is a more coherent way of understanding our condition than absurdity. But it is another thing to suppose that unless cosmic teleology is true, there are no grounds for substantive responsibility. There are many thinkers—I have in mind, e.g., the evolutionary biologist Stephen Jay Gould[22]—who reject the idea that nature exhibits an overarching purpose but who surely feel that we are lucky to be alive on Earth and argue forcefully that we ought to respect the delicate natural environment into which we happen to be thrown. Living within a nature that does not care about us or to which we do not make a difference need not be an abyss so long as *we* care: perhaps for its sake as well as ours, but not necessarily because we take ourselves to be special from a cosmic point of view.

Against Jonas's Kantian account of responsibility—which insists that ethics requires a metaphysical good-in-itself sanctioning obligation beyond the web of our natural sentiments—I can imagine a more Humean story that would build on feelings, like most parents have for their children and like field ecologists often have for the niches they come to know, in order to motivate a desire to care about the future habitability of our planet. An empiricist ethic of this sort does not have the systematic force of Jonas's cosmic deontology, but it may be more concrete and generally persuasive.

Finally, a question about the application of Jonas's primary ethical commandment: the duty to perpetuate the existence and essence of human life. What would it mean to undermine our condition in such a fundamental way that our essence had been violated? How do we draw the line between meliorism, which seeks to improve our lot without risking our essence, and utopianism, which would wager "the genuine present" for a "new and improved" humankind? When do proposed improvements violate the legitimate demands of justice, charity, and reason? Few would disagree with Jonas's general commandment. Instead they would plead innocent to the charge of being utopians, and would call themselves meliorists and their critics neo-Luddites. As ecologist Garrett Hardin points out, "Even if the scenario ending in doom is correct, at every point short of the ultimate step, the technological optimist wins out in competition with the technological pessimist."[23] One worries that in spite of Jonas's critique of formalism, his commandment remains as formal as Kant's categorical imperative, and so just as subject to conflicting contents. It would be an unfortunate outcome if the power and glory of Jonas's ontological arguments succeeded in commanding a consensus, while concealing deep disagreements over the fundamental existential and policy choices we face as we approach the twenty-first century. Even if we need an ontological grounding of ethics, there is no shortcut around paying the closest attention to the ontic domain in which real conflicts persist, for this is where each of us will figure out what it means to *live* like a good Jonasian today.

Prologue

Philosophy at the End of the Century: Retrospect and Prospect

I

My task is to speak to you about philosophy in this century and on the threshold of the next. I do not intend to speak here about Philosophy with a capital P, for it is doubtful whether such an identifiable entity exists. Just compare it with the natural sciences: physics, chemistry, astronomy, geology—each has its well-defined *subject matter*, whereas philosophy can deal with anything and everything. Then, too, these sciences of nature all have a clearly recognized *method* that each of them is strictly bound to follow. Philosophy, on the other hand, which is so fond of reflecting on the method of every other science, has yet to produce any binding method of philosophizing and possibly never will.

Above all, however, every branch of natural science can state at any given time what is valid in it and what is forever out of the question in the certainty that the latest findings are also the most correct up to that moment. The past is, at the most, of historical interest. No physicist of today, for example, can rescue "phlogiston" from history's graveyard. But Plato and Aristotle, the Stoics and Epicureans, Hume and Kant, Hegel and Nietzsche offer continual subjects for debate for modern philosophers and can still find adherents among them. Whereas there can no longer be an alchemist or astrologer whom we take seriously, we can still take seriously an Aristotelian or Hegelian. In philosophy we cannot have a

A lecture delivered on 25 May 1992 in the Prinzregenten Theater in Munich as part of the series, "The End of the Century," sponsored by the Directors of the Bavarian State Theater and by the Literatur Handlung in Munich (Frankfurt: Suhrkamp, 1993). This is a slightly amended version of a translation that first appeared in *Social Research* 61 (Winter 1994).

binding consensus about what is true and what is false. We cannot even desire one; it would spell the death of philosophy.

That is why it is impossible to describe the "state" of philosophy at any given time with the same exactitude with which one can describe, for example, the state of physics. It is a partially vexing, partially welcome fact that there are as many philosophies and also as many views of philosophy as there are philosophers. Those who invited me to deliver this lecture were certainly not unaware of this, and they must therefore consent to my painting a very personal and perhaps thoroughly unrepresentative picture of the field of philosophy at the close of this century and of the challenge awaiting it in the one to come.

In any case, what I have to offer is more a contribution to the never-ending discussion of philosophy than a report on its present state—a confession, in the last analysis, of a personal nature. The advantage that I have been "on the scene" for the past seventy years is balanced by the disadvantages that my participation has been selective and that I have kept my distance from some important currents, especially from the powerful one of analytic philosophy. Thus, the picture I present will be historically incomplete, for I shall speak only from the experience of my own thinking. Now to the subject at hand.

II

For philosophy—in its classic homeland of Germany—the century began without the fanfare associated, in the field of physics, with the names of Planck and Einstein. In spite of the significant impact of Husserl's *Logical Investigations*, which began to appear in the year 1900, his work cannot be compared with the work of those physicists. Nietzsche's influence was beginning to be noticeable, Kierkegaard was being discovered, from France the voice of Bergson was heard, and in Vienna logical positivism started to show signs of life. But in the universities the dominant philosophical interest was clearly epistemology. This field was practically identical with "the theory of cognitive consciousness," as set forth, for example, in the several varieties of neo-Kantianism. Deferring to the powerful position of the natural sciences, professors of philosophy had long since given up the attempt to formulate a philosophy of *nature.*

It was not until shortly after the First World War that an earthquake shook the field of philosophy, and here I can speak from my own experience because, by the accident of my year of birth, I found myself in the midst of it. In 1921 when, at the age of eighteen, I went to the University of Freiburg to study philosophy, the leading figure there was the already graying Edmund Husserl. "Phenomenology," which he so passionately preached, was a program of self-examination of consciousness as the site of the appearance of all things possibly present to thought. A "pure" phenomenology of "pure" consciousness was to become the basis of all philosophy. "Pure" of what? Of the adventitious nature of all factual and individual elements, whereby an inner awareness of essences is deemed able to extract that which is valid for all subjects in equal measure. A Platonizing element is unmistakable here, but—what is novel—it is applied to the field of subjectivity. The method, correspondingly, involves observation and description, not causal explanation as in psychology. The main accent rests on those functions of consciousness that constitute objects, that are cognitive and ultimately observing, and, in turn, can also be quite well observed themselves. Husserl was almost religiously convinced that the phenomenology he prescribed had finally made possible "philosophy as a rigorous science" and that he had brought to its culmination a major theoretical trend present in modern philosophy since Descartes.

There is not time to examine this theory more closely, but perhaps the following anecdote I recall hearing is indicative of its spirit. Someone—an outsider—once asked Husserl in person whether phenomenology had anything to say about God. The philosopher is said to have answered, "If we encounter him as a datum in consciousness, then we will certainly describe him." That sounds almost flippant, yet it is a fact that for many people Husserl's phenomenology became a path to God, mainly via Catholicism. I am thinking of Edith Stein and also of Max Scheler.

For myself, I confess gratefully that for the beginning philosopher phenomenology is a wonderful school in which to learn his trade. Respect for phenomena, practice in observing them, the rigorous task of describing them call for high standards one must strive to live up to. Yet even all this could not make philosophy into a "rigorous science"—that was a dream which Husserl brought with him from his early days as a mathematician and for which he had to be excused. But for his students the development of intuition was a lifelong gain; it freed the area of intuition from the aura of irrationality that had clung to it ever since the days of the Mystics. On the other hand, I had my doubts about the adequacy of his theory, especially about its restrictive emphasis on pure consciousness. What about the existence of our *body*, I asked myself. Can we reduce it as well to a "datum of consciousness" without robbing the datum to be described of its real import—namely, that what is at stake is the existence or nonexistence of the subject itself?

It is now my duty as speaker to announce that the theme of "corporeality" is a leitmotif that will sound throughout the remainder of my address; it will accompany us far beyond the special case of phenomenology and will be with us until the end of these remarks. What did the phenomenology of a Husserl have to say about the statement "I am hungry"? Assuming there were a phenomenology of the sensations of hunger and satiety, would it say anything at all to me about what these sensations involve? About *why* human beings must eat? And about *how much*? Biology, along with physics and chemistry, enlightens us about the why, about the inexorable "must." As for how much—good heavens, phenomenology's strictly qualitative awareness of essences cannot even begin to pose questions of a quantitative nature; yet the real, completely empirical size of our bodies has something to do with the answer. And in its turn the answer to "how much" leads to such unphilosophical questions as whether there is enough food and how to obtain it, and these then raise more questions concerning the just and unjust distribution of property as well as good and bad forms of society: here we find ourselves in the very midst of the burning questions of the time, which phenomenology, in keeping with its self-definition, must remain aloof from. Thus, it had nothing to say about the possible truth of Bert Brecht's brash lines written in those same years, "First comes the grub / Then comes morality." In this respect, among our nonphilosophical fellow students, the Marxists—in taking such questions seriously—were ahead of us.

III

But it was not from the Marxists that we nonpolitical disciples of philosophy were to learn that "pure consciousness" is too pure for this world and that "direct awareness" is not the primary modality of our relationship to world and self. The new orientation sprang up in close proximity to phenomenology itself: it was the existential philosophy of Martin Heidegger. The appearance of *Sein und Zeit* (*Being and Time*) in the year 1927 turned out to be that earthquake affecting the philosophy of our century referred to earlier. It shattered the entire quasi-optical model of a primarily *cognitive* consciousness, focusing instead on the willful, striving, feeble, and mortal ego. And this happened not, as one might assume, within the framework of psychology but out of the age-old question, rescued from oblivion, concerning the meaning of "*Sein.*" No one will expect me to give an outline of Heidegger's philosophy here, but something must be said about the experience of the great shift in thinking that it brought with it.

Take, for example, the *language* of *Being and Time*, specifically— even more prominent than its strikingly metaphorical quality—the purely grammatical aspects of its conceptual style. What stands out immediately is the preference for using verbal forms as nouns: "*In-der-Welt-sein*" (being-in-the-world), "*Geworfensein*" (thrownness), "*Miteinandersein*" (being-with-others), "*Zuhandensein*" (being-at-hand), "*Sich-Vorwegsein*" (being-ahead-of-oneself), "*Vorlaufen zum Tode*" (the anticipating of death) . . . In German these are predominantly compounds containing the infinitive *Sein* (to be). The "time" in the book's title becomes "*Zeitlichkeit*" (temporality) and "*Zeitigung*" (temporalization) in the text, and instead of past and future we find "*Gewesenheit*" (pastness) and "*Zukünftigkeit*" (futurity). None of these are terms for objects but for events and for executions of actions: they do not refer to things but to ways of being; the concept of substance disappears, everything is always "in process," so to speak, and what was formerly called the subject is now called "*Dasein*." This extremely general and abstract infinitive becomes the technical designation for being in its specifically *human* forms, indeed for individual concrete persons as they experience themselves from within. Wherever "*Dasein*" occurs in Heidegger, "you" or "I" can be substituted, but always as the agent of a specific kind of being. "*Da-sein*" is also a compound: the "*da*" indicates that this special form of being surrounds itself with a horizon toward which it lives. Thanks to this verbal usage, a singular dynamism, indeed an element of drama, permeates the description of every relationship between ego and world; and the expectation of dynamic circumstances thus awakened by grammatical usage is fulfilled by the concrete imagery with which Heidegger—almost like a poet—describes the attributes of *Dasein*. For instance, "thrown" (or "projected") into the world, *Dasein* "projects" itself into the future.

Passing now from the question of language to that of meaning, let us examine the *definition* of "*Dasein*" with its new significance. To wit: *Dasein* is that form of being which in its being is concerned with this very being. "It is concerned with something": this is certainly no longer the transcendental consciousness met with in idealism. The end-oriented character of all subjectivity takes priority; it is essentially purpose-oriented, and its prime purpose is itself. "For the sake of" dominates all of *Dasein*'s relations with the world. The "intentionality" of consciousness, which in Husserl's case quite neutrally indicates that it has an object, now turns out to be permeated with "interest"; will outweighs awareness, and the world is in practical terms primarily "there" for *Dasein*. Here lies a certain relationship with Anglo-Saxon utilitarianism and pragmatism, a connection that has not gone unnoticed.

But why must *Dasein* always be concerned with something and, in the last analysis, with itself? The answer: because without this concern it would perish, since it is constantly exposed to nothingness. Thus, along with its end-orientation, its overall purposiveness, Heidegger's definition of *Dasein* articulates its precarious and threatened quality: because it is *mortal* it must be concerned with existing as such. And this existing must at every moment be wrested from the constant imminence of death. For this reason the basic mode of *Dasein*'s being is described as "care."

With the positing of care as the primary aspect of *Dasein*'s being we have reached the heart of Heidegger's so-called "existentialism" (he himself did not use this term). It is in the perspective of care that the world can confront us as the quintessence of "at-handness" and the things of this world as potential "stuff" or "equipment," as something that can be of service in the end-means situation. That one's own being is the constant object of care does not mean that it is the only or even the foremost one. Much else that is transitory is encompassed by care: other persons—for example in the mode of "care-for" or "solicitude," perhaps to the point of self-abnegation—and even inanimate things, such as the uncompleted work to which the artist devotes his life. Here too it is a matter of one's own being in the sense that it can find fulfillment in total devotion to other beings.

Obviously, we are now at a threshold leading from an ontology of *Dasein* to the area of ethical conduct. Heidegger never really crosses it in *Being and Time*, nor, as far as I know, does he do so in his later works. To be sure, he does distinguish between "authenticity" and "inauthenticity" of existence, and it is clear that this is a value judgment—that, in other words, there are latent imperatives of "should" and "shouldn't" present in the distinction. But Heidegger left it at that: namely, for him "authentic" and "inauthentic" are simply descriptions of alternative ways of being and of conditions present in every *Dasein*. First of all and most of the time, people do not live as themselves but speak, think, and act as "one" speaks, thinks, and acts; it is only the "anticipating of death," i.e., reflecting on one's own mortality, that awakens in people the resolution to be their own selves, i.e., to exist "authentically." Doubtless this state is superior to trivial "everydayness," but what this resolution favors or opposes is not stated. That it is enveloped by "dread" *is* stated, however, and here as well as elsewhere we find the influence of Kierkegaard, from whom the word "existence" had received a new definition, applicable only to human beings. The foregoing must suffice to recall the gist of *Being and Time*, and this book, his most famous and influential, must stand for all of Heidegger, although the immense scope of his later work progressed beyond it in many respects.

I have two criticisms that trouble me here. The first goes back to one already provoked by the case of Husserl. Heidegger's concept of *Dasein* as "care" and as mortal is certainly more in keeping with our being's subjugation to nature than is Husserl's "pure consciousness." The adjective "mortal" in particular calls attention to the *existence* of the body with all its crass and demanding materiality. And the world can be "at hand" only for a being who possesses hands. But is the body ever mentioned? Is "care" ever traced back to it, to concern about nourishment, for instance—indeed, to *physical* needs at all? Except for its interior aspects, does Heidegger ever mention that side of our nature by means of which, quite externally, we ourselves belong to the world experienced by the senses: that world of which we, in blunt objective terms, are a part? Not that I know of. Somehow German philosophy with its idealistic tradition was too high-minded to take this into account.

Thus, Heidegger too failed to bring the statement "I am hungry" within the purview of philosophy. In the last analysis, it was a very abstract mortality that we were meant to contemplate and that was meant to make us recognize the gravity of existence. By ignoring the concrete basis of *ethics*, Heidegger's interpretation of inwardness denied itself an important means of access to this field; with this lack, ethics for him remained empty of real content. It was crucial for human beings to choose, but *what* choices they should make was not stated.

Behind all of this, however, quite apart from Heidegger's particular case, lay an age-old one-sidedness from which philosophy has suffered: a certain disdain for nature, to which the mind or spirit felt itself superior. This was the heritage of the metaphysical *dualism* that has polarized Western thought since its origins in Platonism and Christianity. Soul and body, mind and matter, the interior life and the external world were, when not hostile, at least alien to each other and could be joined together theoretically only with difficulty. The split went right through the human individual, yet thinkers were in agreement as to which side the individual really belonged on. It was on this side that their gaze was fixed, and it was here that there was a world to be discovered which the eye does not see nor the hand grasp. It is to the long reign of dualism with its one-sided focus that we in the West owe the exploration of the realm of the soul, indeed the enrichment of the soul itself through constant reflection—an invaluable gain, exemplified by names like Augustine and Pascal, but one whose price was high: mutual alienation between two parts of one whole.

Dualism's most recent form had been Descartes's splitting of reality into "extension" and "thought." Extension, expressible in mathematical terms—in other words, the entire material world stripped of all inwardness—was handed over to the nascent natural sciences to become their exclusive domain. This was still philosophy's deed; it thereby renounced, however, its right to express itself any longer on matters pertaining to nature, reserving for itself henceforth only the cultivation of the field of consciousness. It was on this salvaged half of the dualistic heritage that German Idealism blossomed. And ever since, philosophy has no longer concerned itself with the whole. The universe of knowledge was divided by the academic world into the natural sciences and the humanities, and philosophy found itself as a matter of course among the latter—whereas rightfully it should have stood above this division. Thus, when I was a student in Germany, concentrators in philosophy were not required to know anything about developments in the natural sciences. It was not until emigration brought me to the Anglo-Saxon world that I found a lively interest among philosophers in the natural sciences and a desire to integrate their findings into the humane disciplines. (I shall mention here only the name of the great Alfred North Whitehead.) For Heidegger, on the other hand, the natural sciences were, if I am not mistaken, little more than the creators of that soulless technology he deplored.

And yet that baffling *Dasein* of his emerged from the supposedly neutral "at-handness" of the external world that science reveals to us—emerged in the first place in the evolution of the species and then repeatedly in every case of conception and birth. That must say something about objective nature, which causes this—and us—to occur. Nature must be questioned, so to speak, about its intentions concerning us. Heidegger himself, after writing *Being and Time*, deemed necessary such a reversal of the question of Being and called it "the turn." The question is no longer what does "world" mean for *Dasein*, which finds itself in it, but what does *Dasein*, i.e., the human being, mean for the world that contains it—contains you and me. In the one case it is the human being, in the other, Being, which is the focal point of the relationship. But Heidegger never brings this question about Being—how it is, namely, that Being contains and maintains the human and what it thereby reveals about itself—into correlation with the testimony of our physical and biological evolution. Instead of taking into account this massively material basis that after all propounds the riddle, he invokes as our underlying determinant a highly spiritual entity that he calls "*das Seyn*" [the German word for "Being" in an archaic spelling]. Here again, as previously in the case of his overlooking the body, this means simply that the question of Being was spared the tremendous impact of considering the reciprocal relationship between human beings and nature—a relationship which at that very moment was entering a new and critical phase, although this was still unrecognized at the time.

This is the first of my two critical comments on the thinking of my great teacher. My second reservation has to do with Heidegger's conduct in the year 1933. Does that have anything to do with philosophy? In my opinion, yes. Since ancient times philosophy, unlike every other branch of learning, has been guided by the idea that its pursuit shapes not only the knowledge but also the conduct of its disciples, specifically in the service of the Good, which is after all the goal of knowledge. At the very least, philosophy's schooling of its adherents in discriminating among values ought to protect them from being infected by the mass mind. The example of Socrates, which has served as a beacon for philosophy since its beginnings, has kept the belief in such an ennobling force from being extinguished. Therefore, when the most profound thinker of my time fell into step with the thundering march of Hitler's brown battalions, it was not merely a bitter personal disappointment for me but in my eyes a debacle for philosophy. Philosophy itself, not only a man, had declared bankruptcy. Had its nimbus perhaps always been a false one? Would it ever be able to win back some of that splendor we had expected of it? The unique caliber of the philosopher in question made his fall from grace an historic event.

The counterexample I shall now adduce only poses a new question. Among my professors was Julius Ebbinghaus, a strict and uncompromising Kantian, not to be compared with Heidegger in significance. He had passed the test admirably; I learned of this and visited him in Marburg in 1945 to pay him my homage. He looked into my eyes with that old fire of absolute conviction and said: "But do you know what, Jonas? Without Kant I wouldn't have been able to do it." I suddenly realized that here theory and life were one. With which man, then, was philosophy in better hands? With the creative genius whose profundity did not keep him from a breach of faith in the hour of decision *or* with his unoriginal but upright colleague, who remained pure? To this day I do not presume to have the answer to this question, but I believe it belongs—unanswered—in a retrospective look at philosophy in this century.

IV

Just as for many other areas, the Second World War represented a watershed for philosophy. The reality of what had been experienced and the tasks it left behind could not be ignored. From the heaven of eternal thought, contemplation—unnerved—descended to the Earth with its conflicting forces and intervened in the course of affairs. Noble abstention from events of the day was a thing of the past. Politics and society became the dual focus of philosophical interest. Moral engagement permeated theoretical investigation. Belatedly, the voices of Marxist philosophers, long excluded from the universities of the West, finally began to be heard as well. In Germany the major example of this turn to the problems of a frightened and guilt-ridden society was afforded by the Frankfurt School, whose members had returned from exile; their "critical theory" is unimaginable without the ethical component, still present in the thinking of the School's second generation as represented by Habermas and Apel. There were parallel developments in France. Concurrently, to be sure, analytic philosophy with its exclusive emphasis on the theory of knowledge, originally born in Vienna, returned to the continent as a new force along with the Anglo-American victors. Its highly specialized branches are actually separate disciplines and as little touched by events of the day as is mathematics. The most prominent name here is that of Ludwig Wittgenstein.

But among the events of the time was "Hiroshima," and this shock, perpetuated by the immediately following nuclear arms race, was the first trigger for a new and anxiety-ridden rethinking of the role of technology in the Western world. With its help, victory had been attained, but at the cost of the constant danger of collective self-destruction. Thus, the philosophical critique of technology that now began stood initially completely in the shadow of terror (as in the case of Günther Anders), and it was not to lose this apocalyptic aspect. To the fear of a sudden catastrophe was soon added the growing realization of the negative sides of technological triumphs in general, a realization that was accompanied by totally new questions for philosophy. For example, advances in biology and medicine led to a novel cooperation between philosophers and representatives of the life sciences for the purpose of clarifying the questions arising from the new discoveries. There is no longer room here for a simple "yes" or "no" as with the problem of nuclear weapons; instead, we find an area of fluid boundaries, subtle value judgments, and controversial decisions. Nor is there a Manichean struggle here between good and evil; no malevolent will is at work, but rather the will to help. And yet inventive skill in the service of human welfare often turns out to be in conflict with human dignity. Biotechnology in particular has introduced into the realm of morality completely new dilemmas, heightened complications, and refined nuances that philosophy must take account of, although it often has nothing to offer except compromises between conflicting principles.

This brings to light an important aspect of the entire technological syndrome: its previously undreamt-of power, a product of the power of the human mind, confronts this same mind with previously undreamt-of challenges.

This situation is magnified by the impact of contemporary humankind's technology on the natural environment. And indeed, as this phenomenon—namely, the threat we pose to the planet's ecology—became more and more apparent during the second half of this century and finally even came to the attention of philosophers, suddenly one of the oldest philosophical questions, that of the relationship between human being and nature, between mind and matter—in other words, the age-old question of dualism—took on a totally new form. Now this question is no longer something to meditate on in the calm light of theory; it is illuminated by the lightning flashes of an approaching storm, warnings of a crisis that we, its unintentional creators, have the planetary duty of trying to avert. Thanks to this exceedingly practical aspect of the problem, the reconciliation between our presumptuous special status as humans and the universe as a whole, which is the source of our life, is becoming a central concern of philosophy. I see in this an urgent task for philosophy to address, both at the present moment and into the coming century. Because of this urgency, I hope you will permit me to devote the remainder of my remarks to this topic.

V

Clearly, philosophy can undertake its new assignment only in closest cooperation with the natural sciences, for they tell us what that material world is with which our mind is to make a new peace. Let us ask, then: What findings of physics, of cosmology, of biology must philosophy keep in view in trying to determine the status of mind in the total scheme of Being? I shall confine myself to a few summary points.

Since Copernicus, to our knowledge it is no longer the entire cosmos that is the dwelling place of life but solely our planet Earth. Nothing in the remainder of the gigantic universe guarantees that there must be such a dwelling place at all. Therefore, we must regard ourselves and all life around us as a cosmic rarity, a stroke of luck that caused a *potentiality*, hidden in matter's womb and as a rule remaining hidden, to become, as an exception, reality. On the other hand, as Darwin taught us, what had become reality, thanks to the unique favorableness of special planetary conditions, demonstrated its ontological force in an aeons-long process of evolution—changeable, without plan or goal, both creative and destructive—which populated the receptive biosphere with unforseeable forms. In comparison with this earthly drama with its immensely complex creations, all the rest of the discernible universe is primitive and monotonous. But it is the same primeval substance, present throughout the universe in galaxies, suns, and planets, that has also brought forth life, pleasure and pain, desire and fear, seeing and feeling, love and hatred. No mere materialism as formulated by the physicists can ever comprehend this. Yet opposing every form of dualism is the monistic testimony of evolution, which, it seems to me, has not been adequately taken into account by any ontology put forward by philosophers. This cannot be the concern of the physical sciences by themselves, which are dependent solely upon physical data. These data taken by themselves can explain, by means of mere mechanistic causality and without postulating any special vital force or the like, even the subtlest complexity of organic structure and function as well as their phylogenetic development. Which makes even greater, then, the enigma of subjectivity that accompanies advancing levels of physical history and speaks an entirely different language. Natural scientists need to be deaf to this language or, if they do hear it, to accuse it of lying, for it speaks of goals and purposes. But this enigma must give no rest to philosophy, which has to listen to both languages, that of the external and internal worlds, uniting them in one statement about Being that does justice to the psychophysical totality of reality. We are still far distant from this welcome kind of ontology and do not know whether it will ever be our portion. Merely striving for it means venturing forth from the Cartesian certainty of exact knowledge into the uncertainty of metaphysical conjecture. I do not believe that in the long run this can be avoided.

Late in the evolution of life we encounter ourselves—human beings. We appeared on the scene only very recently. In the history of life, our entrance was an event with immense consequences, and it has not yet been determined whether we are equal to them. With us, the power of thought intervened in Earth's further development and severely impaired those biological mechanisms in effect until then that ensured the equilibrium of ecological systems. No longer did organisms with genetically fixed patterns of behavior struggle for their portion of habitat, with the result that each portion remained approximately constant; now the inventive genius of *homo faber*, free and responding to the perceived needs of the moment, dictated—one-sidedly, again and again, more and more rapidly—the conditions of future symbiosis. The span of time from the Paleolithic Age to the era of scientific technology is a long one in human history but very short in evolutionary terms, and since the rise of the modern natural sciences in the seventeenth century the tempo of change has accelerated exponentially. What we are experiencing today is the paradox of excessive success that threatens to turn into a catastrophe by destroying its own foundation in the natural world.

What has philosophy to do with all this? Until now it has posed questions about the good life of the individual, about the good society, about the good state. Since its beginnings, it has always concerned itself with human actions insofar as these occurred between human beings, but scarcely ever with the human individual as an acting force in nature. But now the time for this has come. To address this problem, a new conception of human beings must be developed that takes into account their mind-body unity, thanks to which they are, on the one hand, a part of nature themselves and, on the other, extend beyond it. In this connection let us not deny that the practical use of the mind—i.e., its power over the body—was, from the beginning and for a long time almost exclusively, in the service of the body: to better meet its needs, to attend to them more fully, to satisfy them for longer periods—and constantly to create *new* needs by making them fulfillable. In serving the body, the human mind wreaks havoc on nature. And in so doing, it increasingly adds to our needs and desires, more dignified than those of the body but possessing an appetite equally as ravenous for the Earth's resources. This is evidenced by the physical prodigality of advanced cultures, which only increases the impact of an already excessively large population upon the shrinking resources of the natural world. Indeed, the mind has made the human being into the most gluttonous of all creatures and this to such a degree that today the entire species is driven to live from the environment's unrenewable capital rather than from its income.

Knowledge about this situation is as new as the situation itself. But the knower here is that same mind which caused the situation in the first place. Thus, the future has not yet been decided. We say this in spite of the disturbingly questionable character of the human mind's present ascendancy. A few remarks about this state of affairs:

As we awake from a hundred years of technology's blithe plundering of the planet and its triumphant celebration of its successes, its utopian dreams of happiness for the entire human race, we are discovering a previously unsuspected tragedy in the gift of the sixth day of creation as reported in Genesis: the granting of self-consciousness and intellect to a creature of physical needs and drives. Nobility and doom join hands in the human intellect, which taken by itself raises the human being into the realm of metaphysics but becomes, in its practical application, the instrument of extremely brutal biological success. In itself the mind represents the fulfillment of human destiny; around itself it spreads destruction. With it we reach the peak of Being's self-affirmation, which became discernible with the first stirrings of a feeling and mortal life, and now it is undermining the foundation that sustains it. At the height of its triumph the mind is placing the species endowed with it before an abyss. But the very fact that it is beginning to see this abyss offers the glimmer of a chance of preventing the plunge over the edge. For the mind, which recognizes itself here as the source of doom, is after all not merely an instrument for attaining power over material objects but also has its own characteristic motivations arising from its perception of values. It forms the concepts of the good, of duty, and of guilt. It prides itself on its freedom of choice and thereby declares itself responsible for its actions. And since these actions now threaten the entire planet, the mind is also capable of recognizing its responsibility for the planet's survival.

It has become one of philosophy's tasks to reinforce this recognition and develop it further. First of all in the role of gadfly, with which Socrates compared his function as philosopher: we cannot keep silent a moment longer about these problems, and we must continually seek to awaken people's consciences. Next, we must work on the idea of a *peace pact* between mind and nature, for the sake of which arrogant humans must renounce much of that to which habit appears to entitle them. In addition to this must come the, properly speaking, philosophical effort to provide as rational a basis as possible for the imperative of responsibility within a comprehensive ontology, and to make the absoluteness of this imperative as convincing as the enigma of creation will permit.

The actual articles of a possible peace pact itself can be worked out only by practical experts—in other words, not by philosophers. All the sciences concerning nature and human beings, concerning economics, politics, and society, must cooperate in drafting a planetary assessment of condition, along with suggestions for arriving at a budget balanced between human beings and nature. Whether so much as a theoretical agreement is attainable I do not know, and even less do I know whether one with the best possible practical grounding has a chance of being translated into action. Perhaps it will not be a matter of planning at all but of improvisations which the escalating emergency will cause humanity's inventive genius to devise from occasion to occasion. I do not know—and probably no one does. Only the great *imperative* is overwhelmingly clear to me along with the fact that the human mind alone, the great creator of the danger, can be the potential rescuer from it. No rescuer god will relieve it of this duty, which its position in the order of things places upon it.

From the abyss that is now becoming visible there arise questions we have scarcely ever asked before. Here, in conclusion, a sampling of them. Can nature continue to tolerate the human mind, which it created from its own substance? Must it eliminate the human mind because it finds that mind too destructive of the natural order? Or can the mind ultimately make itself tolerable for nature once it has become aware that it is intolerable? Is peace possible when war was the primeval law governing the relationship between the two? Or was tragedy perhaps the original purpose behind the birth of mind? Is the drama, in spite of its tragic ending, worth performing for the sake of the unfolding of the plot? And how can we make the drama worthwhile in itself, regardless of the ending? How much of its worthwhileness can we sacrifice in order to attempt to avert catastrophe? Is it permissible for us to be inhumane so that humans can continue to live on Earth? And so on.

All of these are questions of the type Wittgenstein forbade us to ask, since there can be no verifiable answers to them. But they help us to recognize the existing situation, which forces these questions upon us, and to see that it is ourselves to whom these questions are addressed. And here we discover that what lies at the heart of these questions is not metaphysical brooding (which undoubtedly has its own justification) but an anguished sense of responsibility for this threatening state of affairs. It is that sense of responsibility which will give rise to answers involving action where there are none involving knowledge. And so the shudder of horror evoked by the last question I raised—that of dehumanization for the sake of saving humankind—can reinforce philosophy in its role as guardian of those basic values we cannot live without, even though it must simultaneously become the advocate of our living without much of value that we have become accustomed to.

In rethinking the concept of responsibility and of its extension— never conceived of before—to the behavior of our whole species toward the whole of nature, philosophy will be taking a first step in the direction of assuming this responsibility. As I take my leave now, it is my wish for philosophy that it persevere in this endeavor, undeterred by all reasonable doubt as to whether it will meet with success. The coming century has a right to this perseverance.

Translated by Hunter and Hildegarde Hannum

THE NEED OF REASON: GROUNDING AN IMPERATIVE OF RESPONSIBILITY IN THE PHENOMENON OF LIFE

1

Evolution and Freedom: On the Continuity among Life-Forms

I

Our Western philosophical tradition, with its gaze fixed on the human subject alone, customarily attributes to him as a unique distinction much of what is actually rooted in organic existence as such. Philosophy thereby refuses to allow those insights afforded by human self-perception to shed light on our understanding of the organic world. For its part, the science of biology—being limited by its methods to external physical facts—must ignore the dimension of inwardness that is a part of life. In so doing, it leaves material life, which it claims to have totally explained, more mysterious than when it was unexplained. The two approaches, philosophy and science, unnaturally separated since Descartes, are in fact complementary and play into each other's hands—to the detriment of their objects, which are shortchanged as a result. Our understanding of man suffers from the separation just as much as our understanding of nonhuman life. A new philosophical reading of the biological text may be able to reclaim the inner dimension—the one most familiar to us—to help us understand organic entities and thus restore life's psychophysical unity to its place in the theoretical totality, lost on account of the divorce of the mental and the material since the time of Descartes. The resulting gain for our understanding of the organic realm will then also be a gain for our understanding of the human realm.

First published as "Evolution und Freiheit" in *Scheidewege* 13 (1983–84).

The great contradictions that man discovers in himself—freedom and necessity, autonomy and dependence, ego and world, connectedness and isolation, creativity and mortality—are present *in nuce* in life's most primitive forms, each of which maintains a perilous balance between being and nonbeing and from the very beginning harbors within itself an inner horizon of "transcendence." This theme, common to all life, can be traced in its development through the ascending order of organic capabilities and functions: metabolism, motility and appetite, feeling and perception, imagination, art, and thinking—a progressive scale of freedom and danger, reaching its pinnacle in man, who can perhaps understand his uniqueness in a new way if he no longer regards himself in metaphysical isolation.

Independently of the findings of research on evolution, the simultaneous diversity of forms of life, especially of animal life, presents itself as an ascending sequence stretching from "primitive" to "developed"; on this scale, complication of form and differentiation of function, acuteness of senses and intensity of drives, control of limbs and capability of action, reflection and the search for truth all have their place. We can interpret this progression in two ways: in terms of the concepts of perception and of action (in other words, of "knowledge" and of "power"). As for "knowledge," we see development in the breadth and clarity of experience and in increasing degrees of sensuous world-awareness, which lead via the animal realm to the most comprehensive and freest objectification of the totality of Being, found in man. As for "power," parallel to "knowledge" and similarly reaching its pinnacle in man, we witness growth in the extent and manner of impact on the world—in other words, progressive degrees of freedom of action. In terms of organic functions these two sides are represented by perception and motility. The reciprocal relationship and interplay of both concepts are a constant theme in the empathic study of animal existence.

In the preceding paragraph the concept of "freedom" appeared in connection with both perception and action. One expects to encounter this concept in the realm of the mind and the will, but not before; we, however, go so far as to maintain that *metabolism,* the basic substratum of all organic existence, already displays freedom—indeed, that it is the first form freedom takes. This must sound strange to most people, for what could have less to do with freedom than the blind automatism of chemical processes within our body? Nevertheless, I shall attempt to demonstrate that in the dark stirrings of primordial organic substance a principle of freedom comes to light for the first time within the vast necessity of the physical universe. This is a principle alien to the myriad suns, planets, and atoms. Clearly, the concept must first of all be divorced from all mental connotations if it is to be made such a comprehensive principle: "freedom" must designate an objectively discernible modality of being, i.e., a manner of existing that typifies the organic realm per se and to that extent is common to all members (but to no nonmembers) of the class "organism." It must be an ontologically descriptive concept that can apply to mere physical evidence at first. The primitive objects described by this concept, however, form the ontological basis for those higher phenomena that more directly deserve the name of "freedom"; and even the highest of these remain bound to humble beginnings in the organic substratum, which represent the conditions of their possibility. Thus, this first appearance of the principle of freedom in its naked and elementary object-form signifies Being's breakthrough into an unlimited realm of possibilities extending into the farthest reaches of subjective life and subsumed in its entirety under the rubric of "freedom."

Understood in this fundamental sense, the concept of *freedom* can serve as an Ariadne's thread for the interpretation of what we call "life." The origin of the universe remains a mystery to us. But once we find ourselves in the area of life itself, we are no longer dependent on hypotheses. Here the concept of freedom is appropriate from the very beginning and is necessary for the ontological description of life's most elementary dynamics.

II

The path leading upward from this beginning is not, however, a simple success story. The privilege of freedom carries with it the burden of need and entails endangered existence. For this privilege depends upon the paradoxical fact that living substance, by a primordial act of separation, detached itself from the overall integration of things within the totality of nature, positioned itself vis-à-vis the world, and thus introduced the opposition between "being" and "nonbeing" into the indifferent assuredness of existence. Living substance accomplished this by assuming a relationship of precarious independence vis-à-vis that same matter which is indispensable for its existence, and by distinguishing its own identity from that of its temporary material basis, which it shares with the entire physical world. With this dual aspect of metabolism—its power and its need—*nonbeing* entered the world as an alternative contained within being itself. Only then did "to be" take on an emphatic meaning: intrinsically qualified by the threat of its negation, being must now assert itself. And existence affirmed is existence as a concern. Therefore, being itself became, instead of a given state, a constant possibility, always to be wrested anew from its ever-present opposite, nonbeing, which inevitably devours it in the end.

Being, thus suspended in possibility, is characterized through and through by *polarity*. Life always manifests this polarity in basic antitheses between which its existence is located: being and nonbeing, self and world, form and matter, freedom and necessity. Of all these polarities, the one between being and nonbeing is the most fundamental. Identity is wrested from it in an extreme and unceasing effort to postpone an end that is inevitable. For nonbeing has generality, or the sameness of all things, on its side. The defiance that the organism shows it must ultimately end in compliance; selfhood eventually vanishes, never to return in the same form. That life is mortal is, to be sure, its basic contradiction, but one that belongs inseparably to its nature, for life cannot even be imagined without it. Life is mortal, not although but *because* it is life, in keeping with its primal constitution, for the relationship between form and matter that characterizes it is of this revocable, unassured nature. Its reality, in continual contradiction to mechanical nature, is at bottom an ongoing crisis, whose resolution is never permanent.

The enormous price of anxiety, which life had to pay from the beginning and which steadily mounted with life's ascent to more ambitious forms, keeps alive the question of the meaning of this hazardous venture. When man asks the question, as bold in its way as was that primal form-seeking substance at the dawn of life, he is simply giving voice, after aeons of mute insistence, to life's original problematic nature.

As to the epistemological position underlying this discussion as well as all that follows, just this comment: it admits to the much-scorned offense of *anthropomorphism*.[1] And this after four centuries of the modern natural sciences! Yet perhaps, in a properly understood sense, man *is* the measure of all things—not, of course, by virtue of laws promulgated by his reason but by the paradigm of his psychophysical wholeness, which reveals the maximum degree of concrete ontological completeness known to us. *From this pinnacle downwards*, the classes of being would then be described in terms of privation, by progressive subtraction down to the minimum of mere elementary matter. In other words, instead of the higher forms of life being reduced to the lowest, beings would be characterized in terms of "a less and less," an ever more distant "not yet." Ultimately, the deterministic nature of lifeless matter would be interpreted as sleeping, not yet awakened freedom.[2]

I would like to mention one point in defense of the "anthropomorphism" just confessed to. The theory of evolution signals the final victory of monism over all earlier forms of dualism, including the Cartesian variety. Yet the very completeness of this victory robbed the monistic, i.e., materialistic, enterprise of the protection that dualism was able to afford it for a time. For evolution destroyed man's special status, which had allowed for the Cartesian, purely physical treatment of the rest of the universe. The *continuity* of descent linking man with the animal world made it henceforth impossible to regard his mind, and mental phenomena in general, as the abrupt intrusion of an ontologically alien principle in the total stream of life. Man's isolation, the last citadel of dualism, disappeared, and he could once again use his knowledge of himself to interpret the totality of which he was a part. For if it was no longer possible to regard his mind as discontinuous with the prehuman history of life, then it was also no longer justified to deny the presence of mind in proportional degrees in his closer or more distant ancestors and therefore in *any* stage of animal life. The evidence of common sense once again came into its own as a result of advanced theory—to be sure, in opposition to the theory's own tenor.

In this manner, Darwinism undermined the Cartesian structure more effectively than any metaphysical criticism had been able to do. The affront to human dignity posed by the theory of man's descent from animals provoked outrage, but this reaction overlooked the fact that the same principle restored a degree of dignity to the phenomenon of life as a whole. If man is related to the animals, then the animals are also related to man and therefore, in degrees, possess that inwardness which man, their most highly advanced relative, is aware of in himself. After the contraction brought about by Christian belief in transcendence and by Cartesian dualism, the realm of the "soul"—with its attributes of feeling, striving, suffering, enjoying—was extended anew in a gradation from man throughout the whole realm of life. Thanks to evolutionary theory, the principle of qualitative continuity, which permits infinite gradations of obscurity and clarity of "perception," became a logical complement to the scientific genealogy of life. At which point, then, in the enormous spectrum of life are we justified in drawing a line, attributing a "zero" of inwardness to the far side and an initial "one" to the side nearer to us? Where else but at the very beginning of life can the beginning of inwardness be located? But if inwardness is coextensive with life, then a purely mechanistic interpretation of life, framed in external terms alone, cannot be sufficient.

III

Thus, it came about that at the very moment when materialism won a total victory, the actual means of achieving this victory, "evolution," burst the boundaries of materialism because of its own inner logic. The idea of evolution raised the ontological question anew, just when it appeared to be resolved. Let us consider this question in the form of a thought-experiment in which we place ourselves in the position of Laplace's hypothetical Divine Mathematician, who, at an arbitrary instant of time, has all the simultaneous particles of the material world before his analytic gaze and integrates all their manifold vectors into a world equation. Let us attempt to see with his eyes when his gaze rests by chance on an organism. What would we "see"?[3]

As a complex physical body (which even bacteria are), the organism would exhibit the same general features as other aggregates. But in and around it, special processes would be observable that make its phenomenal unity more questionable than that of ordinary bodies and almost completely undo its material identity in the course of time. I am speaking of its *metabolism*, its exchange of matter with the environment. In this remarkable process of being, the material parts of which the organism consists at a given moment are for the analytic observer only temporary contents, whose own identity does not coincide with the identity of the whole they pass through. On the other hand, this whole maintains *its* identity by means of foreign material passing through its spatial system, its living form. It is never materially the same, and yet it persists as this identical self by the very fact that it does not remain the same matter. If ever any two of its "slices of time" do become identical with each other, then it has ceased to live: it is dead.

We must keep in mind the all-pervasiveness of metabolism within the living system. The image of "input" and "output" does not capture the radical nature of this fact. In the case of a motor we have input of fuel and output of waste products, but the motor parts through which the fuel passes do not themselves participate in the process. Thus, the machine remains a self-identical inert system as opposed to the changing identity of the matter "feeding" it, and it exists as the same entity if feeding is omitted; it is then the same machine at a standstill. In contrast to this, when we designate a living body as a "metabolizing system," we must take into account that the system itself is totally and constantly the result of its metabolic activity and, further, that no part of the "result" ceases to be the object of metabolism while simultaneously carrying out the process. For that reason alone it is wrong to compare an organism to a machine.[4]

Can the living body perhaps be compared, then, to the movement of waves in a medium of matter such as the surface of water? The oscillating units, which make up the water's successive forward motion, perform their movements singly, and each participates only momentarily in the composition of the individual wave, which nevertheless, as the comprehensive form of the radiating disturbance, has its own well-defined unity, its own history, and its own laws. And this transcending form—an event structure—is of a different order from that of a crystal structure, where the form is an inseparable part of the persisting material. Is something similar perhaps true for the temporal continuity of form in those entities *we* know as "organisms"? Here too the analysis of Laplace's Divine Mathematician, unclouded by the merging summations of the senses, must ultimately be directed to those transient elements, which, in their own permanence, alone offer the immediate identities for the mechanical construction of the compound and alone remain as the residues of its analysis. The life process will then present itself as a series of events on the part of these persisting units of general substance: *they* are the real agents, moving—each for causal reasons of their own—through given configurations. *One* such configuration would then be the organism. Just as the wave is nothing but the morphological sum of the successive entry of new units into the total movement, which thanks to it moves forward, so too the organism could be regarded as an integral function of metabolism instead of metabolism being seen as a function of the organism. And all the features of a self-related autonomous entity will ultimately appear as merely phenomenal, i.e., fictitious.

Would we, as is usually the case, grant that this result of strictly physical analysis is *truer* than our naively sensuous view of the object? Definitely not, in this case. And here we are on firm ground, for, being living bodies ourselves, we happen to have inside knowledge. On the strength of the direct witness of our body we can say what no disembodied observer would be capable of saying: that the Divine Mathematician, with his homogeneous analytical view, misses the decisive point—the point of life itself: namely, that life is self-centered individuality, existing for itself and distinct from all the rest of the world, with an essential boundary between "inside" and "outside," in spite of—even on the basis of—the actual exchange that takes place between the two. For every other aggregate form it may be that the visible unity, which makes it appear as a whole, is nothing other than the product of our sensuous perception and thus does not have ontological but purely phenomenological status. But then in living things nature presents us with an ontological surprise. The accident of terrestrial conditions brings about an entirely new possibility of being: systems of matter that are unities of a manifold, not as a result of a synthesizing perception whose object they happen to be, nor by the mere concurrence of forces binding their parts together, but by virtue of themselves, for the sake of themselves, and continually sustained by themselves. Here, wholeness is actively self-integrating; form is not the result but the cause of the material collections in which it successively exists. Here, unity is self-unifying by means of ever-changing multiplicity. Sameness is continual self-renewal through process, borne on the stream of continual otherness. It is this active self-integration of life that first provides the ontological, as opposed to the merely phenomenological, concept of the individual or subject.

IV

This ontological individual, its existence at each moment, its duration and its sameness in duration, are thus essentially its own function, its own concern, its own constant achievement.[5] In this process of self-sustaining being, the relationship of the organism to its own material substance is of a twofold nature: dependent on the availability of this substance, the organism is nonetheless independent of matter's particular identity. Its own functional identity does not coincide with the substantial identity of its material components, which nevertheless constitute it completely at any given moment. In a word, the organic form stands in a dialectical relationship of *needful freedom* to matter. The usual ontological relationship is reversed: priority of matter gives way to priority of form—but only, to be sure, at the cost of simultaneous dependence. For here too the specific concrete unity of matter and form exists naturally, namely in the coincidence of form with the material basis of every moment. But whereas in lifeless matter the temporal moment of a material totality— every temporal moment—reflects this totality completely and can be replaced equivalently by any other, the temporal moment of an organism, no matter how complete in terms of matter, reflects everything except its essential character, which is life, whose form is to be found only across time and in its functional wholeness. Time, not simultaneous space, is the medium of the formal totality of the living, and its temporality is not the indifferent separation which time is for the movements of matter and for the sequence of its conditions but the qualitative mode of presentation of the life-form itself.

    Self-identity, then, which in dead beings is a merely logical attribute and nothing more than a tautology, is in the case of living beings an ontologically meaningful characteristic, one that is constantly being *achieved*. The *basic freedom* of the organism consists accordingly in a certain independence of form vis-à-vis matter. Its appearance at life's beginnings signifies an ontological revolution in the history of "matter." The development and increase of this independence or freedom constitutes the principle of all progress in the evolution of life, which in its course gives birth to new revolutions, each one a further step in the direction already taken, i.e., the opening up of a new horizon of freedom. The first step was the emancipation of form, by means of metabolism, from immediate identity with matter. At the same time this means emancipation from the fixed, empty self-identity characteristic of matter in favor of a different, mediate, and functional kind of identity. What is the nature of this identity?

A particle of matter, identifiable in its space-time position, is simply what it is, without any action on its part; it is immediately identical with itself and without the need to assert this self-identity as an act of its existence. The self-identity of its moment in time is the empty logical one of A = A; that of its successive moments or duration is an empty remaining, not a reaffirmation. Its uninterruptedly traceable "path" in the space-time continuum is the only criterion here of sameness in duration, and since there is no trace of its existence being *threatened*, we have no grounds beyond this external finding to confer any conative inwardness on its persistence.

Organic identity, on the other hand, has to be of an entirely different kind. In the precarious, metabolic continuity of organic form, with its constant turnover of constituent parts, there is no persisting substratum— no individual "path" or "bundle" of paths—available as a pole of reference for external identity. An *inner* identity of the whole, transcending the collective identity of any particular appearing and disappearing substratum, must span the ever-changing succession. Such internal identity is implicit in the adventure of form and is spontaneously inferred from its external morphological evidence, which is all that is accessible to observation. What kind of inference is this? And who makes it? How can the unprepared observer deduce what no mere analysis of physical findings will ever reveal? Indeed, the unprepared observer cannot do so: the observer of life must be prepared by life itself. In other words, organic existence, with the experience it brings, is required of the observer so that he may be able to make that "induction," which he constantly makes de facto. This is the advantage—so stubbornly denied or maligned in the history of epistemology—of our having a *body*, i.e., of being a body. In brief, we *are* prepared by what we are. Only by means of this interpolation of internal identity can the mere morphological (and as such meaningless) *fact* of metabolic continuity be understood as an unceasing *act*; i.e., can continuity be understood as self-continuation.

V

The introduction of the concept of "self," unavoidable when describing even the most elementary instance of life, signifies that, with life as such, *inner* identity entered the world—and, consequently, its self-isolation from the rest of reality. Radical singularity and heterogeneity within a universe of homogeneously interrelated beings characterize the organism's selfhood. An identity that creates itself from moment to moment and continually reasserts itself, defying the leveling forces of physical sameness around it, is basically pitted against everything else. In the perilous polarization that emerging life takes upon itself, that which is not it and which borders from without on the area of its internal identity immediately takes on the character of absolute otherness. The challenge of selfhood qualifies everything beyond the boundaries of the organism as foreign and somehow oppositional: as "world"—in which, through which, and against which it must preserve itself. Without this universal opposition of otherness there could be no selfhood. And in this polarity of self and world, of inner and outer, which complements the polarity of form and matter, the underlying condition of *freedom* is potentially established, with all its daring and difficulties. Let us describe this underlying condition somewhat before we move on to its higher manifestations in evolution.

To begin with, a word about the thoroughly *dialectical* nature of organic freedom, about the fact that it is balanced by a correlative *necessity* that adheres to it as inseparably as its own shadow and recurs as its intensified shadow at each stage of its ascent to higher degrees of independence. We already encounter this double aspect on organic freedom's primary level, that of metabolism, which on the one hand indicates an *ability* of organic form—namely, to alter its matter—but at the same time the unremitting *necessity* for it to do this. Its "can" is a "must," since this activity is identical with its being. "Can" becomes "must" since it is a question of being, and being is what all life is about. Metabolism—the organism's distinguishing capability, which gives it its sovereign position in the world of matter—is therefore at the same time its inescapable duty. Possessing this ability, the organism must activate it in order to be, and it cannot cease doing so without ceasing to be: a freedom to do, but not a freedom to fail to do. This state of neediness, so foreign to the self-sufficiency of mere matter, is no less a unique distinction of life than is its power, of which neediness is only the reverse side. Being's freedom is itself Being's peculiar necessity. This is the antinomy of the freedom that exists at life's very roots and in its most elementary form, that of metabolism.

A second observation immediately follows. In order to alter matter, living form must have matter at its disposal, which it finds outside itself in the alien "world." Life is thereby turned toward the world in a special relationship of dependence and capability. Its need reaches out to where the means of satisfying it lie. Its self-concern, active in acquiring new matter, is essentially openness for encountering external reality. In its need dependent on the world, it is turned toward the world; turned toward it (open to it), life is related to the world; in this relationship it is ready for encounter; in its readiness for encounter, it is capable of experience; in its active self-concern, primarily apparent in its active acquisition of matter, it continually brings about encounter and actualizes the possibility of experience; experiencing, it "has world." Thus, "world" is there from the very beginning: a horizon opened up by the transcendence of need, which breaks the isolation of inner identity to embrace a circumference of vital relationship. In other words, life's self-transcendence consists in having a world in which it must reach beyond itself and expand its being within a horizon. This self-transcendence is rooted in an organic need for matter, and this need is based in turn on its formal freedom from matter. In its ability to sustain a relationship with the world, i.e., in its behavior, this freedom takes control of its own necessity.

Third, this transcendence includes *inwardness* or *subjectivity*, imbuing all encounters occurring within its horizon with the quality of felt selfhood, no matter how faint its voice. It must be there in order for satisfaction or frustration to make a difference. Whether we give this inwardness the name of feeling, receptiveness or response to stimuli, volition, or something else—it harbors, in some degree of "awareness," the absolute interest of the organism in its own being and continuation. That is, the organism is "egocentric," and yet its self-concern bridges the qualitative break with the rest of things by modes of selective *relationship*. With their specific nature and their urgency for the organism, these modes of relationship replace the general integration of material objects into their physical environment. But this open horizon signifies both the state of being affected and spontaneity, outward *exposure* no less than outward *reach*. Only by being sensitive can life be active. In being affected by what is foreign, that which is affected feels itself; its selfhood is aroused and, as it were, illuminated in opposition to the otherness of what is outside, thereby setting itself off in its isolation. At the same time, however, beyond and through this inner, self-related state of excitation, the *presence* of the affecting agent is felt, its message of otherness incorporated within. With the first glimmer of subjective stimulation, with the most rudimentary experience of contact, a crack appears in the opacity of divided being, unlocking a dimension in which things take on a new and manifold existence qua objects. This is the dimension of *interpretive* inwardness. Self-transcendence is, to be sure, based on organic need and thus is one with the drive toward activity: it is movement toward the outside. But perceptual receptivity for what comes from outside, the passive side of this same transcendence, enables life to be selective and "informed" instead of being mere blind dynamism. Therefore, inner identity, by being open to what is outside, becomes the subject-pole of a communication with things which is more intimate than that between merely physical units. In this way the exact opposite of isolation emerges from the isolation of the organic subject.

And a final remark: when we refer to the "transcendence" of life, we mean that it has a horizon beyond its discrete identity. So far we have considered the horizon of the environment along with the presence of things or the extension of relations into simultaneous *space*. But self-concern, driven by need, likewise opens up a horizon of *time*, which encompasses inner imminence instead of outer presence: the imminence of that immediate future toward which organic continuity moves at every moment in order to satisfy that moment's want. Life thus faces forward as well as outward; just as its Here extends into There, its Now extends into Not Yet, and life exists "beyond" its own immediacy in both horizons at once. Indeed, it faces outward only because it faces forward due to the necessity of its freedom, with the result that spatial presence is illuminated, so to speak, by temporal imminence. Both then merge into either fulfillment or its opposite, disappointment. Here the element of transcendence we discerned in the primitive forms of metabolizing existence has found fuller articulation.

VI

Only with the appearance of animal life do the characteristics described above as basic to organic existence emerge fully into light.[6] Three traits distinguish animal from plant life: freedom of movement, perception, and feeling. All three abilities are the expression of one underlying principle.

The simultaneous emergence of *perception* and *movement* opens a significant chapter in the history of freedom, which began with organic existence as such and first manifested itself in the primeval restlessness of metabolizing substance. The progressive development of these two abilities within evolution signifies the increasing disclosure of world and the increasing individuation of self. Openness toward the world is basic to all life. Its elementary manifestation is the irritability, the sensitivity to stimuli, displayed by the simple cell.

True relatedness-to-world arises, however, only with the development of specific senses, defined motor structures, and a central nervous system. The differentiation of sentience, in alliance with the central integration of its manifold data, provides the beginnings of a true object-world. Active dealings with this world by the use of motility subject the world as perceived by the senses to the self-assertion of freedom, which thus responds on a higher plane to the fundamental necessity of the organism. It is the main characteristic of *animal* evolution as distinguished from plant life that *space*, as the dimension of dependence, is progressively transformed into a dimension of freedom, specifically by the parallel development of the following two abilities: to move about and to perceive at a distance. Indeed, only by means of these abilities is space truly opened up to life. Similarly, the other dimension of "transcendence," *time*, is opened up by the parallel development of a third ability, namely emotion, according to the same principle: that of the "distance" between self and its object, except that here the distance is a temporal one. Let us try to demonstrate the indissoluble interconnection among these three animal abilities, particularly the link between movement and emotion, and to interpret its meaning in the larger framework of a general theory of life.

An animal's movement from place to place is directed toward or away from an object, i.e., it is either pursuit or flight. Extended pursuit, when the animal matches its powers of movement against those of its intended prey, betrays not only developed motor and sensory faculties but also articulated powers of feeling. The span between start and capture represented by this series of actions must be bridged by continual emotional intent. The appearance of directed mobility over long distances (as shown by vertebrates) thus indicates the emergence of emotional life. Desire is at the root of the chase, fear at the root of flight. If appetite spurred on by need is the basic precondition for motility, then pursuit (i.e., advancement toward an object) is the primary movement. This movement is the first sign of the difference between animal and plant: the placing of *distance* between drive and fulfillment, i.e., the possibility of reaching a distant goal. Perception of distance is required in order to discern such a goal; consequently, the development of the senses is involved, and controlled continuous movement is required to attain the goal. Therefore, the development of motility is involved, too.

But in order to experience what is perceived at a distance *as* goal and to keep its goal-quality alive so that the movement needed for the span of effort and time is sustained, appetite is required, and this involves the development of feeling. Fulfillment not yet at hand is the essential precondition for appetite, which for its part makes deferred fulfillment possible. For appetite represents the temporal aspect of that same situation of which perception represents the spatial one. In both cases distance is revealed as well as bridged: perception presents the object as "not here but over there"; appetite presents the goal as "not yet but to be expected." Motility, steered by perception and driven by appetite, transforms *there* into *here* and *not yet* into *now*. Without the tension caused by distance and the delay it imposes, there would be no reason at all for appetite or emotion. The great secret of animal life lies precisely in the interval it can tolerate between its immediate intent and its mediate satisfaction, i.e., in the loss of immediacy, which corresponds to a gain in scope.

Sentience, feeling, and motility are different manifestations of the *principle of mediacy*—in other words, of the essential "distancing nature" of animal existence. If feeling implies distance between need and its satisfaction, then it is based on the original separation between subject and object, thereby paralleling the situation of perception and motility, which likewise implies the element of distance. "Distance" in all these cases involves the subject-object split. This split is at the root of the entire phenomenon of animality and of its divergence from the vegetative form of life.

Let us now try to understand the nature of this divergence. The evolutionary precondition is an environment contiguous with the organism: an environment with which the chemical exchanges of metabolism take place directly. This situation permits constancy of the exchange process and thereby direct satisfaction of the organism's continual need. In this state of continuous nourishment there is no room for appetite. Environment and self still make up an independently functioning coherent unity; not until a split between the two occurs can desire and fear arise. Life itself produces this split, and with it evolve the ability and necessity to relate to an environment no longer adjoining it and no longer directly available for its metabolic needs.

Through its ability to synthesize inorganic material directly into organic compounds, the plant is capable of drawing its nourishment from the soil's ever-available mineral supply, whereas the animal is dependent upon the unguaranteed presence of highly specific organic bodies that are not always available. But this very capability of direct synthesis enjoyed by plants is the reason for the absence of all those other features that animals were forced to develop via their more precarious form of metabolism. In order to survive, the animal must always close an interval that does not exist for the plant. This ability is the source of its greater yet more perilous freedom.

The closing of the "interval" in space and time takes place by means of the uniquely animal phenomenon of mediate activity, i.e., of *action* separate from its purpose. Typical plant activity is part of the metabolic process itself. In the movements of animals, on the other hand, activity is fueled by the surplus left over from earlier metabolism and is intended to ensure its continuation in the future. This activity diverges from the ongoing vegetative one and is freely expended. It is therefore "activity" in a completely new sense: external action, which is superimposed on the inner action of the vegetative system and parasitic on it. Only the results of this activity are intended to ensure the continuation of those primary functions.

This mediacy of vital action by means of external movement is the distinguishing feature of animal life. The arc of its *detour* is the seat of the freedom and risk of animal life. Outer-directed movement is an expenditure that is repaid only through ultimate success. But this success is not assured. In order for external activity, which has the reserves of the nutritive system at its disposal, to have a possibility of success, it must also be able to fail. The possibility of error or failure is correlative with that of success under the conditions of mediate action.

The mediacy of animal existence lies at the root of motility, perception, and feeling. It creates the isolated individual pitted against the world, a world simultaneously inviting and threatening, containing those things needed by the solitary animal, which must set out and seek them. It contains as well objects of fear, which the animal must flee. Survival becomes a matter of performing discrete actions; it is not assured by organic functioning, but requires alertness and effort, whereas plant life can slumber on. The animal may know the satisfaction of fulfillment or the distress of failure, and a susceptibility to suffering is not a defect detracting from the faculty for enjoyment but is its necessary complement. Animal existence is essentially passionate existence.

VII

Measured in terms of mere biological security, the advantages of animal as opposed to plant life are highly questionable and in every case dearly bought. But survival alone is an inadequate measure for the evaluation of life. If it had been only a question of ensuring duration, life ought not to have begun at all. It is by its very nature precarious and transitory, an adventure in mortality, and none of its possible forms is assured of duration as an inorganic being can be. Not duration as such but "duration of what?" is the question here; in other words, such "means" of survival as perception and feeling are never to be judged only as means but also as qualities of the life to be preserved and therefore as aspects of the purpose of survival. It is one of life's paradoxes that means are used to modify its ends and themselves become parts of those ends. Feeling, perception, and motility are faculties accompanying the phenomenon of self-preservation they serve. They preserve a "self" of which they are a part, and one can just as well say that metabolism exists for their sake as that they exist for its sake. Without these faculties there would be much less to preserve, and this "less" of what is to be preserved is the same as the "less" by means of which it is preserved.

From this perspective we see where the true progress represented by animal development lies. The mediate manner in which animals relate to the world is an increase in the mediacy already peculiar to organic existence on its most primitive (metabolizing) level, compared to the direct self-identity of inorganic matter. This increased mediacy brings about a gain in scope, both internal and external, at the price of greater risk, both internal and external. A more differentiated self must face a more differentiated world. Every further stage of separation (here we think of ourselves) pays in its own coin—the same coin with which it also acquires fulfillment. The kind of coin determines the value of the venture. The split between subject and object—opened up by perception at a distance and by a greater radius of movement, and reflected in the acuteness of appetite and fear, satisfaction and disappointment, enjoyment and pain—was never to be closed again. But in its growing expansion, life's freedom found room for all those ways of relating—perceptive, active, and emotional—that justify the split by spanning it and that indirectly regain the lost unity.

Translated by Hunter and Hildegarde Hannum

2

Tool, Image, and Grave: On What Is beyond the Animal in Man

|

Darwin's theory of evolution was not the first system of thought to inform us that human beings have much in common with animals. That we physically belong to the animal kingdom was already as familiar to Aristotle as it would later be to Linnaeus. It is obvious, moreover, from human anatomy, for man is a vertebrate, warm-blooded, placental mammal. Closer morphological comparison places him—with or without the theory of evolution—in, or at least closest to, primates, a specific family of animals.

Recognizing these similarities, however, has never been an obstacle to distinguishing human beings immediately from all the animals—in other words, from perceiving in him something that is beyond mere animality and locating his essential nature in that difference. It remains open whether what is peculiar to man—the *differentia specifica* defining him—is a single quality or several qualities; and if several, whether one or the other can be assigned the prime position. A famous definition based on one such quality is Aristotle's, which sees man as "the animal that possesses language (or reason)": *zóon lógon échon, homo—animal rationale.* The Bible, for its part, emphasizes the human ability to distinguish between good and evil, which is seen to be the main meaning of the phrase

First published as "Werkzeug, Bild und Grab: Vom Transanimalischen im Menschen," in *Scheidewege* 15 (1985–86).

"imago dei." This ability assumes the existence of language and reason, but does not simply coincide with them. By transcending animality while at the same time remaining bound to it, man is regarded as a citizen of two worlds, as midway between animal and angel—in short, as a *partly* supranatural being rising above nature, even animate nature.

Why, then, when man had always known on the basis of his body that he was related to the animal, was Darwin's theory of man's *descent* from the animals such a cultural shock? If we disregard the obvious explanation which first comes to mind—that those who believed in the Creation story as told in Genesis were scandalized—there is still a more strictly philosophical trauma. With Darwin's immanent explanation of man's origins according to purely biological rules, which did not require the intervention of a new principle, the last earthly home of all previously believed-in transcendence was destroyed by the almighty monism of purposeless, mechanical nature. The *way* man had become what he had, defined what he had become. This last disenchantment, following all those having to do with the rest of the world, appeared to undermine the very foundations of the previous image of man.

Or so it appears according to what is called "the genetic fallacy." Since the principle of natural selection consists exclusively in the advantage of various modes of behavior for survival, man's difference from animals is viewed from an increasingly pragmatic perspective and seen to lie in his superior skill in achieving success. His mental faculties are interpreted purely instrumentally as means to this success, and the value, even the meaning, of what is specifically human is defined in terms of it. Indeed, we can ask what aspect of each human characteristic qualified it for natural selection, for passing through the biological sieve. Consequently, this *explanation* of its origin—that is, of nature's approval and nurture of it—can be mistaken for knowledge of its essence; the criteria favoring its development can be mistaken for the substance of what it has become. This fails to explain the enormous surplus of those characteristics that have emerged in man beyond what is needed for purposes of survival, the luxury of his highly autonomous, *self-generated* purposes, which are no longer biological at all.

The same approach, moreover, is exemplified by the genetic logic that characterizes much of modern psychology and sociology. Terms like "sublimation" and "superstructure" are applications of "evolutionary theory" in those fields and represent further examples of reductive interpretation beyond the field of biology. All these interpretations, insofar as they are true, are justified as correctives of a previous extreme view, of the absolute gulf opened up between man and animal—indeed, between man and nature in general—by the Judaic story of Creation, the Greek metaphysics of reason, and—encompassing both—Christian transcendentalism. As a result, the trauma of Darwinism was specifically Christian and Western, a shock that avenged a long historical one-sidedness. In the battle that raged around Darwinism, certainly those who rejected the view that man was denigrated by his relationship to animals were right; they were also right in repudiating the accompanying affront to animal nature.

But given the way we are, one truth can get in the way of another; the correction of one extreme can easily lead to the opposite extreme. The new monistic one-sidedness threatens to leave us with an impoverished self-image that will obscure valuable insights afforded by the rightly supplanted dualism. Our disenchantment, eye-opening at first, is beginning to make us blind. In order to find the golden mean between the extremes, it is time—and the task of a philosophical anthropology— to give thought to what is essentially beyond the animal in man without denying the features common to both. On the contrary, we can see everything surpassing animality as a new stage of mediate relationship to the world that is already beginning to take form in animals and, in turn, is already based upon the mediate nature of all organic existence as such.[1] Upon this basis the intensified mediacy of man's relationship to world and self is built—but as something essentially new, not as something that simply emerges gradually. The meaning of this statement will become clearer in what follows.

My method will be to investigate the significance of several selected human traits. There are many such traits, extending from the external ones of the body to the internal ones of the mind. But the increase in man's brain size, his hand, his erect posture reveal their significance in what they allow us to accomplish, and the same applies to his internal traits, such as reason and imagination. I have thus chosen for evidence visible artifacts made by man, specifically those occurring early in prehistoric times, which were widely dispersed, cannot be attributed to any animal, and already display in their most primitive and simple form the essential nature of the human trait reflected in them. In making my choice I have consciously bypassed speech, for philosophically speaking it is anything but "simple," though since time immemorial it has been correctly acknowledged to be man's most outstanding trait. Also, its prehistoric beginnings are not directly accessible to us, whereas the visible artifacts I shall treat here already indirectly attest to speech (or the ability for it), since their creators must have been speaking subjects. Although a thematic analysis of this basic human trait is thus bypassed, its pervasive presence cannot be overlooked. Let us therefore restrict ourselves to paradigmatic categories of what man has *produced* since earliest times and ask what each of them has to tell us about what is uniquely peculiar to him.

II

My choice falls upon tool, image, and grave, all of which appear among the remnants of the past long before the time of historical cultures, before the great temples of the gods and the written tablets. These three artifacts leave no doubt as to their human origin and reveal various decisive human qualities. Taken together, they provide us with something approaching essential coordinates of a philosophical anthropology. I shall begin with the *tool*, which is certainly the earliest of the three and comes the closest to serving vital animal needs.

What is a tool? A tool is an artificially devised, inert object interpolated as a means between the acting bodily organ (usually the hand) and the extracorporeal object of the action. It is given permanent form for recurring use and can be set aside in readiness for this use. Thus, a stick or a stone employed as a momentary aid is not yet a tool. Intended for working on something, the tool itself is worked on. Its production is free and therefore differs according to differing purposes, of which there are many; in the beginning there are typically recurring uses, but new ones can always be added. The point of a spear is shaped differently from an ax, a scraper, a knife, or a pestle. The production of all these may in turn call for additional tools—a double mediation in dealing with the world that can be multiplied again and again: a mediation in increasing degrees.

The tool is a human device by virtue of having in itself nothing to do with man. It neither arises from any organic function nor is subject to any biological programming. Thus, the spider web, "artful" as it is, is not a tool—not truly "artificial" but simply "natural" (as are bird nests and termite hills). The non-organ nature of the artificial tool is the other face of the *freedom* necessary for its invention. In spite of the roles that groping attempts and fortunate discoveries may play, its invention ultimately has an eidetic element: its form, present in the imagination, is forced upon matter; what is seen in a successful model is widely replicated. This presupposes an eidetic power of imagination and eidetic control of the hand (and of voluntary motility in general), bringing us to man's image-making ability, which is not simply synonymous with "thinking" but rather supports and enhances it through playful imagination (something that makes true thinking easily distinguishable from what computers do).

Before we move on to the theme of image-making, it should first be said that the free nature of tool creation, lying beyond the ability of animals as it does, is still—in terms of its motivation and intent, of its whole utilitarian character—very closely connected with the realm of animal necessity, even while it serves animal needs in a supra-animal manner. It should also be noted that here we can most readily speak of fluid boundaries between animal and human capabilities.

III

The same is not true of *image*-making, a capability which, from its very beginnings in its most primitive and awkward products, displays a total, rather than a gradual, divergence from the animal's. Later refinement adds nothing to this divergence—fluid boundaries are not even conceivable here. With this intuitive evidence, *homo pictor,* the maker and viewer of images, teaches us that *homo faber,* the maker and user of tools, is as such not yet the complete *homo sapiens.*

Wherever we come upon rock drawings, even if it should be on another planet, why are we so sure that only man can have made them (granting that in an extraterrestrial case "man" would be a creature lacking any morphological similarity to us)? The biological uselessness of any form of representation is enough to convince us immediately that no mere animal would or could produce an image. Animal artifacts have direct physical application to the pursuit of vital ends such as nourishment, procreation, concealment, and hibernation. The artifacts themselves have a purposive connection to something else. The depiction of something, however, changes neither the environment nor the condition of the organism itself. An image-making creature is therefore one that either indulges in the production of useless things, or has purposes beyond the biological, or can pursue the latter in a different way than through the instrumental application of things. In any case, by depicting images the object is appropriated in a new, nonpractical manner, and the very fact that interest in it can be attached to its *eidos* is evidence of a new kind of object-relationship.

What kinds of abilities and attitudes are involved in the creation of images (and in the recognition of images)? In the first place, what *is* an image? It is an intentionally produced likeness with the visual appearance of a thing (at rest or in action) in the static medium of the surface of another thing. It is not meant to repeat the original or to pretend that it is the original but to "re-present" it. For this purpose the suggestion of a few "representative" features suffices: the rendition of something requires selectivity and permits, on the one hand, extreme frugality through omission and simplification and, on the other, even exaggeration, distortion, stylization. As long as the intent remains recognizable, the image of what is portrayed can do with a minimum of likeness. Since only the view of a thing, not the thing itself, is reproduced in an image, there can be any number of repetitions (copies) of the same image. Since there can be countless views of the same thing, there can be any number of different images of it, although certain views will be favored at different times. Above all, however, since form as such is "general," the same picture can represent any number of individual phenomena: the antelope in the drawings of Bushmen is not this or that specific one but every antelope that can be remembered, anticipated, or referred to as "an antelope"; the figures of hunters are any group of hunting Bushmen in the past, present, or future. Since representation occurs through form, it is essentially general. Generality is a conspicuous feature of the image, interpolated between the individuality of the image qua thing and that of the things depicted.

If these are the characteristics of the image, what characteristics are necessary for a subject to create or comprehend images? In the first place, of course, the perception of likeness—but as *mere* likeness without it being mistaken for what it is only supposed to represent. Perception in itself, however, knows nothing of representation; it recognizes only simple presentation, where everything stands for itself and nothing stands for anything else. Perception is a direct rendering of what is present in its presentness. Depiction, which renders what is absent, is in fact a conceptual dimension of its own, in which all degrees of visible likeness can occur in a representational way. This dimension contains in its structure a threefold differentiation: the image, its physical carrier, and the depicted object. The intermediary, poised between two physical realities—image qua thing and depicted thing—is the *eidos* as such, which becomes the real object we experience.

The principle involved here on the subject's part is the intentional separation of form from matter. Here we have a specifically human situation and the reason why we do not expect animals to make or comprehend images. The animal is concerned with the present object. If it is sufficiently "like" another object, then it is an object of the same kind. Reality alone counts, and reality knows nothing of representation. For example, the "sign" animals can leave behind, the trace of their scent, is not an image of the animal. Therefore, in our search for the conditions of image-making, we must move from the merely physical ability to discern likeness to the nonmaterial one of separating *eidos* from concrete reality or form from matter.

What step does man's image-making ability take when he proceeds to translate a visual aspect into a material likeness? We see at once that in this step a new level of mediacy is reached, beyond that already present in vision as such. The image is separated from the object, that is, the presence of the *eidos* is made independent of the presence of the thing. Having vision already involves a stepping back from the urgent pressures of the environment and created the freedom of an overview from a distance.[2] A stepping back of the second order occurs when appearance is grasped *as* appearance, is distinguished from reality, and—with its presence in our control—is interpolated between the self and reality, whose presence is beyond our control.

This control is first attained in the internal exercise of imagination, which, as far as we know, distinguishes human memory from animal recall. Memory transcends mere recall by means of imagination's capacity for free reproduction, which has the images of things at its disposal. That human beings can alter images at will follows almost necessarily from the fact that we possess them detached from actual sensation and thereby from the stubborn factuality of objects' own being. Imagination separates the remembered *eidos* from the event of the individual encounter with it, thus freeing it from the accidents of space and time. The freedom gained in this manner—to ponder things in the imagination—is one based upon both distance and mastery.

The remembered form can then be translated from inner imagination into an external image, which in turn is an object of perception: a perception, not of the original object, however, but of its representation. It is externalized memory and not repetition of the experience itself. To a certain extent this image makes actual experience superfluous by making some of its essential content available without the experience itself.

The control involved here proceeds via re-creation to new creation. As the re-creator of things "in their own image," *homo pictor* submits to the criterion of truth. An image can be more or less true, i.e., faithful to the original. The intention to depict an object acknowledges it as it is and accepts its verdict on the adequacy of the pictorial homage thus expressed. The *adequatio imaginis ad rem* preceding the *adequatio intellectus ad rem* is the first form of theoretical truth—the precursor of verbally descriptive truth, which is in turn the precursor of scientific truth.

The re-creator of objects is potentially also the creator of new objects, and the one power is no different from the other. The freedom that has chosen to render a likeness can just as easily choose to deviate from it. The first intentionally drawn line opens up that dimension of freedom in which faithfulness to the original or to any model is only *one* decision: this dimension transcends actual reality as a whole and offers its range of endless variation as a realm of the *possible*, which man can actualize however he chooses. The same ability can bring about both what is true and what is new.

Pictorial activity is yet another example of human freedom. Images must, after all, be produced, not only conceived. Thus, their outer existence as the result of human activity also reveals a *physical* aspect of the power inherent in the image-making ability: the kind of command man has over his body. Only by means of this command can imagination proceed to depiction, and the motor freedom activated here repeats the imaginative one; the transition from imagination to depiction and the latter's *allowing* itself to be directed by the former are just as free as was the imaginative act itself. The most familiar example of this "translation" of an eidetic pattern or scheme into movement of the limbs is writing. The use of the hand in general demonstrates that this motor translation of imagined form in its fullest extent is the condition of all human creativity and therefore also of all technology, as we already saw in the case of tools.

What we have here is a uniquely human ability beyond that of animals: the eidetic control of motility, i.e., muscular action governed not by set stimulus-and-response patterns but by freely chosen, inwardly imagined, and purposely projected form. Eidetic control of motility, with its freedom of external execution, thus complements eidetic control of the imagination, with its freedom of internal projection. *Homo pictor,* who illustrates both capacities in *one* indivisible example, represents the point at which *homo faber* and *homo sapiens* coincide—indeed, the point at which they prove to be one and the same.

We can deduce something more from the examples of the earliest images: those who created them also possessed speech. What we assumed in the case of tools we can be sure of in the case of images, which do in visible fashion what names do invisibly: give things a new existence qua symbol. The Bible (Genesis 2:19) tells us that God created the beasts of the Earth and the fowl of the air but left it to Adam to name them. The naming of creatures is here regarded as the first feat of newly created man and as a distinctively human act. It is a step beyond Creation; the one who took it thereby proved his superiority to his fellow creatures and proclaimed his future mastery over nature. By giving names to "every living creature" created by God, man created a species name for the multiplicity of specimens that would later develop. The name, becoming general in this way, preserves the archetypical order of Creation in the face of its manifold replications in individual cases. Thus, the symbolic duplication of the world through names is at the same time an ordering of it according to its generic prototypes. Every horse is the original horse, every dog the original dog.

The generality of the name is the generality of the image. The prehistoric hunter did not draw this or that bison but *the* bison—every possible bison was thereby evoked, anticipated, remembered. Drawing an image of something is analogous to calling it by name, or rather is its unabridged form, since it makes physically present that inner image of which the phonetic sign is an abbreviation and whose generality alone makes it applicable to the many individual specimens. Image-making repeats each time the creative act whose residue is concealed in the name: the symbolic "making-again" of the world. It demonstrates what the use of names takes for granted: the availability of the *eidos*, as something beyond particular things, for human comprehension, imagination, and speech. In the ideogram, then, the two—image and word—visibly meet.[3]

IV

We now turn to the *grave* as the third artifact, after tool and image. If biological superfluity or even uselessness is to be taken as a sign of what is beyond the animal in man, then in this respect grave surpasses image, which after all can serve purposes of communication, instruction, and even invention. To this extent the image could still be explained, as the tool certainly can be, by the evolutionary system of rewards. That the grave is an exclusively human phenomenon is empirically demonstrated to us by the fact that no animal buries or gives further consideration to its dead. According to this criterion alone, it would not rank any higher than tool and image. But the commemoration of the dead perpetuated in the cult of the grave and in other visible ways is uniquely human in a sense that surpasses both of the previous examples. For it is linked to *beliefs*, whose content—varying at different times and places, sometimes known and sometimes merely conjectured—we need not concern ourselves with here. Common to them all is that they somehow defy our apparent mortality, pointing beyond what is visible to the invisible, from the material to the immaterial. The grave bears visible testimony to this defiance.

Among all beings, man is the only one who knows that he must die, and in considering "the afterwards" and "the there," he also considers "the now" and "the here" of his existence—that is, he reflects about himself. With graves, the question takes on concrete form: "Where do I come from; where am I going?" and ultimately, "What am I—beyond what I do and experience at a given time?" With these questions *reflection* emerges as a new mode of dealing with the world, beyond tool and image. It is not only man's relationship to the world which is indirect but also his relationship to himself. He arrives at his own being only via the detour of ideas about it. Knowing of his mortality, he must live as a human being with a self-image that is by no means self-evident but is the tentative result of questioning and speculation. This speculation necessarily expands from the individual ego to the whole of existence, in which the ego finds itself situated. Thus, metaphysics arises from graves. But so does that commemoration of the past which we call history, as the cult of ancestors first makes clear. Preserving the link with our forebears merges the transitory "now" of the single existence with the continuity of the succession of generations, and the memory of the temporal becomes just as suprapersonal as the commemoration of the eternal. In both respects the self attains distance from itself, thus discovering itself—with the ultimate sacrifice of immediacy—for the first time.

V

With this attainment of distance and the bridging of it by means of never-ending reflection, the principle of mediacy, with which life began and whose growth can be traced through all of organic evolution, reaches it pinnacle.[4] Man, who represents this pinnacle, emerges in his fullest sense when he who depicted the bison and its hunter turns his gaze upon the nondepictable image of his own being and fate. By the distancing of this wondering, searching, and comparing gaze, a new entity, "I," is established. This is the greatest step of all hazarded by mediacy and objectification, and the knowledge of death may very well have been the impetus for it. Henceforth, like it or not, man—each one of us—must live the idea or "image" of man, an image that is constantly being modified. It never leaves him, however much he sometimes yearns for the animal felicity he has lost. Only via the immeasurable distance of being-an-object-to-himself can man "have" himself. But he does have himself, whereas no animal has itself. In the gulf opened up by the confrontation of the self with itself, the greatest heights and the deepest depressions of human experience have their place. Man alone is open to despair; he alone can commit suicide. *Quaestio mihi factus sum*, "I have become a question to myself": religion, ethics, and metaphysics are never-completed attempts to confront this question within the framework of an interpretation of the totality of existence and to find an answer to it.

Let us summarize what the human products we selected have to say to us about man. The *tool* tells us that a being, forced to deal with matter out of need, meets this need in an artificially mediated way that depends on invention and is open to improvement. The *image* tells us that a being, using a tool on matter for an immaterial purpose, depicts the contents of his visual perception, varies them and transforms them, thereby creating a new world of depicted objects beyond the material world that is there to satisfy his needs. The *grave* tells us that a being, subject to mortality, reflects about life and death, defies appearances, and raises his thinking to the realm of the invisible, utilizing tool and image for this purpose. With these basic forms we respond to and surpass, in uniquely human fashion, what is simply a given for man and all animals: in the tool, physical necessity is met with invention; in the image, visual perception with representation and imagination; in the grave, inevitable death with faith and piety.

All three, going beyond the immediate, are modes of mediacy and freedom, which we today share with those who preceded us, and are thus valid for all time as diverse means, emanating from one source, of understanding the world. We may not always know the purpose of a specific tool, but we know that it had one, conceived in terms of end-means and cause-effect relations and produced as a result of that conception. If we follow this type of causal thinking further, we arrive at technology and physics. We may not always understand the significance of a given image, but we know that it is an image, was supposed to depict something, and by this depiction reproduced a heightened and validated reality. If we follow in this direction we arrive at art. We may not know the specific ideas behind a cult of the dead (and if we did know them, we would probably find them extremely strange), but we do know that ideas were involved here—the mere fact of the grave and its rituals tell us so—and that these ideas represented reflection about the mystery of existence and what lay beyond the realm of appearance. Following in the direction of such reflection we arrive at metaphysics. Physics, art, and metaphysics, adumbrated in primitive times by tool, image, and grave, are not discussed here as already existing or as developments that must occur universally but as original dimensions of the human relationship to the world, whose expanding horizon includes them as *potentialities* in its far reaches.

Just as little as potentiality guarantees realization, so little, too, does this enumeration of horizons mean that even their primitive adumbrations must be found in every human group at all times. Their presence is significant, but their absence is not necessarily so. For understandable reasons, tools will probably be found everywhere. But image and grave, both representing a greater luxury for human beings struggling with the exigencies of nature, may for various reasons be missing here and there. Yet we consider the ability to produce them part of being fully human, and they are not missing entirely in any *culture*. Our culture today places the greatest emphasis on what was foreshadowed in the tool: technology and the natural sciences that serve it. Tools, which—of the three—best served the purposes of biology and its dynamics of selection, first appeared in response to the constraints of nature. Continually surpassing themselves with their undreamed-of successes in recent times, they now completely dominate our entire external existence, overshadowing everything else that distinguishes us "from all beings that we know" (Goethe). In spite of this, let us not forget that those other human creations pointing beyond the animal—even including the field of metaphysics, in such disrepute today—although less amenable to progress, still belong to the total picture of man.

Translated by Hunter and Hildegarde Hannum

3

The Burden and Blessing
of Mortality

S ince time immemorial, mortals have bewailed their mortality, have longed to escape it, groped for some hope of eternal life. I speak, of course, of human mortals. Men alone of all creatures know that they must die; men alone mourn their dead, bury their dead, remember their dead. So much is mortality taken to mark the human condition, that the attribute "mortal" has tended to be monopolized for man: in Homeric and later Greek usage, for example, "mortals" is almost a synonym for "men," contrasting them to the envied, ageless immortality of the gods. *Memento mori* rings through the ages as a persistent philosophical and religious admonition in aid of a truly human life. As Psalm 90 puts it, "Teach us to number our days, that we may get a heart of wisdom."

Over this incurably anthropocentric emphasis, not much thought was spent on the obvious truth that we share the lot of mortality with our fellow creatures, that all life is mortal, indeed that death is coextensive with life. Reflection shows that this must be so; that you cannot have the one without the other. Let this be our first theme: mortality as an essential attribute of life as such—only later to focus on specifically human aspects of it.

Two meanings merge in the term *mortal*: that the creature so called *can* die, is exposed to the constant possibility of death; and that, eventually, it *must* die, is destined for the ultimate necessity of death. In the continual possibility I place the burden, in the ultimate necessity I place

This paper was first presented to the Royal Palace Foundation in Amsterdam on 19 March 1991. It was also delivered at a conference in honor of Hans Jonas sponsored by Hebrew University, Jerusalem in January 1992.

the blessing of mortality. The second of these propositions may sound strange. Let me argue both.

|

I begin with mortality as the ever-present *potential* of death for everything alive, concurrent with the life process itself. This "potential" means more than the truism of being destructible, which holds for every composite material structure, dead or alive. With sufficient force, even the diamond can be crushed, and everything alive can be killed by any number of outside causes, prominent among them other life. However, the inmost relation of life to possible death goes deeper than that: it resides in the organic constitution as such, in its very mode of being. I have to spell out this mode to lay bare the roots of mortality in life itself. To this end I now beg you to keep me company on a stretch of ontological inquiry. By this, we philosophers mean an inquiry into the manner of being characteristic of entities of one kind or another—in our case, of the kind called "organism," as this is the sole physical form in which, to our knowledge, life exists. What is the way of being of an organism?

Our opening observation is that organisms are entities whose being is their own doing. That is to say that they exist only in virtue of what they do. And this in the radical sense that the being they earn from this doing is not a possession they then own in separation from the activity by which it was generated, but is the continuation of that very activity itself, made possible by what it has just performed. Thus, to say that the being of organisms is their own doing is also to say that doing what they do is their being itself; being for them consists in doing what they have to do in order to go on to be. It follows directly that to cease doing it means ceasing to be; and since the requisite doing depends not on themselves alone, but also on the compliance of an environment that can either be granted or denied, the peril of cessation is with the organism from the beginning. Here we have the basic link of life with death, the ground of mortality in its very constitution.

What we have couched so far in the abstract terms of being and doing, the language of ontology, can now be called by its familiar name: *metabolism*. This concretely is the "doing" referred to in our opening remark about entities whose being is their own doing, and metabolism can well serve as the defining property of life: all living things have it, no nonliving thing has it. What it denotes is this: to exist by way of exchanging matter with the environment, transiently incorporate it, use it, excrete it again. The German *Stoffwechsel* expresses it nicely. Let us realize how unusual, nay unique a trait this is in the vast world of matter. How does an ordinary physical thing—a proton, a molecule, a stone, a planet— endure? Well, just by being there. Its being now is the sufficient reason for its also being later, if perhaps in a different place. This is so because of the constancy of matter, one of the prime laws of nature ever since, soon after the Big Bang, the exploding chaos solidified into discrete, highly durable units. In the universe hence evolving, the single stubborn particle, say a proton, is simply and fixedly what it is, identical with itself over time, and with no need to maintain that identity by anything it does. Its conservation is mere remaining, not a reassertion of being from moment to moment. It is there once and for all. Saying, then, of a composite, macroscopic body— this stone in our collection—that it is the same as yesterday amounts to saying that it still consists of the same elementary parts as before.

Now by this criterion a living organism would have no identity over time. Repeated inspections would find it to consist less and less of the initial components, more and more of new ones of the same kind that have taken their place, until the two compared states have perhaps no components in common anymore. Yet no biologist would take this to mean that he is not dealing with the same organic individual. On the contrary, he would consider any other finding incompatible with the sameness of a living entity qua living: if it showed the same inventory of parts after a long enough interval, he would conclude that the body in question has soon after the earlier inspection ceased to live and is in that decisive respect no longer "the same," that is, no longer a "creature" but a corpse. Thus we are faced with the ontological fact of an identity totally different from inert physical identity, yet grounded in transactions among items of that simple identity. We have to ponder this highly intriguing fact.

It presents something of a paradox. On the one hand, the living body is a composite of matter, and at any one time its reality totally coincides with its contemporary stuff—that is, with one definite manifold of individual components. On the other hand, it is not identical with this or any such simultaneous total, as this is forever vanishing downstream in the flow of exchange; in this respect it is different from its stuff and not the sum of it. We have thus the case of a substantial entity enjoying a sort of *freedom* with respect to its own substance, an independence from that same matter of which it nonetheless wholly consists. However, though independent of the sameness of this matter, it is dependent on the exchange of it, on its progressing permanently and sufficiently, and there is no freedom in this. Thus, the exercise of the freedom which the living thing enjoys is rather a stern *necessity*. This necessity we call "need," which has a place only where existence is unassured and its own continual task.

With the term *need* we have come upon a property of organic being unique to life and unknown to all the rest of reality. The atom is self-sufficient and would continue to exist if all the world around it were annihilated. By contrast, nonautarky is of the very essence of organism. Its power to use the world, this unique prerogative of life, has its precise reverse in the necessity of having to use it, on pain of ceasing to be. The dependence here in force is the cost incurred by primeval substance in venturing upon the career of organic—that is, self-constituting—identity instead of merely inert persistence. Thus the need is with it from the beginning and marks the existence gained in this way as a hovering between being and not-being. The "not" lies always in wait and must be averted ever anew. Life, in other words, carries death within itself.

Yet if it is true that with metabolizing existence not-being made its appearance in the world as an alternative embodied in the existence itself, it is equally true that thereby to be first assumes an emphatic sense: intrinsically qualified by the threat of its negative it must affirm itself, and existence affirmed is existence as a *concern*. Being has become a task rather than a given state, a possibility ever to be realized anew in opposition to its ever-present contrary, not-being, which inevitably will engulf it in the end.

With the hint at inevitability, we are ahead of our story. As told so far in these musings of mine, we can sum up the inherent dialectics of life somewhat like this: committed to itself, put at the mercy of its own performance, life must depend on conditions over which it has no control and which may deny themselves at any time. Thus dependent on the favor or disfavor of outer reality, life is exposed to the world from which it has set itself off and by means of which it must yet maintain itself. Emancipated from the identity with matter, life is yet in need of it; free, yet under the whip of necessity; separate, yet in indispensable contact; seeking contact, yet in danger of being destroyed by it and threatened no less by its want—imperiled thus from both sides, importunity and aloofness of the world, and balanced on the narrow ridge between the two. In its process, which must not cease, liable to interference; in the straining of its temporality always facing the imminent no-more: thus does the living form carry on its separatist existence in matter—paradoxical, unstable, precarious, finite, and in intimate company with death. The fear of death, with which the hazard of this existence is charged, is a never-ending comment on the audacity of the original venture upon which substance embarked in turning organic.

But we may well ask at this point: Is it worth the candle? Why all the toil? Why leave the safe shore of self-sufficient permanence for the troubled waters of mortality in the first place? Why venture upon the anxious gamble of self-preservation at all? With the hindsight of billions of years and the present witness of our inwardness, which surely is part of the evidence, we are not without clues for a speculative guess. Let us dare it.

The basic clue is that life says "yes" to itself. By clinging to itself it declares that it values itself. But one clings only to what can be taken away. From the organism, which has being strictly on loan, it can be taken and will be unless from moment to moment reclaimed. Continued metabolism is such a reclaiming, which ever reasserts the value of Being against its lapsing into nothingness. Indeed to say "yes," so it seems, requires the copresence of the alternative to which to say "no." Life has in it the sting of death that perpetually lies in wait, ever again to be staved off, and precisely the challenge of the "no" stirs and powers the "yes." Are we then, perhaps, allowed to say that mortality is the narrow gate through which alone *value*—the addressee of a "yes"—could enter the otherwise indifferent universe? That the same crack in the massive unconcern of matter that gave value an opening had also to let in the fear of losing it? We shall presently have to say something about the kind of value purchased at this cost. First allow me one further step in this speculation that roams beyond proof. Is it too bold to conjecture that in the cosmically rare opportunity of organismic existence, when at last it was offered on this planet by lucky circumstance, the secret essence of Being, locked in matter, seized the long-awaited chance to affirm itself, and in doing so to make itself more and more worth affirming? The fact and course of evolution point that way. Then organisms would be the manner in which universal Being says "yes" to itself. We have learned that it can do so only by also daring the risk of not-being, with whose possibility it is now paired. Only in confrontation with ever-possible not-being could Being come to feel itself, affirm itself, make itself its own purpose. Through negated not-being, "to be" turns into a constant choosing of itself. Thus, it is only an apparent paradox that it should be death and holding it off by acts of self-preservation which set the seal upon the self-affirmation of Being.

If this is the burden life was saddled with from the start, what then is its reward? What *is* the value paid for with the coin of mortality? *What in the outcome was there to affirm?* We alluded to it when we said that, in organisms, Being came to "feel" itself. Feeling is the prime condition for anything to be possibly worthwhile. It can be so only as the datum for a feeling and as the feeling of this datum. The presence of feeling as such, whatever its content or mode, is infinitely superior to the total absence of it. Thus, the capacity for feeling, which arose in organisms, is the mother-value of all values. With its arising in organic evolution, reality gained a dimension it lacked in the form of bare matter and which also thereafter remains confined to this narrow foothold in biological entities: the dimension of subjective inwardness. Perhaps aspired to since creation, such inwardness found its eventual cradle with the advent of metabolizing life. Where in its advance to higher forms that mysterious dimension actually opened we cannot know. I am inclined to suspect the infinitesimal beginning of it in the earliest self-sustaining and self-replicating cells—a germinal inwardness, the faintest glimmer of diffused subjectivity long before it concentrated in brains as its specialized organs. Be that as it may. Somewhere in the ascent of evolution, at the latest with the twin rise of perception and motility in animals, that invisible inner dimension burst forth into the bloom of ever more conscious, subjective life: inwardness externalizing itself in behavior and shared in communication.

The gain is double-edged, like every trait of life. Feeling lies open to pain as well as to pleasure, its keenness cutting both ways; lust has its match in anguish, desire in fear; purpose is either attained or thwarted, and the capacity for enjoying the one is the same as that for suffering from the other. In short, the gift of subjectivity only sharpens the yes-no polarity of all life, each side feeding on the strength of the other. Is it, in the balance, still a gain, vindicating the bitter burden of mortality to which the gift is tied, which it makes even more onerous to bear? This is a question of the kind that cannot be answered without an element of personal decision. As part of my pleading for a "yes" to it, I offer two comments.

The first is about the relation of means and ends in an organism's equipment for living. Biologists are wont to tell us (and, I think, with excellent reasons) that this or that organ or behavior pattern has been "selected" out of chance mutations for the *survival* advantage it bestowed on its possessors. Accordingly, the evolution of consciousness must bespeak its utility in the struggle for survival. Survival as such would be the end, consciousness an incremental means thereto. But that implies its having causal power over behavior, and such a power is—by the canons of natural science—attributable only to the physical events in the brain, not to the subjective phenomena accompanying them; and those brain events in turn must be wholly the consequence of physical antecedents. Causes must be as objective throughout as the effects—so decrees a materialist axiom. In terms of causality, therefore, a nonconscious robot mechanism with the same behavioral output could do as well and would have sufficed for natural selection. In other words, evolutionary mechanics, as understood by its proponents, explains the evolution of brains, but not of consciousness. Nature, then, is credited with throwing in a redundancy, the free gift of consciousness, now debunked as useless and, moreover, as deceptive in its causal pretense.

There is but one escape here from absurdity, and that is to trust the self-testimony of our subjective inwardness, namely, that it is (to a degree) causally effective in governing our behavior, therefore indeed eligible for natural selection as one more *means* of survival. But with the same act of trust, we have also endorsed its inherent claim that, beyond all instrumentality, it is for its own sake and an end in itself. There is a lesson in this about the general relation of means and ends in organic existence.

To secure survival is indeed one end of organic endowment, but when we ask "Survival of what?" we must often count the endowment itself among the intrinsic goods it helps to preserve. Faculties of the psychological order are the most telling cases in point. Such "means" of survival as perception and emotion, understanding and will, command of limbs and discrimination of goals are never to be judged as means merely, but also as qualities of the life to be preserved and therefore as aspects of the end. It is the subtle logic of life that it employs means which modify the end and themselves become part of it. The feeling animal strives to preserve itself as a feeling, not just metabolizing, creature. That is, it strives to continue the very activity of feeling; the perceiving animal strives to preserve itself as a perceiving creature . . . and so on. Even the sickest of us, if he wants to live on at all, wants to do so thinking and sensing, not merely digesting. Without these subject faculties that emerged in animals, there would be much less to preserve, and this less of what is to be preserved is the same as the less wherewith it is preserved. The self-rewarding experience of the means in action make the preservation they promote more worthwhile. Whatever the changing contents, whatever the tested utility, awareness as such proclaims its own supreme worth.

But must we assent? This question leads over to my second comment. What if the sum of suffering in the living world forever exceeds the sum of enjoyment? What if, especially in the human world, the sum of misery is so much greater than that of happiness as the record of the ages seems to suggest? I am inclined in this matter to side with the verdict of the pessimists. Most probably the balance sheet, if we could really assemble it, would look bleak. But would that be a valid ground to deny the worth of awareness, that things would be better if it were not in the world at all? There one should listen to the voice of its victims, those least bribed by the tasting of pleasures. The votes of those least lucky may be ignored, but those of the suffering unlucky count double in weight and authority. And there we find that almost no amount of misery dims the "yes" to sentient selfhood. Greatest suffering still clings to it, rarely is the road of suicide taken, never is there a "survival" without feeling wished for. The very record of suffering mankind teaches us that the partisanship of inwardness for itself invincibly withstands the balancing of pains and pleasures and rebuffs our judging it by this standard.

More important still, something in us protests against basing a metaphysical judgment on hedonistic grounds. The presence of any worthwhileness in the universe at all—and we have seen that this is bound to feeling—immeasurably outweighs any cost of suffering it exacts. Since it is in the last resort mortality which levies that cost, but is equally the condition for such to exist that can pay it, and existence of this sort is the sole seat of meaning in the world, the burden of mortality laid on all of us is heavy and meaningful at once.

II

Up to this point we have been dealing with mortality as the *possibility* of death lurking in all life at all times and countered continually by acts of self-preservation. Ultimate *certainty* of death, intrinsic limitation of individual life spans, is a different matter, and that is the meaning we have mostly in mind when we speak of our own "mortality." We are then speaking of death as the terminal point on the long road of *aging.* That word has so far not appeared in our discourse; and indeed, familiar and seemingly self-evident as the phenomenon is to us, aging—that is, internal organic attrition by the life process itself—is not a universal biological trait, not even in quite complex organisms. It is surprising to learn how many and how diverse species are nonsenescent, for example, in groups such as bony fishes, sea anemones, and bivalve mollusks. Attrition there is left entirely to extrinsic causes of death, which suffice to balance population numbers in the interplay with reproduction and amount to certainty of death for each individual within a time frame typical for the species. However, throughout the higher biological orders, aging at a species-determined rate that ends in dying is the pervasive rule (without exception, for example, in warm-blooded animals) and it must have some adaptive benefits, else evolution would not have let it arise. What these benefits are is a subject of speculation among biologists. On principle, they may derive either directly from the trait itself or from some other traits to which senescence is linked as their necessary price. We will not join in this debate, but rather say a word about the general evolutionary aspect of death and dying in their remorseless actuality, whether from extrinsic or intrinsic necessity. The term *evolution* itself already reveals the *creative* role of individual finitude, which has decreed that whatever lives *must* also die. For what else is natural selection with its survival premium, this main engine of evolution, than the use of death for the promotion of novelty for the favoring of diversity, and for the singling out of higher forms of life with the blossoming forth of subjectivity? At work to this effect—so we saw—is a mixture of death by extrinsic causes (foremost the merciless feeding of life on life) and the organically programmed dying of parent generations to make room for their offspring. With the advent and ascent of man, the latter kind of mortality, inbuilt numbering of our days, gains increasing importance in incidence and significance, and from here on our discourse will keep to the human context alone and consider in what sense mortality may be a blessing specifically for our own kind.

Reaching ripe old age and dying from mere attrition of the body is, as a common phenomenon, very much an artifact. In the state of nature, so Hobbes put it, human life is nasty, brutish, and short. Civil society, according to him, was founded mainly for protection from violent— and that means premature—death. This is surely too narrow a view of the motives, but one effect of civilization, this comprehensive artifact of human intelligence, is undeniably the progressive taming of the extraneous causes of death for humans. It has also mightily enhanced the powers of their mutual destruction. But the net result is that at least in technologically advanced societies, more and more people reach the natural limit of life. Scientific medicine has a major share in this result, and it is beginning to try to push back that limit itself. At any rate the theoretical prospect seems no longer precluded. This makes it tempting to hitch the further pursuit of our theme to the question of whether it is right to combat not merely premature death but death as such; that is, whether lengthening life indefinitely is a legitimate goal of medicine. We will discuss this on two planes: that of the common good of mankind and that of the individual good for the self.

The common good of mankind is tied to civilization, and this with all its feats and faults would not have come about and not keep moving without the ever-repeated turnover of generations. Here we have come to the point where we can no longer postpone complementing the consideration of death with that of birth, its essential counterpart, to which we have paid no attention so far. It was of course tacitly included in our consideration of individual mortality as a prerequisite of biological evolution. In the incomparably faster, nonbiological evolution the human species enacts within its biological identity through the transgenerational handing-on and accumulation of learning, the interplay of death and birth assumes a very new and profound relevance. "Natality" (to use a coinage of my long-departed friend Hannah Arendt) is as essential an attribute of the human condition as is mortality. It denotes the fact that we all have been born, which means that each of us had a beginning when others already had long been there, and this ensures that there will always be such who see the world for the first time, see things with new eyes, wonder where others are dulled by habit, start out from where they had arrived. Youth with its fumbling and follies, its eagerness and questioning, is the eternal hope of mankind. Without its constant arrival, the wellspring of novelty would dry up, for those grown older have found their answers and gotten set in their ways. The ever-renewed beginning, which can only be had at the price of ever-repeated ending, is mankind's safeguard against lapsing into boredom and routine, its chance of retaining the spontaneity of life. There is also this bonus of "natality": that every one of the newcomers is different and unique. Such is the working of sexual reproduction that none of its outcome is, in genetic makeup, the replica of any before and none will ever be replicated thereafter. (This is one reason humans should never be "cloned.")

Now obviously, just as mortality finds its compensation in natality, conversely natality gets its scope from mortality: dying of the old makes place for the young. This rule becomes more stringent as our numbers push or already exceed the limits of environmental tolerance. The specter of overpopulation casts its pall over the access of new life anyway; and the proportion of youth must shrink in a population forced to become static but increasing its average age by the successful fight against premature death. Should we then try to lengthen life further by tinkering with and outwitting the naturally ordained, biological timing of our mortality— thus further narrowing the space of youth in our aging society? I think the common good of mankind bids us answer "no." The question was rather academic, for no serious prospect is in sight for breaking the existing barrier. But the dream is taking form in our technological intoxication. The real point of our reflection was the linkage of mortality with creativity in human history. Whoever, therefore, relishes the cultural harvest of the ages in any of its many facets and does not wish to be without it, and most surely the praiser and advocate of progress, should see in mortality a blessing and not a curse.

However, the good of mankind and the good of the individual are not necessarily the same, and someone might say: Granted that mortality is good for mankind as a whole, and I am grateful for its bounty paid for by others, but for myself I still ardently wish I were exempt from it and could go on interminably to enjoy its fruit—past, present, and future. Of course (so we might imagine him to add) this must be an exception, but why not have a select few equally favored for companions in immortality? For *interminably* you are free to substitute "twice or triple the normal maximum" and qualify *immortality* accordingly.

Would that wish at least stand the test of imagined fulfillment? I know of one attempt to tackle that question: Jonathan Swift's harrowing description in *Gulliver's Travels* of the Struldbrugs or "Immortals," who "sometimes, though very rarely" happen to be born in the kingdom of Luggnagg. When first hearing of them, Gulliver is enraptured by the thought of their good fortune and that of a society harboring such fonts of experience and wisdom. But he learns that theirs is a miserable lot, universally pitied and despised; their unending lives turn into ever more worthless burdens to them and the mortals around them; even the company of their own kind becomes intolerable, so that, for example, marriages are dissolved at a certain age, "for the law thinks . . . that those who are condemned without any fault of their own to a perpetual continuance in the world should not have their misery doubled by the load of a wife"—or a husband, I hasten to add. And so on—one should read Gulliver's vivid description.

For the purposes of our question, Swift's fantasy has one flaw: his immortals are denied death but not spared the infirmities of old age and the indignities of senility—which of course heavily prejudges the outcome of his thought-experiment. Our test of imagined fulfillment must assume that it is not the gift of miraculous chance but of scientific control over the natural causes of death and, therefore, over the aging processes that lead to it, so that the life thus lengthened also retains its bodily vigor. Would the indefinite lengthening then be desirable for the subjects themselves? Let us waive such objections as the resentment of the many against the exception of the few, however obtained, and the ignobility of the wish for it, the breach of solidarity with the common mortal lot. Let us judge on purely egotistical grounds. One of Gulliver's descriptions gives us a valuable hint: "They have no remembrance of anything but of what they learned and observed in their youth and middle age." This touches a point independent of senile decrepitude: we are finite beings and even if our vital functions continued unimpaired, there are limits to what our brains can store and keep adding to. It is the mental side of our being that sooner or later must call a halt, even if the magicians of biotechnology invent tricks for keeping the body machine going indefinitely. Old age, in humans, means a long past, which the *mind* must accommodate in its present as the substratum of personal identity. The past in us grows all the time, with its load of knowledge and opinion and emotions and choices and acquired aptitudes and habits and, of course, things upon things remembered or somehow recorded even if forgotten. There is a finite space for all this, and those magicians would also periodically have to clear the mind (like a computer memory) of its old contents to make place for the new.

These are weird fantasies—we use them merely to bring out the mental side of the question concerning mortality and the individual good. The simple truth of our finiteness is that we could, by whatever means, go on interminably only at the price of either *losing* the past and therewith our real identity, or living *only* in the past and therefore without a real present. We cannot seriously wish either and thus not a physical enduring at that price. It would leave us stranded in a world we no longer understand even as spectators, walking anachronisms who have outlived themselves. It is a changing world because of the newcomers who keep arriving and who leave us behind. Trying to keep pace with them is doomed to inglorious failure, especially as the pace has quickened so much. Growing older, we get our warnings, no matter in what physical shape we are. To take, just for once, my own example: a native sensibility for visual and poetic art persists, not much dulled, in my old age; I can still be moved by the works I have learned to love and have grown old with. But the art of our own time is alien to me, I don't understand its language, and in that respect I feel already a stranger in the world. The prospect of unendingly becoming one ever more and in every respect would be frightening, and the certainty that prevents it is reassuring. So we do not need the horror fiction of the wretched Struldbrugs to make us reject the desire for earthly immortality: not even the fountains of youth, which biotechnology may have to offer one day to circumvent the physical penalties of it, can justify the goal of extorting from nature more than its original allowance to our species for the length of our days. On this point then, the private good does concur with the public good. Herewith I rest my case for mortality as a blessing.

Mind you, this side of it, which is perceived only by thought and not felt in experience, detracts nothing from the burden that the ever-present contingency of death lays on all flesh. Also, what we have said about "blessing" for the individual person is true only after a completed life, in the fullness of time. This is a premise far from being realized as a rule, and in all too many populations with a low life expectancy it is the rare exception. It is a duty of civilization to combat premature death among humankind worldwide and in all its causes—hunger, diseases, war, and so on. As to our mortal condition as such, our understanding can have no quarrel about it with creation unless life itself is denied. As to each of us, the knowledge that we are here but briefly and a non-negotiable limit is set to our expected time may even be necessary as the incentive to number our days and make them count.

4

Toward an Ontological Grounding of an Ethics for the Future

I

"An ethics for the future" means a contemporary ethics concerned with a future we seek to protect for our descendants from the consequences of our actions in the present. This task has become necessary because our actions today, in the form of global technology, threaten not only the near but even the distant future. Thus, moral responsibility demands that we take into consideration the welfare of those who, without being consulted, will later be affected by what we are doing now. Without our choosing it, *responsibility* becomes our lot due to the sheer extent of the *power* we exercise daily in the service of our short-term concerns but unintentionally allow to have long-range effects. Our sense of responsibility must be commensurate with the magnitude of our power and therefore involves, *like it*, the entire future of humanity on this Earth. Never has the present day had such power at its disposal, which it constantly and automatically utilizes; never has it borne such responsibility, a responsibility that can be exercised only with *knowledge*.

The knowledge required here is twofold: on an objective level, that of physical causes; on a subjective one, that of human goals. An ethics for the future imposes urgent demands on the present; nevertheless, it needs to take into account futurology—the scientifically informed projection of what our present acts *can* causally lead to—so that we do not face the

This text is a revision and translation of a lecture presented in Bonn in October 1985 at a conference, "Industrial Society and an Ethics for the Future," under the auspices of the Friedrich-Ebert-Stiftung.

future blindly, but with our eyes open. Futurology as *wish fulfillment* is familiar to us as utopianism; but now we must learn futurology as *warning* in order to bring our unleashed abilities under our control. This warning, however, can affect only those people who, besides being aware of the scientific laws of causality, also have an *image of man* that entails certain duties they consider entrusted to their care.

Duty needs to be perceived in order to be followed, but it exists even if not perceived and must therefore possess its own independent ground. This is what the rather unusual term "ontological," used in the title of this essay, is aiming at. To start with, then, a few words about what is meant by "ontological grounding." As an example let us take two statements characterized by different types of logic and therefore by different levels of truth: "We must eat"; "We must work in order to eat." That we must eat has an ontological ground in our nature as metabolizing creatures. We exist only by virtue of our ongoing exchange of matter with the external world. That we must work in order to eat has its variable grounds in the conditions of that same external world (nature and society); our access to food depends on these conditions. Whereas the ontological necessity of having to eat is absolute and admits of no exception, the necessity of having to work is determined by circumstances and, as we know, admits of exceptions: privilege or wealth, for instance—in general terms "unearned income"—can free people from it.

An ontological grounding (such as our example of having to eat) is based on a quality that belongs inseparably to the *being* of something, as metabolism belongs to the organism, even exclusively to it and to no other thing; in such a case, therefore, the statement "All organisms are metabolic" is just as valid as "All metabolic creatures are organisms." The distinction can be illustrated by one and the same quality. That Socrates is mortal because all men are mortal is an empirical grounding whose certainty extends as far as our certain knowledge about "all" men past and future. That Socrates is mortal because mortality is part of being human is an ontological grounding which is valid a priori if "the being of man" assumed here was correctly understood. (This distinction is not the same as that between synthetic and analytic judgments.)

There are thus facts with an ontological basis and hence ontological reasons for the expression of such facts. But is a duty also a fact? Can "thou shalt" be deduced from "it is thus"? Can the validity of a commandment be deduced from the truth of something known? Does it make any sense to speak of value per se and its binding character? In short, is there an ontological grounding for the *concept* of responsibility and for its *warrant* to make demands on us? These questions are ultimately concerned with whether there is logically a bridge from being to moral obligation—from "what is" to "what ought to be"—and therefore an objective morality.[1] The answer will no doubt always be open to debate. Yet this very admission permits, even requires, the debate to continue and keeps the matter from being shelved prematurely, i.e., before the end of time. Invulnerable, then, both to unreasonable expectations and inevitable disappointments, I enter this now abandoned arena with a certain good cheer, ready to encounter metaphysics, so often declared dead. Better to have it lead one to new defeats than no longer to hear its song at all. Before attempting to ground a metaphysics for the future, let me first make my metaphysical belief known: *Being, in the testimony it gives of itself, informs us not only about what it is but also about what we owe to it.* Ethics too has an ontological ground, which is multilayered. We find it first of all in the being of man but further at the base of Being in general. Let us begin with ourselves.

II

Man is the only being known to us who can assume responsibility. The fact that he *can* assume it means that he *is* liable to it. This capacity for taking responsibility already signifies that man is subject to its imperative: the ability itself brings moral obligation with it. But the capacity for taking responsibility, an *ethical* capacity, lies in man's *ontological* capability to choose knowingly and willingly between alternative actions. Responsibility, therefore, is complementary to *freedom*; it is an acting subject's burden of freedom. With my act as such, I am responsible (and just as responsible if I omit it), regardless of whether someone is present—now or in the future—who holds me responsible. Responsibility, therefore, exists with or without God and, naturally even more so, with or without an earthly court of justice. Yet besides being responsibility *for* something, it is also responsibility *to* something—to an ultimate authority to which an accounting must be given. This authority, it will probably be said (if belief in divine authority is no longer present), is the human conscience. But in saying this, we are only replacing one question with another: namely, where does conscience get its criteria, or what source authorizes *its* decisions? To whom or what are we responsible in our conscience? Let us examine whether we can perhaps deduce what we are responsible *to* from what we are responsible *for*.

What I am responsible for are naturally the consequences of my actions—to the degree that they affect a being. Thus, the actual object of my responsibility is this *being* itself that I have affected. This, however, has an ethical sense only when this being is of some value: toward a being

that is value-indifferent I can defend any action at all, and that is the
same as saying that I need take no responsibility. If now (and whenever)
there is the assumption—again an *ontological* one—that what exists is of
value, then *its* being will have a claim on me; and since the valuableness
of Being as a whole speaks to me via this special instance, then ultimately
this whole does not appear solely as that *for* which I *become* responsible
with my actions in this particular case but also as that *to* which I *have*
always *been* responsible with all my possible actions—since its *value* has a
justified claim on me. This means that a commandment can proceed from
the being of things themselves—not initially from the will of a personal
Creator God on their behalf—and can be intended for me.

This "being intended for me" or "justified claim on me" is in the
first place and quite generally a claim on my perception and subsequently
on my respect. All of us are under an obligation to all value with our
perception, i.e., as *contemplative* subjects. "Value," however—this is part
of the concept—contains an immanent claim on reality that says it is
better for value to *be* than not to be. This is simply a part of the meaning
of "the Good" per se, and the abstract *recognition* of its prerogative to be is
the first thing "the Good" requires of me when I perceive it. But the claim
of a value-possessing being on me as a *practical* subject becomes concrete
(1) when this being is a vulnerable one, as living beings with their intrinsic
fragility always are; *and* (2) when it, with this vulnerability, enters the field
of my actions and is at the mercy of my power—either by accident or, what
is even more binding on me, by my own choice. Then the universal call
issuing from all transitory and valuable being is very concretely meant
for me and becomes an imperative for me. At the mercy of my power, it is
at the same time entrusted to it. In such a situation this being is naturally
subject to a *ranking* of values as soon as it is necessary to make a decision
between values (i.e., pro or con), as is almost always the case under real
conditions. By acting we must also incur guilt.

Not only passively, then, as the changing object of my actions, but
also actively as the permanent subject of a claim upon my duty, it is *Being*
which responsibility has to do with, in every individual case and always.
It is the being of this or that thing *for which* the individual act incurs
responsibility; the Being of the whole in its integrity is the authority
to which our act is responsible. This act itself, however, presupposes
freedom. Between these two ontological poles of human freedom and
the valuableness of Being lies responsibility as the ethical mediator. It is
complementary to each and the common function of both. This is basic
to what responsibility, as I understand it, is in its *essence*.

In its *full dimensions*, however — in all it applies to — responsibility
is a function of our *power* and proportional to it. For the magnitude of

our power determines the extent to which we can affect reality and in fact do so in our actions. Thus, as power increases so does responsibility.

Expansion of power also means expansion of its effects on the *future*. It follows from this that we can *exercise* our increased responsibility— which we *have* in any case, whether we want it or not—only if foreseeing the consequences of our actions increases proportionally. Ideally, the span of foresight should equal the span of the chain of consequences. But this kind of prognostication, both in the human domain—indeed in the vital realm as a whole—is impossible for many reasons. To be sure, increased power per se does in fact also encompass increased knowledge, for power is itself the fruit and application of such knowledge, and therefore the methods, acuity, and breadth of our foreknowledge have grown with it. But our increased knowledge has not kept pace with the far-reaching *effects* of our power, for in projecting the future there are always consequences—the farther ahead they lie, the more numerous they are— beyond those we can know and foresee. Perhaps it has always been thus, even when our power was much more limited, but it was just because of its limited extent that we could afford to speculate, make guesses, and wager on the unknown. That is no longer the case. Today human power *and its excesses*, which far outstrip any certain foreknowledge of its consequences, have taken on such enormous dimensions that even the daily exercise of our powers, which makes the routine of modern civilization possible and which we all depend on, becomes an ethical problem.[2]

III

This brings us to the present day and to the duties enjoined upon us by an ethics for the future appropriate to our contemporary situation; from this point on, our argument will be more concrete. The increased power mentioned earlier refers of course to modern technology. Both quantitatively and qualitatively it totally surpasses everything man has been able to do up to now both with nature and with himself. We do not need to waste many words on this subject, nor do we need to emphasize here that technology is double-faced, able to lead to either good or evil. Indeed, its good has the potential of turning into something bad due to its sheer growth, and it is the enormity of this growth that will affect man's lot on Earth far into the future. Although we have not known this for long, we are aware of it now with ever-increasing certainty. Two preliminary tasks follow from the need to ground an ethics that takes responsibility for the future of humanity: (1) to maximize our *knowledge* of the consequences of our actions in view of the way they are able to determine and imperil the future lot of mankind; and (2) in light of this knowledge of something unprecedentedly new that *might* come about, to develop a new knowledge of what is permissible and not permissible, of what to allow and what to avoid: in other words, in the last analysis and in positive terms, a knowledge of *the Good*, of what man ought to be. Here the anticipatory glimpse of what is *not* permissible, but now for the first time appears to be *possible*, can be of help to us. The first task is to develop an understanding of facts, the second an understanding of values. We need both as a compass for the future.

On the first point, the need for maximal *information* about probable long-term consequences of our collective actions, I refer the reader to what I have often already said on the subject,[3] stressing here only that intellectual deduction must be coupled with vividness of imagination in order for what we know about the future to win power over our present behavior. First of all, our foreknowledge of the out-of-control aspects of technology must try to catch up with our power so that we can subject its perhaps harmless immediate objectives to criticism based on its long-range consequences. Then, a serious *futurology*, such as the goal of responsibility demands, will become an independent and ongoing branch of research requiring the cooperation of numerous experts from the most divergent fields. By confronting our power with its future ramifications, futurology will have a sobering effect on those drunk with their own abilities and protect them from themselves. Still, in order for what is foreseen to determine our actions, we need a bridge of feeling that will awaken in us a vision of what is to come. Looking into the future for the sake of establishing an ethics has therefore an intellectual and an emotional function: it must instruct our mind and motivate our will. We must make clear what has to be averted; our horror of it must bring us to our senses; that understanding of causal connections which enabled us to deduce these horrors must be used to avert them. More will be said later about the role of feeling in this process.

The second preliminary task leads directly to the ontological problem to which this investigation is devoted: a concept of the *human being* that informs us what the human *Good* is, what human beings should be, what we are all about, and what is advantageous for us—which at the same time involves what we must *not* be, what diminishes and distorts us. We need this knowledge in order to be on guard that the human *Good*—which has always been imperiled, given its nature—does not fall victim to the deluge of technological advances. The dangers are new, but the Good is old.

Knowledge of the human Good must be derived from the essence of what is human. We have two sources for this: *history* and *metaphysics*. History teaches us what man can be—the range of his possibilities, those aspects about him to be preserved and those to be extirpated. For throughout the course of his history, *"man" has already shown himself*—in his heights and his depths, his greatness and wretchedness, in the sublime and the ridiculous. All theories of an "authentic" and "true" man whom we are to await or create or make possible or even force into existence are eschatological dreams of a political and anthropological nature that can only lead us to disaster. All such utopian dreams must be countered by the fact that "man" has always been present with everything in him that should be avoided and all that cannot be surpassed. From this we become aware of what is worthwhile in man, *that* there is something worthwhile about him and that our existence is worthy of a future—of an always new chance to develop our *potentiality* for the Good. And all we can attempt to do is to assure that this *potentiality* continues to exist.

IV

But it is metaphysics, with its utterly different *ontological*, not phenomenological, knowledge of existence that instructs us about the *ground* of what is truly human and man's *"ought*-to-be." Today it stands in ill repute, but we cannot do without it and must dare to turn to it again. For it alone can inform us *why* man ought to be at all, why he must not bring about his own disappearance from the world or unwittingly allow this to happen; it also tells us *how* he ought to be so that he honors and does not invalidate the ground of why he ought to be. The "Why," obligating humanity to *existence,* forbids first of all the physical suicide of the species (which is not forbidden by any biological imperative); the "How," which obligates humanity to a certain *quality* of life—i.e., which fills out the purely "That" with a "What"—forbids us to make out of this existence a wasteland for the soul. Technology's blind progress, however, is a threat to us in both regards. Thus, the new need for metaphysics, which must arm us against our blindness with its vision.

Needing metaphysics does not yet mean *having* it, and it is further removed from our positivistic way of thinking than ever. Needless to say, I don't possess it either. Still, a modest beginning, it seems to me, would be contained in the sentence with which we began our personal attempt at a grounding of ethics: Man is the only being known to us who *can* assume responsibility. We immediately recognize this "can" as more than a simply empirical fact. We recognize it as a distinguishing and decisive feature of human existence. Thus, we have in this fact a basic principle of philosophical anthropology, i.e., of the ontology of the being "Man," and with it already a principle of metaphysics—but only of the metaphysics of man.

Perhaps we may proceed from there as follows: we intuitively recognize in this ontological distinction of man—his capacity for responsibility —not only its *essentiality* but also a *value*. The appearance of this value in the world does not simply add another value to the already value-rich landscape of *being* but surpasses all that has gone before with something that generically transcends it. This represents a qualitative intensification of the valuableness of *Being as a whole*, the ultimate object of our responsibility. Thereby, however, the capacity for responsibility as such— besides the fact that having it obligates us to exercise it from case to case as the objects of our actions shift—becomes *its own object* in that having it obligates us to perpetuate *its presence in the world*. This presence is inexorably linked to the existence of creatures having that capacity. Therefore, the capacity for responsibility per se obligates its respective bearers to make existence possible for future bearers. In order to prevent responsibility from disappearing from the world—so speaks its immanent commandment—there ought to be human beings in the future. Thus, responsibility, behind all its ever differing *contingent* objects, always has itself as *ontological* object, even though this object becomes relevant only in the case of ontic endangerment. Then, for its own sake and for the sake of its presence in being, responsibility must make the preservation of its representation in the world an eminent concern. The first condition of this representation is the physical existence of man, i.e., of humanity, which leads to the prohibition of mankind's physical suicide or to the commandment to prevent it.

But that is only the first commandment. For although the ontological capacity for responsibility cannot be lost, psychological openness to it is an historically acquired, vulnerable possession that can be lost collectively, even if calculative reasoning and the power arising from it survive with the biological subject. Our responsibility to see that the capacity for responsibility survives in the world involves not only the *existence* of future human beings but also the *way* they exist; we must make sure the *conditions* of their existence do not cause this capacity (which depends upon the freedom of the subject) to disappear. Here the principle invoked earlier would come into effect: the "How" of existence must not contradict the *ground* of our obligation to it. That this could happen, externally and internally, is illustrated by such dystopias as the one described in Aldous Huxley's *Brave New World*, in which man, stripped of his nobility, survives in a not at all uncomfortable fashion. In *Beyond Freedom and Dignity*, B. F. Skinner goes so far as to portray such a world as a utopia.

What we have attempted in the foregoing is the metaphysical deduction of a specific duty of responsibility for the future of mankind from the phenomenon of responsibility itself—a seemingly circular "ontological argument." We have extracted a condition of existence from formal being, have deduced from the original experiential datum—the capacity for responsibility—the duty of responsibility to preserve the capacity for responsibility in general.

It is just this underlying empirical fact that saves our argument from the logical vicious circle of the famous "ontological proof" for the existence of God, which states that from the mere *concept* of God, which essentially assumes a necessary (noncontingent) existence—from conceptual "essence" therefore—actual existence necessarily follows. In contrast, the capacity for responsibility, upon which our argument is based, is primarily *given* as a fact of experience. When further conclusions are deduced from its essence, including the duty to perpetuate its existence, this is an argument proceeding from essence to *obligatory* existence, but not a vicious circle proceeding from essence to *given* existence. Thus, our argument is not an empty one.

But neither does it establish *proof.* For it is dependent on certain unproved, axiomatic premises: namely, that the capacity for responsibility per se is a *good*, something whose presence is preferable to its absence, and that there are *"values per se,"* which are anchored in Being—that the latter is thus *objectively* valuable.

Especially in the case of the former axiom, we cited direct intuition in our support. The validity of such intuition can, however, be debated; indeed, any individual can deny having it. And everyone is free to regard "values" *in general* as merely subjective preferences, either biological or determined by circumstances—and in particular to regard a feeling of responsibility (like every form of moral illusion) as a purposive attribute, favored by evolution and necessary for the survival of the species, which as such naturally gives the species no greater right to survival than does any other purposive attribute of any other kind of animal. The individual certainly does not *owe obedience* to the "imperative" of such biological programming, as little as he does to the imperative of other evolutionary endowments such as the sex drive or the aggressive drive. Nor does this disposition, with which so many others compete, obligate him to the *idea* of an everlasting existence of humanity after him; it is simply one determinant among others, all of which either do their work or do not. An "ought" is not to be inferred from them.

This combination of biologism and subjectivism of values (closely related to historical relativism) cannot really be refuted. One can only counter that *it* too is based on unproved, axiomatic premises, which I cannot enumerate here. My premises are, I believe, somewhat better thought out and do more justice to the total phenomenon of man and Being in general. But in the last analysis my argument can do no more than give rational grounding to an *option* it presents as a choice for a thoughtful person—an option that of course has its own inner power of persuasion. Unfortunately I have nothing better to offer. Perhaps a future metaphysics will be able to do more.

V

But to return to our subject: Modern megatechnology contains both of the threats we have named—that of physical annihilation and that of existential impoverishment: the former by means of its unquestionably negative potential for catastrophe (such as atomic war), the latter by means of its positive potential for manipulation. Examples of this manipulation, which can lead to our ethical powerlessness, are the automation of all work, psychological and biological behavior control, various forms of totalitarianism, and—probably most dangerous of all—the genetic reshaping of our nature. Finally, as far as *environmental* destruction is concerned—i.e., not a sudden nuclear apocalypse but a gradual one by means of a completely peaceful technology in the service of humanity— the physical threat itself becomes an existential one if the end result is global misery that allows only for an imperative of naked survival devoid of all feeling of ethical responsibility.

With this, we return to the other desideratum for the grounding of an ethics for the future in a technological age: the *factual* knowledge afforded by "futurology." We said earlier that this knowledge must awaken the right feelings in us in order to motivate us to act with responsibility. A few words are appropriate here about this emotional side of a vision of the future called for by ethics.

If we first think, as we cannot help but do, of the fate man has imposed on the planet, a fate staring at us out of the future, then we are right to feel a mixture of fear and guilt: fear because what we see ahead is something terrible; guilt because we are conscious of our own causal role in bringing it about. But can something frightful, which will not affect *us* but those who come much later, frighten us? Even watching a tragedy on the stage can do this, as we know. This analogy adds to our "fear" and anticipatory "pity" for later generations damned in advance, yet we do not have the consolation afforded by a stage drama that this is mere fiction; the reality of futurology's warning denies us that. Above all, however, its accusation that future generations are our victims makes the selfish distancing of our feelings, which something remote otherwise permits, morally impossible for us. Our horror at what the future holds cries out to us: "That must not be! We must not permit that! We must not bring that about!" An unselfish fear of what will eventuate long after us, anticipatory remorse on its account, and shame on our own account overcome us as sheer reflexes triggered by decency and by solidarity with our species. Here no metaphysical sanction is even necessary, yet it is anticipated in these reflexes and finds in those spontaneous feelings a natural ally for its demands. For this very reason the dismal conclusions of scientific futurology ought to be widely disseminated. In the end, then, it is the "ontological imperative," discussed earlier, of man's "ought-to-be," whether clearly recognized or dimly perceived, which absolutely forbids us to have the contemptible attitude of "after us the deluge." Given the validity of this imperative (which many surely can agree upon without any philosophical substantiation), the responsibility we bear because of our power becomes a compelling law.

The role of power in this entire context is complicated and in part paradoxical. On the one hand, it is the cause of the catastrophe we fear; on the other, the sole means of its possible prevention. This prophylaxis demands massive application of the same knowledge which is the source of our fateful power. By struggling against the effects of this power, we are strengthening its roots. Fear of our power has taken the place of the natural euphoria that once accompanied its possession, its enjoyment, and above all its self-engendered growth. It is no longer nature, as formerly, but our power over it which now fills us with fear—for the sake of nature and for our own sakes. Our power has become our master instead of our servant. We must now gain control over it. We have not yet done so, even though our power is entirely the result of our knowledge and our will. Knowledge, will, and power are collective, and therefore control of them must also be collective: it can come only from forces within the public sector. In other words, it must be political, and that requires in the long run a broad, grass-roots consensus.

But what sort of consensus would this be, and how could it be achieved? It would be a consensus to sharply reduce our habits of excessive consumption, to lower our celebrated "Western" standard of living of recent times, whose greed, along with its impact, is a major culprit in the global despoiling of the environment. Further, it would be a consensus to accept the at least temporary economic suffering such a contraction would bring with it; a consensus also to allow public intervention in the most private sphere of all, that of reproduction, which the population problem might make necessary. All this is inescapable, and the later it occurs the worse it will be, due to the simple truths that an Earth with its limited resources is incompatible with unlimited growth and the Earth will inevitably have the last word. As easy as this is to grasp, it is nevertheless still a complete mystery how consent to the necessary restraints is to be attained and then maintained through difficult times. For it is incomparably easier to offer a theoretical grounding for the ethics of a collective responsibility toward the future, as we have attempted to do here, than to map out the ways to accomplish it. Nevertheless, the call for such a theoretical grounding and the subsequent awakening of our awareness and education of our feelings that can emerge from a futurology infused with this purpose are crucial first steps.

VI

When faced with the dangers technological power holds for the planet's future, we have been concerned up to now mainly with its threats to the *environment*, to the *external* conditions of life in the future. In other words, we have envisaged consequences that affect man himself only indirectly and that can become catastrophic if they take on global proportions. This power deals in a direct way with nonhuman *things* (as has been true until now for all technology with the exception of medicine). When we assess how such power can critically change the overall condition of the Earth—where, for instance, the critical threshold values lie or how far we can go in this or that direction—quantitative considerations play the main role, and in attempting to weigh them we are still for the most part groping in the dark.

Recently, however, new technologies have been developed that have *man* as their direct object and that concern the being of *persons*. In this case *qualitative* questions arise in which numbers do not play a role and whose answers need not wait for the integral environmental science we would need in order to answer quantitative ecological questions in a competent way. When it is a matter of our own being, all we need is the always available knowledge of the *nature* of man, which tells us what the human *Good* is and, of course, what runs counter to it. I am thinking here primarily of developments in the field of *human biology*, with the completely new practical possibilities they open to medicine. The possibilities already realized or still on the horizon concern the beginning and the end of our existence—our birth, the length of our life, and our death—and our genetic constitution. They touch thereby upon ultimate questions having to do with our being human: i.e., the concept of the "bonum humanum," the meaning of life and death, the dignity of the individual, the integrity of the human image (in religious terms, the *imago dei*).

We must answer such questions in the light of a *valid* image of man, not simply one prevailing at the moment, and for this we need in turn a metaphysics. This time it must not be a merely formal one such as that attempted previously, which tells us why man should exist at all and why we bear the responsibility for his existence, but a material metaphysics of substance, which protects responsibility-taking existence from concrete distortions. In its light we can approach the questions of human technology in an *anticipatory* and also categorical way, free from hypothetical guessing games about numbers and complex global causalities, which now dominate the effects of our actions on the large scale. Here, where just one single example can tell the whole truth from the standpoint of Being, an encounter between an ethics for the future and technology can occur far in advance of the development of that technology's capability and can lead to binding decisions. The simple rule of thumb of "a heuristics of fear"—in the case of varying prognoses, to give ear to those that warn of catastrophe—is replaced by a sure judgment (not dependent on a *quantitative* calculation of the consequences) that this or that—whether in large or small measure—absolutely must not take place. If, for example, experimenting with the human genetic substance is in itself a crime, then it is so the first, single time it is done and not only when applied on a massive scale; otherwise the scale is the determining factor when evaluating the ravages of technology as well as excessive biological experimentation. Then, even research would not be free to perform such experiments, to set itself the goal of (or even explore the possibility of) genetic alteration in man. Here the so highly prized *freedom of science* would encounter a barrier, both in terms of its goal and its path.

With this look ahead at an ethics for the future, we are touching at the same time upon the question of the future of freedom. The unavoidable discussion of this question seems to give rise to misunderstandings. My dire prognosis that not only our material standard of living but also our democratic freedoms would fall victim to the growing pressure of a worldwide ecological crisis, until finally there would remain only some form of tyranny that would try to save the situation, has led to the accusation that I am defending dictatorship as a solution to our problems. I shall ignore here what is a confusion between warning and recommendation. But I have indeed said that such a tyranny would still be better than total ruin; thus, I have ethically accepted it as an alternative. I must now defend this standpoint, which I continue to support, before the court that I myself have created with the main argument of this essay.

For are we not contradicting ourselves in prizing physical survival at the price of freedom? Did we not say that freedom was the condition of our capacity for responsibility—and that this capacity was a reason for the survival of humankind? By tolerating tyranny as an alternative to physical annihilation are we not violating the principle we established: that the How of existence must not take precedence over its Why? Yet we can make a terrible concession to the primacy of physical survival in the conviction that the *ontological capacity* for freedom, inseparable as it is from man's being, cannot really be extinguished, only temporarily banished from the public realm. This conviction can be supported by experience we are all familiar with. We have seen that even in the most totalitarian societies the urge for freedom on the part of some individuals cannot be extinguished, and this renews our faith in human beings. Given this faith, we have reason to hope that, as long as there are *human beings* who survive, the image of God will continue to exist along with them and will wait in concealment for its new hour. With that hope—which in this particular case takes precedence over fear—it is permissible, for the sake of physical survival, to accept if need be a temporary absence of freedom in the external affairs of humanity.

This is, I want to emphasize, a worst-case scenario, and it is the foremost task of responsibility at this particular moment in world history to prevent it from happening. This is in fact one of the noblest of duties (and at the same time one concerning self-preservation), on the part of the imperative of responsibility to avert future coercion that would lead to lack of freedom by acting freely in the present, thus preserving as much as possible the ability of future generations to assume responsibility. But more than that is involved. At stake is the preservation of Earth's entire miracle of creation, of which our human existence is a part and before which man reverently bows, even without philosophical "grounding." Here too faith may precede and reason follow; it is faith that longs for this preservation of the Earth (*fides quaerens intellectum*), and reason comes as best it can to faith's aid with arguments, not knowing or even asking how much depends on its success or failure in determining what action to take. With this confession of faith we come to the end of our essay on ontology.

Translated by Hunter and Hildegarde Hannum

PART 2

A LUXURY OF REASON: THEOLOGICAL SPECULATIONS AFTER AUSCHWITZ

5

Immortality and the Modern Temper

For H. A.

In the following reflections I shall start from what I consider an undeniable fact, namely, that the modern temper is uncongenial to the
idea of immortality.[1] It is that over and above the objections which the
modern intellect entertains against it on theoretical grounds. These—
which for brevity I will simply grant en bloc—are by themselves indecisive.
As transcendental, the object of the idea—immortality itself—is beyond
proof or disproof: it is not an object of knowledge. But the idea of it is.
Therefore, the intrinsic merits of its meaning become the sole measure of
its credibility, and the appeal of that meaning remains as the sole ground
of possible belief—as certainly the lack of such an appeal is sufficient
ground for actual disbelief. But since what is meaningful depends, beyond
the mere condition of logical consistency, largely on the dispositions and
insights of the mind that judges it, we must interrogate these for their
prevalent unresponsiveness as well as for any possible hold which the idea,
even in its present eclipse, may still have, or reclaim, on our secularized
estate. Thus, an examination of the problem at this hour will be as much
an examination of ourselves as an examination of the issue of immortality;

Originally delivered as the Ingersoll Lecture of 1961 at Harvard University and subsequently published in the *Harvard Theological Review* 55 (1962), 1–20 [and then reprinted as
essay 11 in *The Phenomenon of Life* (New York: Delta, 1966). —ED.].

and even if it should throw no new light on the latter, on which in more than two thousand years probably everything has been said there is to say, it may yet throw some light on the present state of our mortal condition.

I

On the inhospitableness of the contemporary mind to the idea of immortality I can, indeed must, be very brief, since much has been said about it in our century, and the area of agreement is broad, and little disputed; whereas on the less noticed, and less obvious, opening which the modern mind does offer to the idea in one of its possible meanings, and does so precisely by its "modern" turn, I shall have to dwell at some length. This "opening," however, stands forth essentially from the negative background without which the modern temper would not be what it is.

First, then, a look at the negative side. Let me start with the oldest and most *empirical* concept of immortality: survival by immortal *fame*. This was most prized in antiquity and considered not only the just reward of noble deeds but a prime incentive to them.[2] The deeds must be visible, that is, public, to be noted and remembered as great. The dimension of this living-on is the dimension itself in which it is earned: the body politic. Immortal fame is thus public honor in perpetuity, as the body politic is human life in perpetuity. Now, already Aristotle pointed out that honor is worth just as much as the judgment of those who bestow it.[3] But then, the desire for it, and a fortiori the desire for its extension into posthumous fame, and ultimately the estimation of this form of immortality in principle, are justified only by the trust we can reasonably place in the integrity of its trustee and master, namely, public opinion: in its enlightenment now, its faithfulness in the future—and, of course, in its own unceasing continuity, that is the indefinite survival of the commonwealth. Now on all these counts the modern temper cannot permit itself the innocent confidence of the Greeks. The selectiveness as such of this "immortality," that it admits few and excludes most, we might accept if only we could believe in the justice of the selection. But for that we know too much of how reputations are made, how fame is fabricated, public opinion engineered, the record of history remade, and even premade, to the order of interest and power. In the age of the party lines, and, for that matter, of Madison Avenue, in the age of the universal corruption of the word, we are sadly aware that speech, the vehicle of this immortality, is the medium of lies as well as of truth, and more often the former than the latter in the public sphere—with a busily fostered growth between them of meaninglessness, not even fit for either, eating away into both; and the older suspicion whether we are not dealing with a tale told by an idiot is overshadowed by the worse that it might be a tale concocted by knaves.

We have also learned that even superhuman heroism can be so effectively shut off from all public knowledge and testimony that in mundane terms it is as if it had never been. Further, if generally the premium put on the spectacular at the expense of the hidden provokes our disdain, the great evildoers we moderns have had the fortune to know face us with the wholly repugnant perspective that the famous and the infamous come to stand on a par. For let no one deceive himself on the fact that to the perversity of those agents, and to that of a posterity responding to theirs, their evil fame is an achievement and not a penalty: and so the Hitlers and Stalins of our era would have succeeded to extract immortality from the extinction of their nameless victims.

Shall we add that only the vain craves immortality of name, while the truly proud and good can do with anonymous survival of his work? This leads to another version of the empirical concept: immortality of *influence*—to some extent the hope of every earnest effort in the service of higher purpose. But, alas, there again we are too worldly wise to trust in the worldly causality of things as a faithful repository of acts, since we can credit it neither with adequate discrimination of worth nor with its conservation in the shifts of time. This much, sober judgment could always have known. But we know something more and never known before: that the repository itself, namely human civilization, is perishable. This new knowledge invalidates both concepts, immortality of name and of influence—even that of great works of art and thought, which most of all resist obliteration by time: for what is itself mortal cannot well be the vehicle of immortality. With the dramatic sharpening which the generally modern awareness of the passing nature of cultures and societies has undergone more recently—to the point where the survival of the human race itself seems in jeopardy—our presumptive immortality, as that of all the immortals before us, appears suddenly at the mercy of a moment's miscalculation, failure, or folly by a handful of fallible men.

II

Let us, then, turn to the *nonempirical* and really substantive concept of immortality: survival of the person in a *hereafter*. This finds itself at even greater odds with the modern temper. I do not concern myself with the persuasive inference from the indubitable organic basis of "person" to its essential nonseparableness therefrom. But, do at least the nonempirical reasonings behind the *postulate* still have our ear? The serious ones, if we dismiss the mere creaturely recoil from death, fall roughly under two heads: justice, and the distinction between appearance and reality, of which the idea of the mere phenomenality of time is a case. Both have this in common: that they accord to man the metaphysical status of moral subject and, as such, of belonging to a moral or "intelligible" order besides the sensible one. This should not be lightly dismissed. But the principle of justice, be it retributive or compensatory justice, does by its own criterion not support the claim to immortality. For temporal merit or guilt calls for temporal, not eternal retribution, and justice thus requires at most a finite afterlife for settling accounts, not an infinity of existence. And as to compensation for undeserved suffering, or denied chances, or missed happiness here, there applies the additional consideration that a *claim* to happiness as such (how much of it?) is questionable to begin with; and that missed *fulfillment* could only be made up for *in its original terms*, that is, in the terms of effort and obstacles and uncertainty and fallibility and unique occasion and limited time—in short, in terms of nonguaranteed attainment and possible miss. These are the very terms of *self*-fulfillments and they are precisely the terms of the world. To try in them our being, and to experience the vicissitudes of our try, not knowing the outcome in advance—this is our genuine claim. Without those terms, without the anxiousness of chance and the zest of challenge and the sweetness of achievement under such terms, no bliss gratuitously granted can be anything but a counterfeit coin for what has been missed. It also would lack all moral worth. Indeed the here cannot be traded for a there—such is our present stance.

This also contains the modern temper's response to the distinction of appearance and reality. I have always felt that the idealistic philosophers who profess it may have been too sheltered from the shock of the external, so that they could regard it as a spectacle, a representation on a stage. They certainly do less than honor to what they demote to mere appearance. We hard-pressed children of the now insist on taking it seriously. Where we find it deceptive we take a harder look at it to make its truth more truly appear. The starkness of a barren mountainside, the beauty of an animated face, are the direct language of reality. And when in horror we look at the pictures from Buchenwald, at the wasted bodies and distorted faces, at the utter defilement of humanity in the flesh, we reject the consolation that this is appearance and the truth is something else: we face the terrible truth that the appearance is the reality, and that there is nothing more real than what here appears.

Most unsympathetic, perhaps, is modern philosophy to the view that time is not ultimately real but only the phenomenal form under which a timeless, noumenal reality appears to a subject which "in itself" is of that noumenal world. This was the tenuous theoretical link to possible personal immortality left by Kant's critical idealism, and it has withered away in the climate of the modern mind. From the discovery of man's basic historicity to the ontological elaboration of the innermost temporality of his being, it has been borne in upon us that time, far from being a mere form of phenomena, is of the essence of such things as selves, and that its finitude for each is integral to the very authenticity of his existing. Rather than dissemble, we claim our perishability: we do not wish to forego the pang and poignancy of finitude. We insist on facing nothingness and on having the strength to live with it. Thus, without a secret lifeline for reassurance, existentialism, this extreme offspring of the modern temper or distemper, throws itself into the waters of mortality. And we, whether of its doctrine or not, share enough of its spirit to have taken our lonely stand in time between the twofold nothing of before and after.

III

And yet, we feel that temporality cannot be the whole story, because in man it has an inherently self-surpassing quality, of which the very fact and fumbling of our idea of eternity is a cryptic signal. If everlastingness is a wrong concept, "eternity" may have other meanings—and a reference to the temporal of which our mortal experience, transcending its mere transience in the stream of events, may sometimes bear witness. The opaqueness of the here and now clears at times as if by sudden precipitation at the critical point: if there is any such transparency of the temporal for the eternal, however rare and brief, then the moments and modes in which it comes to pass can give us a clue as to what of our being, if not the substance of our selves, may be said to reach into the deathless and, therefore, be our stake in immortality. In what situations and in what forms do we encounter the eternal? When do we feel the wings of timelessness touch our heart and immortalize the now? In what manner does the absolute enter the relativities of our everyday existence?

I shall not invoke the testimony of mystical experiences that are not mine and, if they were, would find their claim come under the invincible suspicion of the psychologizing modern mind. Nor should the unsolicitable encounters of love or of beauty, which we might grant to be flashes of eternity, be summoned as evidence in discourse as if they were at our call, to the complacence of him who can claim them, and the discomfiture of him who cannot. Rather, in keeping with the modern temper, I turn to the one kind of evidence that depends on ourselves because we are active there, not receptive: wholly subject and in no way object.

In *moments of decision,* when our whole being is involved, we feel as if acting under the eyes of eternity. What can we mean by it—nay, by our willing that it be so? We may express our feeling in different symbols according to articulate beliefs which we hold or to the images we cherish. We may say, for instance, that what we do now will make an indelible entry in the "Book of Life," or leave an indelible mark in a transcendent order; that it will affect that order, if not our own destiny, for good or for evil; that we shall be accountable for it before a timeless seat of justice, or if we are not there for the accounting, because we have flowed down the river of time—that our eternal image is determined by our present deed, and that through what we do to that image of ours here and now, we are responsible for the spiritual totality of images that evergrowingly sums up the record of being and will be different for our deed. Or, less metaphysically, we may say that we wish to act so that, whatever the outcome here in the incalculable course of mundane causality—whether success or miscarriage—we can live with the spirit of our act through an eternity to come, or die with it the instant after this. Or, that we are ready to see ourselves, in an eternal recurrence of all things, when our turn comes round, and again we stand poised as now, blind as now, unaided as now—to see ourselves making the same decision again, and ever again, always passing the same imaginary test, endlessly reaffirming what is yet each time only once. Or, failing that certainty of affirmation, that at least the agony of infinite risk may be rightfully ours. And in this, eternity and nothingness meet in one: that the "now" justifies its absolute status by exposing itself to the criterion of being the last moment granted of time. To act as if in the face of the end is to act as if in the face of eternity, if either is taken as a summons to unhedging truth of selfhood. But to understand the end in this way is really to understand it in a light from beyond time.

BOTH DECISIONIST + EXISTENTIALIST

IV

What shall we make of these feelings and metaphors, and what, if anything, do they contribute? What hints do they furnish toward the issue of immortality? It will be noted that the symbols referred to speak, not of immortality, but of eternity—which, to be sure, is deathlessness but not necessarily mine, yet must have such a relation to my mortality that with something in or of my being I can, even must, share in it. What can that be? Let us further note that in all those symbols it was not the realm of feeling but that of acting, not the matter of bliss and pain but the spirit of decision and deed, in short, not our passive but our active nature, which came to stand in a relation to eternity. Let us take that hint. It seems a paradox at first. For is it not feeling which has duration, which spreads over time and, as a time-filling content, can at least be thought spread out indefinitely—whereas decision is of all the most transient occupant of time, an infinitesimal magnitude in extension, entirely lodged in the moment and irretrievably carried off with its fleeting now? And is it not feeling which craves immortality, which wishes to last, which tells to the moment "O stop and stay!"—while the act presses on, self-liquidating, looking beyond itself, not even wishing to stay, nay, wishing to end?

The paradox is that in what is self-negating, not in what is self-affirming with respect to lastingness, we should look for the relation—as yet undefined—to eternity. But perhaps the paradox contains its own hint. For that which has extension may have more or less of it, but must have an end: duration feeds on the boon of quantity, but is also enclosed in its limits: its benefit from the largess of a sensible continuum is at the same time its confinement—the confinement to its own immanence. Lasting as long as it does, it cannot outlast itself. On the other hand, the critical divide of the existential "now," in which free action is born, has dimension only by accident and is not measured by it. The evanescence as much as the protraction of its sensible span is defied by a transcendence of meaning which is indifferent to the long or the short of duration. Thus it may well be that the point of the moment, not the expanse of the flux, is our link to eternity: and the "moment" not as the *nunc stans*, the "standing now," in which the mystic tastes release from the movement of time, but moment as the momentum-giving motor of that very movement. On the threshold of deed holding time in suspense, but not a respite from time, it exposes our being to the timeless and with the turn of decision speeds us into action and time. Swiftly reclaimed by the movement it actuates, it marks man's openness to transcendence in the very act of committing him to the transience of situation, and in this double exposure, which compounds the nature of total concern, the "moment" places the responsible agent between time and eternity. From this place-between springs ever new the chance of new beginning, which ever means the plunge into the here and now.

Thus, to say it again, not what lasts longest in our experiences but what lasts shortest and is intrinsically most adverse to lastingness, may turn out to be that which binds the mortal to the immortal. From its testimony, then, we can perhaps extract a better meaning of what, inadequately, is called the "immortality of man," than the literal ones we have found wanting. Let us at least proceed on that expectation and by that hint.

To look in this direction for a tenable concept of immortality is in keeping with the modern temper, which we found so keenly conscious of the essential temporality of our being, of its intrinsic reference to finite situation, and so suspicious of the possibility and the very sense of endless self-persistence. And it is also in keeping with the most meaningful, if misapplied, aspects in traditional ideas of immortality. It was the meteoric flash of deed and daring which was to be immortalized by worldly fame; the life-sum of purpose, acts, and failure to act, on which retribution in an afterlife was to be visited; our moral being, from which alone Kant held immortality of the person to be arguable—as a postulate of "practical" (not an inference of theoretical) reason. Dubious as the vehicle of fame has been found, faulty as the correlation of temporal merit with eternal reward or punishment, and invalid as the argument of infinite perfectibility and the supposed right thereto is—the aspect of justice as such in these ideas of immortality, as against the wholly untenable argument from indestructible substance, still commands in us a stirring of acknowledgment by the transcendent dignity it confers on the realm of decision and deed. Let us then follow the intimations of our acting experience, of our freedom and responsibility, and take the tentative term of an "immortality of deeds" for our lead in interrogating some of the quoted metaphors which must themselves have sprung from intimations of just that kind. I wish to choose two of those we encountered: the "Book of Life," and the transcendent "Image."

V

What can the symbol of the Book of Life tell us? In Jewish tradition it means a kind of heavenly ledger wherein our "names" shall be inscribed according to our deserts: we shall qualify by our deeds to be inscribed "for life," namely ours. And this, of course, implies individual immortality. But instead of seeing deeds in the light of deserts, to be accounted to the agent, we can choose to see them as counting in themselves—and then adopt a different concept of the Book whereby it fills with deeds rather than names. We are, in other words, speaking of the possibility that deeds inscribe *themselves* in an eternal memoir of time; that whatever is here enacted somehow registers—beyond its registering and eventual dissipating in the causal patterns of time—in a transcendent realm by rules of effect quite different from those of the world, ever swelling the unfinished record of being and forever shifting the anxious balance of its reckoning. Might it not even be, to venture yet a step further, that what we thus add to the record is of surpassing import—not indeed for a future destiny of ours, but for the concern of that spiritual account itself kept by the unified memory of things—and that, although we mortal agents have no further stake in the immortality which our acts go to join, these acts of ours, and what through them we make of our lives, may just be the stake which an undetermined and vulnerable eternity has in us? And with our freedom, what a precarious stake! Are we, then, perhaps an experiment of eternity? Our very mortality—a venture of the immortal ground with itself? Our freedom—the summit of the venture's chance and risk?

We turn for further advice to another simile, that of the transcendent "Image" filled in, feature by feature, by our temporal deeds. We encounter it in gnostic literature, especially of the Iranian branch, in several versions.

One is the conception of a celestial double of the terrestrial self, which the departing soul will meet after death: "I go to meet my image and my image comes to meet me: it caresses and embraces me as if I were returning from captivity"—thus a Mandaean source.[4] And in the beautiful Hymn of the Pearl, this "double" (first described as a "raiment"), when meeting the returning "prince," is recognized by him as the image of his own self, and in turn acknowledges him as the one "for whom I was reared in my Father's house, and I perceived in myself how my stature grew in accordance with his labors."[5] According to this version, then, everyone seems to have his alter ego, "kept safe" in the upper world while he labors down below, yet as to its state ultimately entrusted to his responsibility: symbolizing the eternal self of the person, it grows with his trials and deeds, and its form is perfected by his toils—perfected or else, we must add, remembering *The Picture of Dorian Gray*, spoiled and defiled by them. In the salvational turn of our texts this sinister but logically necessary alternative is regularly omitted. There, the encounter as such marks the successful conclusion of the soul's earthly journey and results in a consummating fusion of the two, a mutual absorption, a reuniting of what was temporarily parted. Again, this symbolism expresses immortality of the individual self.

However, there is a collective as well as individualized version of the image symbolism, which connects our deeds not with a perpetuity of our separate selves but with the consummation of the divine self. I quote from one of Mani's writings, discovered about 1930 in a Coptic translation in Egypt:

At the end, when the cosmos is being dissolved, the Thought of Life shall gather himself in and shall form his Self in the shape of the Last Image.[6] . . . With his Living Spirit he shall catch the Light and the Life that is in all things, and build it onto his body.

He gathers in his own Soul unto himself and forms himself in the shape of this Last Image. And thou shalt find him as he sweeps out of himself and casts out the impurity which is alien to him, but gathers in to himself the Life and the Light that is in all things and builds it onto his body. Then, when this Last Image is perfected in all its members, then it shall . . . be lifted out of the great struggle through the Living Spirit . . . who comes and . . . fetches the members out of . . . the dissolution and the end of all things.[7]

It would take us far beyond our present purpose to expound the precise dogmatic meaning of this symbolism. It must suffice to say that what is here called "the last image," emerging at the end of time, is according to Manichaean doctrine built up progressively over and through the world process as a whole: all history, of life in general and of man in particular, incessantly works at it and, in the "final image," restores to its pristine fullness that immortal but passible deity, an emanation from the First God (called "Primal Man"), whose initial self-surrender to the darkness and danger of becoming made the material universe possible— and necessary at the same time. Now, neither the reasons which Mani gives for this initial divine surrender, nor their more sophisticated alternatives in other gnostic speculations, nor, in general, the denigration of corporeal nature as such common to all these versions, will be acceptable to the modern mind in its resolutely antidualistic temper. Nor will the finite eschatology, positing a determinate goal and end of time, suit our conviction of indefinite continuation of cosmic change and our profound disbelief that the mechanics of it would provide for any ending within or of it to coincide with consummation. Yet the motif of the total "Image" can speak to us across these barriers of doctrine and mood. Let us note what in it is potentially significant for us.

I for one would note these features. In the temporal transactions of the world, whose fleeting now is ever swallowed by the past, an eternal presence grows, its countenance slowly defining itself as it is traced with the joys and sufferings, the triumphs and defeats of divinity in the experiences of time, which thus immortally survive. Not the agents, which must ever pass, but their acts enter into the becoming Godhead and indelibly form his never decided image. God's own destiny, his doing or undoing, is at stake in this universe to whose unknowing dealings he committed his substance, and man has become the eminent repository of this supreme and every betrayable trust. In a sense, he holds the fate of deity in his hands.

This, I contend, makes sense. As a hypothetical background of metaphysical fact it can validate those subjective feelings about an eternal issue which we experience in the call of conscience, in the moments of supreme decision, in the total commitment of deed, and even in the agony of remorse—and these may well be the only empirical signs of an immortal side to our being which our present critical consciousness will still be ready to consider in evidence.

VI

But into what complete metaphysics would such a hypothetical fragment fit? If, as one sometimes cannot resist doing, I permit myself the license of ignorance, which in these matters is our lot, and the vehicle of myth or likely imagination, which Plato allowed for it, I am tempted to thoughts like these.

In the beginning, for unknowable reasons, the ground of being, or the Divine, chose to give itself over to the chance and risk and endless variety of becoming. And wholly so: entering into the adventure of space and time, the deity held back nothing of itself: no uncommitted or unimpaired part remained to direct, correct, and ultimately guarantee the devious working-out of its destiny in creation. On this unconditional immanence the modern temper insists. It is its courage or despair, in any case its bitter honesty, to take our being-in-the world seriously: to view the world as left to itself, its laws as brooking no interference, and the rigor of our belonging to it as not softened by extramundane providence. The same our myth postulates for God's being in the world. Not, however, in the sense of pantheistic immanence: if world and God are simply the same, the world at each moment and in each state represents his fullness, and God can neither lose nor gain. Rather, in order that the world might be, and be for itself, God renounced his own being, divesting himself of his deity—to receive it back from the Odyssey of time weighted with the chance harvest of unforeseeable temporal experience: transfigured or possibly even disfigured by it. In such self-forfeiture of divine integrity for the sake of unprejudiced becoming, no other foreknowledge can be admitted than that of *possibilities* which cosmic being offers in its own terms: to these, God committed his cause in effacing himself for the world.

And for aeons his cause is safe in the slow hands of cosmic chance and probability—while all the time we may surmise a patient memory of the gyrations of matter to accumulate into an ever more expectant accompaniment of eternity to the labors of time—a hesitant emergence of transcendence from the opaqueness of immanence.

And then the first stirring of life—a new language of the world: and with it a tremendous quickening of concern in the eternal realm and a sudden leap in its growth toward recovery of its plenitude. It is the world-accident for which becoming deity had waited and with which its prodigal stake begins to show signs of being redeemed. From the infinite swell of feeling, sensing, striving, and acting, which ever more varied and intense rises above the mute eddyings of matter, eternity gains strength, filling with content after content of self-affirmation, and the awakening God can first pronounce creation to be good.

But note that with life together came death, and that mortality is the price which the new possibility of being called "life" had to pay for itself. If permanence were the point, life should not have started out in the first place, for in no possible form can it match the durability of inorganic bodies. It is essentially precarious and corruptible being, an adventure in mortality, obtaining from long-lasting matter on its terms—the short terms of metabolizing organism—the borrowed finite careers of individual selves. Yet it is precisely through the briefly snatched self-feeling, doing, and suffering of *finite* individuals, with the pitch of awareness heightened by the very press of finitude, that the divine landscape bursts into color and the deity comes to experience itself. If, then, mortality is the very condition of the separate selfhood which in the instinct of self-presentation shows itself so highly prized throughout the organic world, and if the yield of this mortality is the food of eternity, it is unreasonable to demand for its appointed executants, the self-affirming selves—immortality. The instinct of self-preservation indeed acknowledges this, for it implies the premise of extinction in its straining each time to ward it off for the nonce.

Note also that with life's innocence before the advent of knowledge God's cause cannot go wrong. Whatever variety evolution brings forth adds to the possibilities of feeling and acting, and thus enriches the self-experiencing of the ground of being. Every new dimension of world-response opened up in its course means another modality for God's trying out his hidden essence and discovering himself through the surprises of the world-adventure. And all its harvest of anxious toil, whether bright or dark, swells the transcendent treasure of temporally lived eternity. If this is true for the broadening spectrum of diversity as such, it is even truer for the heightening pitch and passion of life that go with the twin rise of perception and motility in animals. The ever more sharpened keenness of appetite and fear, pleasure and pain, triumph and anguish, love and even cruelty—their very edge is the deity's gain. Their countless, yet never blunted incidence—hence the necessity of death and new birth—supplies the tempered essence from which the Godhead reconstitutes itself. All this, evolution provides in the mere lavishness of its play and the sternness of its spur. Its creatures, by merely fulfilling themselves in pursuit of their lives, vindicate the divine venture. Even their suffering deepens the fullness of the symphony. Thus, this side of good and evil, God cannot lose in the great evolutionary game.

Nor yet can he fully win in the shelter of its innocence, and a new expectancy grows in him in answer to the direction which the unconscious drift of immanence gradually takes.

And then he trembles as the thrust of evolution, carried by its own momentum, passes the threshold where innocence ceases and an entirely new criterion of success and failure takes hold of the divine stake. The advent of man means the advent of knowledge and freedom, and with this supremely double-edged gift the innocence of the mere subject of self-fulfilling life has given way to the charge of responsibility under the disjunction of good and evil. To the promise and risk of this agency the divine cause, revealed at last, henceforth finds itself committed; and its issue trembles in the balance. The image of God, haltingly begun by the universe, for so long worked upon—and left undecided in the wide and then narrowing spirals of prehuman life—passes with this last twist, and with a dramatic quickening of the movement, into man's precarious trust, to be completed, saved, or spoiled by what he will do to himself and the world. And in this awesome impact of his deeds on God's destiny, on the very complexion of eternal being, lies the immortality of man.

With the appearance of man, transcendence awakened to itself and henceforth accompanies his doings with the bated breath of suspense, hoping and beckoning, rejoicing and grieving, approving and frowning—and, I daresay, making itself felt to him even while not intervening in the dynamics of his worldly scene: for can it not be that by the reflection of its own state as it wavers with the record of man, the transcendent casts light and shadow over the human landscape?

VII

Such is the tentative myth which I would like to believe "true"—in the sense in which myth may happen to adumbrate a truth which of necessity is unknowable and even, in direct concepts, ineffable, yet which, by intimations to our deepest experience, lays claim upon our powers of giving indirect account of it in revocable, anthropomorphic images. In the great pause of metaphysics in which we are, and before it has found its own speech again, we must entrust ourselves to this, admittedly treacherous, medium at our risk. The myth, if only it is conscious of its experimental and provisional nature and does not pose as doctrine, can from the necessity of that pause bridge the vacuum with its fleeting span. I at any rate felt driven to it for once under the constraint of a task which philosophy even in its helplessness must not deny.

To continue, then, in the same speculative vein, there follow certain ethical conclusions from the metaphysics which my myth has adumbrated. The first is the transcendent importance of our deeds, of how we live our lives. If man, as our tale has it, was created "for" the image of God, rather than "in" his image—if our lives become lines in the divine countenance—then our responsibility is not defined in mundane terms alone, by which often it is inconsequential enough, but registers in a dimension where efficacy follows transcausal norms of inner essence. Further, as transcendence grows with the terribly ambiguous harvest of deeds, our impact on eternity is for good *and* for evil: we can build and we can destroy, we can heal and we can hurt, we can nourish and we can starve divinity, we can perfect and we can disfigure its image: and the scars of one are as enduring as the lustre of the other. Thus, the immortality of our deeds is no cause for vain rejoicing—what most often ought to be wished for is rather their leaving no trace. But this is not granted: they have traced their line, though not as the individual's destiny. The individual is by nature temporal, not eternal; and the person in particular, mortal trustee of an immortal cause, has the enjoyment of selfhood for the moment of time as the means by which eternity lays itself open to the decisions of time. *As* enacted in the medium of becoming, that is, as transient, are personal selves eternity's stake. Thus it is that in the irrepeatable occasions of finite lives the issue must be decided time and again: infinite duration would blunt the point of the issue and rob occasion of its urgent call.

Nor, apart from this ontological consideration, does man have a moral claim to the gift of immortality. Availing himself of the enjoyment of selfhood, he has endorsed the terms on which it is offered, and rather than having it as a title for more, he owes thanks for the grant of existence as such—and for that which made it possible. For *there is no necessity of there being a world at all.* Why is there something rather than nothing?—this unanswerable question of metaphysics should protect us from taking existence for an axiom, and its finiteness for a blemish on it or a curtailment of its right. Rather is the fact of existence the mystery of mysteries—which our myth has tried to reflect in a symbol. By foregoing its own inviolateness the eternal ground allowed the world to be. To this self-denial every creature owes its existence, and with it has received all there is to receive from beyond. Having given himself whole to the becoming world, God has no more to give: it is man's now to give to him. And he may give by seeing to it in the ways of his life that it does not happen, or not happen too often, and not on his account, that "it repented the Lord"[8] to have made the world. This may well be the secret of the "thirty-six righteous ones" whom, according to Jewish tradition, the world shall never lack:[9] that with the superior valency of good over evil, which, we hope, obtains in the noncausal logic of things there, their hidden holiness can outweigh countless guilt, redress the balance of a generation and secure the serenity of the invisible realm.

But does that serenity, or its contrary, matter to our life on Earth? Does it touch it? Let me join this question with another one, in conclusion of my groping journey. What about those who never could inscribe themselves in the Book of Life with deeds either good or evil, great or small, because their lives were cut off before they had their chance, or their humanity was destroyed in degradations most cruel and most thorough such as no humanity can survive? I am thinking of the gassed and burnt children of Auschwitz, of the defaced, dehumanized phantoms of the camps, and of all the other, numberless victims of the other man-made holocausts of our time. Among men, their sufferings will soon be forgotten, and their names even sooner. Another chance is not given them, and eternity has no compensation for what has been missed in time. Are they, then, debarred from an immortality which even their tormentors and murderers obtain because they could *act*—abominably, yet accountably, thus leaving their sinister mark on eternity's face? This I refuse to believe. And this I like to believe: that there was weeping in the heights at the waste and despoilment of humanity; that a groan answered the rising shout of ignoble suffering, and wrath—the terrible wrong done to the reality and possibility of each life thus wantonly victimized, each one a thwarted attempt of God. "The voice of thy brother's blood cries unto me from the ground": Should we not believe that the immense chorus of such cries that has risen up in our lifetime now hangs over our world as a dark and accusing cloud? that eternity looks down upon us with a frown, wounded itself and perturbed in its depths?

And might we not even feel it? I think it possible, in spite of what I have said about the closed immanence of the worldly realm. For the secret sympathy that connects our being with the transcendent condition and makes the latter depend on our deeds, must somehow work both ways—

or else there would not even be that inward testimony for us to invoke on which our whole case for the eternal was grounded. If so, the state of transcendence, as we have let it become, will in turn have a resonance in ours—sometimes felt, though mostly not, and presently felt, perhaps, in a general malaise, in the profound distemper of the contemporary mind. Things human do not prosper under our hands. Happiness eludes our pursuit, and meaning mocks our desperate need. Could it be that, superinduced upon the many-layered, but never completely explaining causes from within our historical existence, also the disturbance of the transcendent order which we have caused by the monstrous crimes of our time, thus reacts on the spiritual mood of men—and thus the modern temper paradoxically might itself reflect the immortality which it disowns? It would be fitting—more I dare not say if the slaughtered had that share in immortality, and on their account a great effort were asked of those alive to lift the shadow from our brow and gain for those after us a new chance of serenity by restoring it to the invisible world.

But even if not their shadow, certainly the shadow of the bomb is there to remind us that the image of God is in danger as never before, and on most unequivocal, terrestrial terms. That in these terms an eternal issue is at stake together with the temporal one—this aspect of our responsibility can be our guard against the temptation of fatalistic acquiescence or the worse treason of *apres nous le deluge.* We literally hold in our faltering hands the future of the divine adventure and must not fail Him, even if we would fail ourselves.

Thus, in the dim light at the end of our wandering we may discern a twofold responsibility of man: one in terms of worldly causality, by which the effect of his deed extends for some greater or shorter length into a future where it eventually dissipates; and a simultaneous one in terms of its impact on the eternal realm, where it never dissipates. The one, with our limited foresight and the complexity of worldly things, is much at the mercy of luck and chance; the other goes by knowable norms which, in the Bible's words,[10] are not far from our hearts. There might even be, as I indicated, a third dimension to our responsibility in terms of the impalpably reciprocal way in which eternity, without intervening in the physical course of things, will communicate its spiritual state as a pervading mood to a generation which will have to live with it.

But the first two are more than enough to summon us to our task. Although the hereafter is not ours, nor eternal recurrence of the here, we can have immortality at heart when in our brief span we serve our threatened mortal affairs and help the suffering immortal God.

The Concept of God after Auschwitz: A Jewish Voice ⟨1984, age 81⟩

NB his mother died in Auschw.

W hen, with the honor of this award, I also accepted the burden of delivering the oration that goes with it, and when I read in the biography of Rabbi Leopold Lucas, in whose memory the prize is named, that he died in Theresienstadt, but that his wife Dorothea, mother of the donor, was then shipped to Auschwitz, there to suffer the fate that my mother suffered there, too, there was no resisting the force with which the theme of this lecture urged itself on my choice. I chose it with fear and trembling. But I believed I owed it to those shadows that something like an answer to their long-gone cry to a silent God be not denied to them.

What I have to offer is a piece of frankly speculative theology. Whether this behooves a philosopher is a question I leave open. Immanuel Kant has banished everything of the kind from the territory of theoretical reason and hence from the business of philosophy; and the logical positivism of our century, the entire dominant analytical creed, even denies to the linguistic expressions such reasonings employ for their purported subject matters this very object-significance itself, that is, any conceptual meaning at all, declaring already—prior to questions of truth

This is my translation of a lecture I delivered in German on the occasion of receiving the Dr. Leopold Lucas Prize for 1984 at Tübingen University. It was published in Fritz Stern and Hans Jonas, *Reflexionen finsterer Zeit* (Tübingen: J. B. C. Mohr, 1984). The lecture expanded and recast an earlier paper with the same title ("The Concept of God after Auschwitz," in *Out of the Whirlwind*, ed. A. H. Friedlander [New York: Union of American Hebrew Congregations, 1968], 465–76), which in turn incorporated portions of my 1961 Ingersoll Lecture, "Immortality and the Modern Temper." [Reprinted as chapter 5 of this volume.—ED.]

and verification—the mere speech about them to be nonsensical. At this, to be sure, old Kant himself would have been utterly astounded. For he, to the contrary, held these alleged nonobjects to be the highest objects of all, about which reason can never cease to be concerned, although it cannot hope ever to obtain a knowledge of them and in their pursuit is necessarily doomed to failure by the impassable limits of human cognition. But this cognitive veto, given the yet justified concern, leaves another way open besides that of complete abstention: bowing to the decree that "knowledge" eludes us here, nay, even waiving this very goal from the outset, one may yet meditate on things of this nature in terms of sense and meaning. For the contention—this fashionable contention— that not even sense and meaning pertain to them is easily disposed of as a circular, tautological inference from first having defined "sense" as that which in the end is verifiable by sense data or from generally equating "meaningful" with "knowable." To this axiomatic fiat by definition only he is bound who has first consented to it. He who has not is free, therefore, to work at the *concept* of God, even knowing that there is no *proof* of God, as a task of understanding, not of knowledge; and such working is philosophical when it keeps to the rigor of concept and its connection with the universe of concepts.

But of course, this epistemological laissez-passer is much too general and impersonal for the matter at hand. As Kant granted to the practical reason what he denied to the theoretical, so may we allow the force of a unique and shattering experience a voice in the question of what "is the matter" with God. And there, right away, arises the question: What did Auschwitz add to that which one could always have known about humans and from times immemorial have done? And what has it added in particular to what is familiar to us Jews from a millennial history of suffering and forms so essential a part of our collective memory? The question of Job has always been the main question of theodicy— of general theodicy because of the existence of evil as such in the world, and of particular theodicy in its sharpening by the riddle of election, of the purported covenant between Israel and its God. As to this sharpening, under which our present question also falls, one could at first invoke—as the prophets did—the covenant itself for an explanation of what befell the human party to it: the "people of the covenant" had been unfaithful to it. In the long ages of faithfulness thereafter, guilt and retribution no longer furnished the explanation, but the idea of "witness" did instead— this creation of the Maccabean age, which bequeathed to posterity the concept of the martyr. It is of its very meaning that precisely the innocent and the just suffer the worst. In deference to the idea of witness, whole communities in the Middle Ages met their death by sword and fire with the Sh'ma Jisrael, the avowal of God's Oneness on their lips. The Hebrew name for this is Kiddush-hashem, "sanctification of the Name," and the slaughtered were called "saints." Through their sacrifice shone the light of promise, of the final redemption by the Messiah to come.

Nothing of this is still of use in dealing with the event for which "Auschwitz" has become the symbol. Not fidelity or infidelity, belief or unbelief, not guilt or punishment, not trial, witness and messianic hope, nay, not even strength or weakness, heroism or cowardice, defiance or submission had a place there. Of all this, Auschwitz, which also devoured the infants and babes, knew nothing; to none of it (with rarest exceptions) did the factory-like working of its machine give room. Not for the *sake* of faith did the victims die (as did, after all, "Jehovah's Witnesses"), nor *because* of their faith or any self-affirmed bend of their being as persons were they murdered. Dehumanization by utter degradation and deprivation preceded their dying, no glimmer of dignity was left to the freights bound for the final solution, hardly a trace of it was found in the surviving skeleton specters of the liberated camps. And yet, paradox of paradoxes: it *was* the ancient people of the "covenant," no longer believed in by those involved, killers and victims alike, but nevertheless just this and no other people, under which the fiction of race had been chosen for this wholesale annihilation—the most monstrous inversion of election into curse, which defied all possible endowment with meaning. There does, then, in spite of all, exist a connection—of a wholly perverse kind—with the God-seekers and prophets of yore, whose descendants were thus collected out of the dispersion and gathered into the unity of joint death. And God let it happen. What God could let it happen?

Here we must note that on this question the Jew is in greater theoretical difficulty than the Christian. To the Christian (of the stern variety) the world is anyway largely of the devil and always an object of suspicion—the human world in particular because of original sin. But to the Jew, who sees in "this" world the locus of divine creation, justice, and redemption, God is eminently the Lord of *history*, and in this respect "Auschwitz" calls, even for the believer, the whole traditional concept of God into question. It has, indeed, as I have just tried to show, added to the Jewish historical experience something unprecedented and of a nature no longer assimilable by the old theological categories. Accordingly, one who will not thereupon just give up the concept of God altogether—and even the philosopher has a right to such an unwillingness—must rethink it so that it still remains thinkable; and that means seeking a new answer to the old question of (and about) Job. The Lord of history, we suspect, will have to go by the board in this quest. To repeat then: What God could let it happen?

For a possible, if groping, answer, I fall back on a speculative attempt with which I once ventured to meet the different question of immortality but in which also the specter of Auschwitz already played its part. On that occasion, I resorted to a *myth* of my own invention—that vehicle of imaginative but credible conjecture that Plato allowed for the sphere beyond the knowable. Allow me to repeat it here.

In the beginning, for unknowable reasons, the ground of being, or the Divine, chose to give itself over to the chance and risk and endless variety of becoming. And wholly so: entering into the adventure of space and time, the deity held back nothing of itself: no uncommitted or unimpaired part remained to direct, correct, and ultimately guarantee the devious working-out of its destiny in creation. On this unconditional immanence the modern temper insists. It is its courage or despair, in any case its bitter honesty, to take our being-in-the-world seriously: to view the world as left to itself, its laws as brooking no interference, and the rigor of our belonging to it as not softened by extramundane providence. The same our myth postulates for God's being in the world. Not, however, in the sense of pantheistic immanence: if world and God are simply the same, the world at each moment and in each state represents his fullness, and God can neither lose nor gain. Rather, in order that the world might be, and be for itself, God renounced his being, divesting himself of his deity— to receive it back from the odyssey of time weighted with the chance harvest of unforeseeable temporal experience: transfigured or possibly even disfigured by it. In such self-forfeiture of divine integrity for the sake of unprejudiced becoming, no other foreknowledge can be admitted than that of *possibilities*, which cosmic being offers in its own terms: to these, God committed his cause in effacing himself for the world.

And for aeons his cause is safe in the slow hands of cosmic chance and probability—while all the time we may surmise a patient memory of the gyrations of matter to accumulate into an ever more expectant accompaniment of eternity to the labors of time—a hesitant emergence of transcendence from the opaqueness of immanence.

And then the first stirring of life—a new language of the world: and with it a tremendous quickening of concern in the eternal realm and a sudden leap in its growth toward recovery of its plenitude. It is the world-accident for which becoming deity had waited and with which its prodigal stake begins to show signs of being redeemed. From the infinite swell of feeling, sensing, striving, and acting, which ever more varied and intense rises above the mute eddyings of matter, eternity gains strength, filling with content after content of self-affirmation, and the awakening God can first pronounce creation to be good.

But note that with life together came death, and that mortality is the price which the new possibility of being called "life" had to pay for itself. If permanence were the point, life should not have started out in the first place, for in no possible form can it match the durability of inorganic bodies. It is essentially precarious and corruptible being, an adventure in mortality, obtaining from long-lasting matter on its terms—the short terms of metabolizing organism—the borrowed, finite careers of individual selves. Yet it is precisely through the briefly snatched self-feeling, doing, and suffering of *finite* individuals, with the pitch of awareness heightened by the very press of finitude, that the divine landscape bursts into color and the deity comes to experience itself.

Note also that with life's innocence before the advent of knowledge God's cause cannot go wrong. Whatever variety evolution brings forth adds to the possibilities of feeling and acting, and thus enriches the self-experiencing of the ground of being. Every new dimension of world-response opened up in its course means another modality for God's trying out his hidden essence and discovering himself through the surprises of the world-adventure. And all its harvest of anxious toil, whether bright or dark, swells the transcendent treasure of temporally lived eternity. If this is true for the broadening spectrum of diversity as such, it is even truer for the heightening pitch and passion of life that go with the twin rise of perception and motility in animals. The ever more sharpened keenness of appetite and fear, pleasure and pain, triumph and anguish, love and even cruelty—their very edge is the deity's gain. Their countless, yet never blunted incidence—hence the necessity of death and new birth—supplies the tempered essence from which the Godhead reconstitutes itself. All this, evolution provides in the mere lavishness of its play and the sternness of its spur. Its creatures, by merely fulfilling themselves in pursuit of their lives, vindicate the divine venture. Even their suffering deepens the fullness of the symphony. Thus, this side of good and evil, God cannot lose in the great evolutionary game.

Nor yet can he fully win in the shelter of its innocence, and a new expectancy grows in him in answer to the direction which the unconscious drift of immanence gradually takes.

And then he trembles as the thrust of evolution, carried by its own momentum, passes the threshold where innocence ceases and an entirely new criterion of success and failure takes hold of the divine stake. The advent of man means the advent of knowledge and freedom, and with this supremely double-edged gift the innocence of the mere subject of self-fulfilling life has given way to the charge of responsibility under the disjunction of good and evil. To the promise and risk of this agency the divine cause, revealed at last, henceforth finds itself committed; and its issue trembles in the balance. The image of God, haltingly begun by the universe, for so long worked upon—and left undecided—in the wide and then narrowing spirals of prehuman life, passes man's precarious trust, to be completed, saved, or spoiled by what he will do to himself and the world. And in this awesome impact of his deeds on God's destiny, on the very complexion of eternal being, lies the immortality of man.

With the appearance of man, transcendence awakened to itself and henceforth accompanies his doings with the bated breath of suspense, hoping and beckoning, rejoicing and grieving, approving and frowning— and, I daresay, making itself felt to him even while not intervening in the dynamics of his worldly scene: for can it not be that by the reflection of its own state as it wavers with the record of man, the transcendent casts light and shadow over the human landscape?[1]

Such is the tentative myth I once proposed for consideration in a different context. It has theological implications that only later unfolded to me. Of these I shall develop here some of the more obvious ones—hoping that this translation from image into concept will somehow connect what so far must seem a strange and rather willful private fantasy with the more responsible tradition of Jewish religious thought. In this manner I try to redeem the poetic liberties of my earlier, roving attempt.

First, and most obviously, I have been speaking of a *suffering God*— which immediately seems to clash with the biblical conception of divine majesty. There is, of course, a Christian connotation of the term "suffering God" with which my myth must not be confounded; it does not speak, as does the former, of a special act by which the deity at one time, and for the special purpose of saving man, sends part of itself into a particular situation of suffering (the incarnation and crucifixion). If anything in what I said makes sense, then the sense is that the relation of God to the world *from the moment of creation*, and certainly from the creation of man on, involved suffering on the part of the God. It involves, to be sure, suffering on the part of the creature too, but this truism has always been recognized in every theology. Not so the idea of God's suffering with creation, and of this I said that, prima facie, it clashes with the biblical conception of divine majesty. But does it really clash as extremely as it seems at first glance? Do not we also in the Bible encounter God as slighted and rejected by man and grieving over him? Do not we encounter him as ruing that he created man, and suffering from the disappointment he experiences with him—and with his chosen people in particular? We remember the prophet Hosea, and God's love lamenting over Israel, his unfaithful wife.

Then, second, the myth suggests the picture of a *becoming God*. It is a God emerging in time instead of possessing a completed being that remains identical with itself throughout eternity. Such an idea of divine becoming is surely at variance with the Greek, Platonic-Aristotelian tradition of philosophical theology that, since its incorporation into the Jewish and Christian theological tradition, has somehow usurped for itself an authority to which it is not at all entitled by authentic Jewish (and also Christian) standards. Transtemporality, impassibility, and immutability have been taken to be necessary attributes of God. And the ontological distinction that classical thought made between "being" and "becoming," with the latter characteristic of the lower, sensible world, excluded every shadow of becoming from the pure, absolute being of the Godhead. But this Hellenic concept has never accorded well with the spirit and language of the Bible, and the concept of divine becoming can actually be better reconciled with it.

For what does the becoming God mean? Even if we do not go so far as our myth suggests, that much at least we must concede of "becoming" in God as lies in the mere fact that he is affected by what happens in the world, and "affected" means altered, made different. Even apart from the fact that creation as such—the act itself and the lasting result thereof—was after all a decisive change in God's own state, insofar as he is now no longer alone, his continual *relation* to the creation, once this exists and moves in the flux of becoming, means that he experiences something with the world, that his own being is affected by what goes on in it. This holds already for the mere relation of accompanying knowledge, let alone that of caring interest. Thus, if God is in any relation to the world—which is the cardinal assumption of religion—then by that token alone the Eternal has "temporalized" himself and progressively becomes different through the actualizations of the world process.

One incidental consequence of the idea of the becoming God is that it destroys the idea of an eternal recurrence of the same. This was Nietzsche's alternative to Christian metaphysics, which in this case is the same as Jewish metaphysics. It is indeed the extreme symbol of the turn to unconditional temporality and of the complete negation of any transcendence that could keep a memory of what happens in time, to assume that, by the mere exhaustion of the possible combinations and recombinations of material elements, it must come to pass that an "initial" configuration recurs and the whole cycle starts over again, and if once, then innumerable times—Nietzsche's "ring of rings, the ring of eternal recurrence." However, if we assume that eternity is not unaffected by what happens in time, there can never be a recurrence of the same because God will not be the same after he has gone through the experience of a world process. Any new world coming after the end of one will carry, as it were, in its own heritage the memory of what has gone before; or, in other words, there will not be an indifferent and dead eternity but an eternity that grows with the accumulating harvest of time.

Bound up with the concepts of a suffering and a becoming God is that of a *caring God*—a God not remote and detached and self-contained but involved with what he cares for. Whatever the "primordial" condition of the Godhead, he ceased to be self-contained once he let himself in for the existence of a world by creating such a world or letting it come to be. God's caring about his creatures is, of course, among the most familiar tenets of Jewish faith. But my myth stresses the less familiar aspect that this caring God is not a sorcerer who in the act of caring also provides the fulfillment of his concern: he has left something for other agents to do and thereby has made his care dependent on them. He is therefore also an endangered God, a God who runs a risk. Clearly that must be so, or else the world would be in a condition of permanent perfection. The fact that it is not bespeaks one of two things: that either the one God does not exist (though more than one may), or that the one has given to an agency other than himself, though created by him, a power and a right to act on its own and therewith a scope for at least codetermining that which is a concern of his. This is why I said that the caring God is not a sorcerer. Somehow he has, by an act of either inscrutable wisdom or love or whatever else the divine motive may have been, forgone the guaranteeing of his self-satisfaction by his own power, after he has first, by the act of creation itself, forgone being "all in all."

And therewith we come to what is perhaps the most critical point in our speculative, theological venture: this is not an omnipotent God. We argue indeed that, for the sake of our image of God and our whole relation to the divine, for the sake of any viable theology, we cannot uphold the time-honored (medieval) doctrine of absolute, unlimited divine power. Let me argue this first, on a purely logical plane, by pointing out the paradox in the idea of absolute power. The logical situation indeed is by no means that divine omnipotence is the rationally plausible and somehow self-recommending doctrine, while that of its limitation is wayward and in need of defense. Quite the opposite. From the very concept of power, it follows that omnipotence is a self-contradictory, self-destructive, indeed, senseless concept. The situation is similar to that of freedom in the human realm; far from beginning where necessity ends, freedom consists of and lives in pitting itself against necessity. Separated from it, freedom loses its object and becomes as void as force without resistance. Absolute freedom would be empty freedom that cancels itself out. So, too, does empty power, and absolute, exclusive power would be just that. Absolute, total power means power not limited by anything, not even by the mere existence of something other than the possessor of that power; for the very existence of such another would already constitute a limitation, and the one would have to annihilate it so as to save its absoluteness. Absolute power then, in its solitude, has no object on which to act. But as objectless power it is a powerless power, canceling itself out: "all" equals "zero" here. In order for it to act, there must be something else, and as soon as there is, the one is not all powerful anymore, even though in any comparison its power may be superior by any degree you please to imagine. The existence of another object limits the power of the most powerful agent at the same time that it allows it to be an agent. In brief, power as such is a *relational* concept and requires relation.

Again, power meeting no *resistance* in its relatum is equal to no power at all: power is exercised only in relation to something that itself has power. Power, unless otiose, consists in the capacity to overcome something; and something's existence as such is enough to provide this condition. For existence means resistance and thus opposing force. Just as, in physics, force without resistance—that is, counterforce—remains empty, so in metaphysics does power without counterpower, unequal as the latter may be. That, therefore, on which power acts much have a power of its own, even if that power derives from the first and was initially granted to it, as one with its existence, by a self-renunciation of limitless power—that is, in the act of creation.

In short, it cannot be that all power is on the side of one agent only. Power must be divided so that there be any power at all.

But besides this logical and ontological objection, there is a more theological, genuinely religious objection to the idea of absolute and un-limited divine omnipotence. We can have divine omnipotence together with divine goodness only at the price of complete divine inscrutability. Seeing the existence of evil in the world, we must sacrifice intelligibility in God to the combination of the other two attributes. Only a completely unintelligible God can be said to be absolutely good and absolutely power-ful, yet tolerate the world as it is. Put more generally, the three attributes at stake—absolute goodness, absolute power, and intelligibility—stand in such a logical relation to one another that the conjunction of any two of them excludes the third. The question then is: Which are truly integral to our concept of God, and which, being of lesser force, must give way to their superior claim? Now, surely, goodness is inalienable from the concept of God, and not open to qualification. Intelligibility, conditional on both God's nature and man's capacity, is on the latter count indeed subject to qualification but on no account to complete elimination. The *Deus absconditus*, the hidden God (not to speak of an absurd God) is a profoundly un-Jewish conception. Our teaching, the Torah, rests on the premise and insists that we can understand God, not completely, to be sure, but something of him—of his will, intentions, and even nature—because he has told us. There has been revelation, we have his commandments and his law, and he has directly communicated with some—his prophets—as his mouth for all men in the language of men and their times: refracted thus in this limiting medium but not veiled in dark mystery. A completely hidden God is not an acceptable concept by Jewish norms.

But he would have to be precisely that if together with being good he were conceived as all powerful. After Auschwitz, we can assert with greater force than ever before that an omnipotent deity would have to be either not good or (in his world rule, in which alone we can "observe" him) totally unintelligible. But if God is to be intelligible in some manner and to some extent (and to this we must hold), then his goodness must be compatible with the existence of evil, and this it is only if he is not all powerful. Only then can we uphold that he is intelligible and good, and there is yet evil in the world. And since we have found the concept of omnipotence to be dubious anyway, it is this that has to give way.

So far, our argument about omnipotence has done no more than lay it down as a principle for any acceptable theology continuous with the Jewish heritage that God's power be seen as limited by something whose being in its own right and whose power to act on its own authority he himself acknowledges.[2] Admittedly, we have the choice to interpret this as a voluntary concession on God's part, which he is free to revoke at will—that is, as the restraint of a power that he still and always possesses in full but, for the sake of creation's own autonomous right, chooses not fully to employ. To devout believers, this is probably the most palatable choice, But it will not suffice. For in view of the enormity of what, among the bearers of his image in creation, some of them time and again, and wholly unilaterally, inflict on innocent others, one would expect the good God at times to break his own, however stringent, rule of restraint and intervene with a saving miracle.[3] But no saving miracle occurred. Through the years that "Auschwitz" raged God remained silent. The miracles that did occur came forth from man alone: the deeds of those solitary, mostly unknown "just of the nations" who did not shrink from utter sacrifice in order to help, to save, to mitigate—even, when nothing else was left, unto sharing Israel's lot. Of them I shall speak again. But God was silent. And there I say, or my myth says: Not because he chose not to, but because he *could* not intervene did he fail to intervene. For reasons decisively prompted by contemporary experience, I entertain the idea of God who for a time—the time of the ongoing world process—has divested himself of any power to interfere with the physical course of things; and who responds to the impact on his being by worldly events, not "with a mighty hand and outstretched arm," as we Jews on every Passover recite in remembering the exodus from Egypt, but with the mutely insistent appeal of his unfulfilled goal.

In this, assuredly, my speculation strays far from oldest Judaic teaching. Several of Maimonides's Thirteen Articles of Faith, which we solemnly chant in our services, fall away with the "mighty hand": the assertions about God ruling the universe, his rewarding the good and punishing the wicked, even about the coming of the promised Messiah. Not, however, those about his call to the souls,[4] his inspiration of the prophets and the Torah, thus also not the idea of election: for only to the physical realm does the impotence of God refer. Most of all, the *Oneness* of God stands unabated and with it the "Hear, O Israel!" No Manichaean dualism is enlisted to explain evil; from the hearts of men alone does it arise and gain power in the world. The mere permitting, indeed, of human freedom involved a renouncing of sole divine power henceforth. And our discussion of power as such has already led us to deny divine omnipotence, anyway.

The elimination of divine omnipotence leaves the theoretical choice between the alternatives of either some preexistent—theological or ontological—*dualism*, or of God's *self*-limitation through the creation from nothing. The dualistic alternative in turn might take the Manichaean form of an active force of evil forever opposing the divine purpose in the universal scheme of things: a two-god theology; or the Platonic form of a passive medium imposing, no less universally, imperfection on the embodiment of the ideal in the world: a form-matter dualism. The first is plainly unacceptable to Judaism. The second answers at best the problem of imperfection and natural necessity but not that of positive evil, which implies a freedom empowered by its own authority independent of that of God; and it is the fact and success of deliberate evil rather than the inflictions of the blind, natural causality—the use of the latter in the hands of responsible agents (Auschwitz rather than the earthquake of Lisbon)—with which Jewish theology has to contend at this hour. Only with creation from nothing do we have the oneness of the divine principle combined with that self-limitation that then permits (gives "room" to) the existence and autonomy of a world. Creation was that act of absolute sovereignty with which it consented, for the sake of the self-determined finitude, to be absolute no more—an act, therefore, of divine self-restriction.

And here let us remember that Jewish tradition itself is really not quite so monolithic in the matter of divine sovereignty as official doctrine makes it appear. The mighty undercurrent of the Kabbalah, which Gershom Scholem in our days has brought to light anew, knows about a divine fate bound up with the coming-to-be of a world. There we meet highly original, very unorthodox speculations in whose company mine would not appear so wayward after all. Thus, for example, my myth at bottom only pushes further the idea of the *tzimtzum*, that cosmogonic centerconcept of the Lurianic Kabbalah.[5] *Tzimtzum* means contraction, withdrawal, self-limitation. To make room for the world, the *En-Sof* (Infinite; literally, No-End) of the beginning had to contract himself so that, vacated by him, empty space could expand outside of him: the "Nothing" in which and from which God could then create the world. Without this retreat into himself, there could be no "other" outside God, and only his continued holding-himself-in preserves the finite things from losing their separate being again into the divine "all in all."

My myth goes farther still. The contraction is total as far as power is concerned; as a whole has the Infinite ceded his power to the finite and thereby wholly delivered his cause into its hands. Does that still leave anything for a relation to God?

Let me answer this question with a last quotation from the earlier writing. By forgoing its own inviolateness, the eternal ground allowed the world to be. To this self-denial all creation owes its existence and with it has received all there is to receive from beyond. Having given himself whole to the becoming world, God has no more to give: it is man's now to give to him. And he may give by seeing to it in the ways of his life that it does not happen or happen too often, and not on his account, that it "repented the Lord"[6] to have made the world. This may well be the secret of the "thirty-six righteous ones" whom, according to Jewish lore, the world shall never lack[7] and of whose number in our time were possibly some of those "just of the nations" I have mentioned before: their guessed-at secret being that, with the superior valency of good over evil, which (we hope) obtains in the noncausal logic of things there, their hidden holiness can outweigh countless guilt, redress the balance of a generation, and secure the peace of the invisible realm.[8]

All this, let it be said at the end, is but stammering. Even the words of the great seers and adorers—the prophets and the psalmists—which stand beyond comparison, were stammers before the eternal mystery. Every mortal answer to Job's question, too, cannot be more than that. Mine is the opposite to the one given by the Book of Job: this, for an answer, invoked the plenitude of God's power; mine, his chosen voidance of it. And yet, strange to say, both are in praise. For the divine renunciation

Goethe!

was made so that we, the mortals, could be. This, too, so it seems to me, is an answer to Job: that in him God himself suffers. Which is true, if any, we can know of none of the answers ever tried. Of my poor word thereto I can only hope that it be not wholly excluded from what Goethe, in "Testament of Old-Persian Faith," thus put into Zarathustra's mouth:

> All that ever stammers praising the Most High
> Is in circles there assembled far and nigh.[9]

Is Faith Still Possible?:
Memories of Rudolf Bultmann
and Reflections on the
Philosophical Aspects of His Work

refatory Note: In July 1976, Rudolf Bultmann, the last of the great Protestant theologians of this century, died in Marburg, Germany, a few weeks before his ninety-second birthday. An almost lifelong friendship, beginning with my being his student in the 1920s, bound me to this man of towering scholarship, clarity of mind, purity of character, and deep—if troubled—piety. In November 1976, the Theological Faculty of Marburg University held a memorial for its longtime professor of New Testament studies, which was attended by many persons from all over Germany and neighboring countries this side of the iron curtain. Of the two academic lectures delivered before that audience, one was by a New Testament theologian and erstwhile student of Bultmann, Professor Erich Dinkler from Heidelberg, the other by me, not a theologian but a philosopher, not a Christian but a Jew. The complete proceedings of the memorial meeting have been published under the title *Gedenken an Rudolf Bultmann* by J. C. B. Mohr in Tübingen, 1977. Only part of what I had prepared in writing was orally presented at the occasion, but the whole was printed. I here submit my own English version of the unabridged German essay, which in the spirit of Bultmann's own openmindedness pushes some of his theoretical concerns beyond the point which he himself had reached.

I

The appraisal of a thinker should perhaps separate the man from the work and confine itself to the substance of his thought. In the case of Rudolf Bultmann, I find this impossible for reasons both of compelling sentiment and of the objective conviction that this would leave out a too essential and precious part of the truth. Bultmann lived with what he thought, and his thought itself was such that this to-be-lived character stood forth as the true meaning of it. Foremost, however, is the fact that I have known him, that he was teacher to me and friend, a moving presence in my life that has shone through the years with a still and steady light. Thus I must speak also of myself if I am to speak of Bultmann and bear witness to the man.

Our relation began in 1924 when in the footsteps of Heidegger I came from Freiburg to Marburg and there entered Bultmann's New Testament seminar in pursuance of the peculiar exchange pattern that sprang up between the disciples of Heidegger and Bultmann, but also in pursuance of my initial interest in the realm of religion, which had kept company with my major commitment to philosophy and until then, according to my origins, had been practiced in Old Testament and Judaic studies.

Rudolf Bultmann opened the New Testament to me. What I know of it and, as a non-Christian, perhaps understand, somehow stems from him. And with the New Testament, he also opened up to me its intellectual environment, the historical stage of primitive Christianity, and therewith the theme that was to hold me in thrall for so long. What accidents of life that become fate! It was the episode of an (immoderately long) seminar presentation by me on "knowing God" in the Fourth Gospel, and Bultmann's lively encouragement to pursue this further, which enticed my unsuspecting youth into the garden of the Gnosis. It was Bultmann also who took a paper (on free will in Augustine) presented in Heidegger's seminar into his prestigious research series.[1] And again it was he who held the publisher—understandably alarmed by a crushing review of this maiden publication—to the agreement to bring out the coming work on Gnosticism by threatening to resign from his editorship if his judgment was not trusted. The famous preface with which he finally sent that work on its way in 1934 still stands as a shining testimony to the courageous generosity of the man in a dark time.

Here then is the point to pass from the teacher and kind patron to the man himself as I have experienced him in the unwavering purity of his being. Two personal episodes may stand for an objective portrayal.

Bultmann was the only one of my academic teachers to whom I paid a farewell visit before my emigration. It was in the summer of 1933, here in Marburg. We sat around the dinner table with his lovely, so richly emotional wife and their three schoolgirl daughters, and I related what I had just read in the newspaper, but he not yet, namely, that the German Association of the Blind had expelled its Jewish members. My horror carried me into eloquence: In the face of eternal night (so I exclaimed) the most unifying tie there can be among suffering men, this betrayal of the solidarity of a common fate—and I stopped, for my eye fell on Bultmann and I saw that a deathly pallor had spread over his face, and in his eyes was such agony that the words died in my mouth. In that moment I knew that in matters of elementary humanity one could simply rely on Bultmann, that words, explanations, arguments, most of all rhetoric, were out of place here, that no insanity of the time could dim the steadiness of his inner light. He himself had not said a word. Ever since, for me this episode has belonged to the image of the inwardly moved but outwardly so unemotional man. (It was certainly not kinship of temperaments that bound me so affectionately and mutually to the restrained, by appearance almost cool, native of Oldenburg.)

As the only one from whom I took leave, he was also (besides Karl Jaspers) the first whom I visited again exactly twelve years later in the devastated Germany of 1945, after we had not heard of each other for years.

This is the second episode I wish to relate, and it is among the most unforgettable of my life. Mrs. Bultmann, who had needed several seconds before she recognized the stranger in British battle dress on her doorstep and then burst into a torrent of words and tears, showed me into his study with the words, "Rudolf, you have a visitor." There he sat, as always, at his desk, pale and emaciated, collar and suit too wide on him, but peace in his face. In instant recognition he hastened to meet me in the middle of the room. And there, barely done with the hurried exchange of first welcomes, scarcely over the emotion of this unexpected reunion— we were both still standing—he said something for which I recount this highly personal story. I had come by military transport from Göttingen and held under my arm a book which the publisher Ruprecht had asked me to take to Bultmann, as civilian mail services had not yet been restored. Bultmann pointed at this parcel and asked, "May I hope [darf ich hoffen] that this is the second volume of the 'Gnosis'?" At that, there entered into my soul too, still rent by the Unspeakable I had just learned about in my erstwhile home—the fate of my mother and of the untold others—for the first time something like peace again: at beholding the constancy of thought and loving interest across the ruin of a world. Suddenly I knew:

one can resume and continue that for which one needs faith in man. Countless times I have relived this scene. It became the bridge over the abyss; it connected the "after" with the "before" which grief and wrath and bitterness threatened to blot out, and perhaps more than anything else it helped, with its unique combination of fidelity and soberness, to make my life whole again. But herewith enough of the personal side.

When I now turn to Bultmann's work[2] with some observations of my own, I wish it to be understood that their subject is at least negatively determined by the fact that, with respect to the specifically Christian focus of Bultmann's theological efforts, I am an outsider—a twofold outsider—neither a Christian nor a theologian, and thus neither entitled nor inclined to interfere in inner Christian matters of faith. But there are *philosophical* aspects to his (as probably to all) theological thought, and these are everybody's domain.

II

I can discern two philosophical aspects in Bultmann's work: the theory of *interpretation*, and the relationship to *modern science*. Both meet in the concept of "*demythologizing*," for this serves simultaneously two quite different, though complementary, purposes: to make the text free for its true, namely, "existential," reading; and to remove the obstacles to faith that arise from the clash of the mythological with the modern worldview. "Mythology" is an obstacle for both concerns, and Bultmann makes it a point that it is not only the coercion by modern science and its claims on intellectual honesty that impels his venture of demythologizing but also, and independently thereof, the cause of Christian truth or true faith itself, which is being obscured by the mythology in which it is couched. In the first sense, the concern is about *saving* the *possibility* of faith; in the second, about *gaining* its *true content*. In the former the interest is defensive; in the latter it is offensive. Naturally, both hang together; the first purpose is effectively attained in the second, and the second has its path cleared by the first.[3]

One could even say: If we knew already how to read the texts properly as they always wanted to be read, then the demythologizing extorted, as it were, from without, by the conflict with science, would not be necessary at all. But the extortion is, after all, an historical fact, and of causal priority at that (even if it should finally turn out to have been a blessing in disguise), and the questions asked according to the two purposes have different directions. In the one sense, according to Bultmann, "the decisive question for demythologizing is this: is the understanding of Jesus Christ as the eschatological event inseparably connected with the ideas of a cosmic eschatology?" (vol. 4, 186). That is, *can* it be detached from this offense to modern thought, so that it does not clash with it? In the other sense, however, the question is this: *Ought* it to be separated from these ideas for its own sake? Is the mythological mode of speech as such legitimate with reference to that which was intended to be said by it? Here Bultmann's well-known answer is, "Myth objectifies the other-worldly to the this-wordly" (vol. 4, 146). Therefore, "Only demythologizing . . . brings to light the true meaning of God's secret" (vol. 4, 162). Against the objectification of the "beyond" to the "here" it wishes "to bring into its own the genuine meaning of the myth" (vol. 4, 134). Bultmann even finds that "demythologizing has its beginning in the New Testament itself," i.e., in Paul and then more radically in John (the Evangelist), "and therefore our task of demythologizing today is justified" (vol. 4, 156; cf. also vol. 3, 8–9). That is, we only continue what the New Testament itself began, and we should do so even if not pressured into it by modern thought (though even in those days an external cause was at work: the delay of the second coming of Jesus). The independent and religiously autonomous nature of the purpose is emphasized in the statement "faith itself demands to be freed of all world views [*Weltanschauungen*], be they mythological or scientific" (vol. 4, 187). Perhaps the strongest statement is this: "Demythologizing is the radical application of the doctrine of justification by faith to the realm of knowing and thinking" (vol. 4, 188). That is, we are bidden to it from the core of Christian doctrine itself, as one mode of complying with it, and therefore demythologizing is essentially more than a mere defensive means to an end. To judge this assertion is up to the Christian theologian, not to the philosopher; but the argument preceding this step into the Christian substance is open to *general* judgment, because it entails a theory of myth and of interpretation and thus falls into hermeneutics as a general philosophical subject. Let us fill it in a bit more.

At the base of the argument lies a conception of mythology in general, namely, "that myth speaks of a reality, but in an inadequate way" (vol. 4, 128). That is, it reveals and falsifies at the same time, and its true meaning must be wrested from it by interpretation. This true meaning, its real intention, is—in the case of Scripture at least—"to speak of the essential reality of man" (vol. 4, 134); it is "the expression of a particular understanding of human existence" (vol. 4, 146), an expression whose language is "metaphorical" or "figurative" (vol. 4, 147–48; 135 speaks of "analogical language"). We have heard before that the general logical principle of this metaphorical mode is *objectification*, and its general effect, therefore, is the conversion of the otherworldly into the this-worldly. This, then, is the falsification, and interpretation becomes in this regard a rectification: in order to lay bare the true meaning, it must go back behind that mode of expression and undo as it were its effect—that is, it must *de*-mythologize.

Thus, demythologizing is a "method of interpretation" (vol. 4, 146), "a hermeneutical procedure that interrogates mythological statements . . . about their reality content" (vol. 4, 128), namely, that which concerns human existence. Such a hermeneutics in itself is not necessarily a theological enterprise, and Bultmann indeed says "philosophical and theological reflection have the task to bring to light this meaning-content [*Sinngehalt*]" (vol. 4, 134). "Bring to light" must then mean to translate into another and more appropriate language, which in turn involves the premise that the same can also be said differently without again lapsing into mythology and metaphor: that, in short, it can also be said directly and in terms adequate to "existence." Of this, Bultmann was indeed convinced, and he never tired of stressing the possibility as well as the necessity of such a translation. "Their meaning," so he says of the symbols and images, i.e., what they were meant to express, "can and must be said without recourse to mythological terms" (vol. 4, 177). This has sometimes almost the ring of a logical postulate whose only alternative would be sheer futility, as when he says, "This [meaning-content which philosophical and theological reflection is to 'bring to light'] must then not again be expressed in mythological language: otherwise its meaning in turn would have to be interpreted, and so on *ad infinitum*" (vol. 4, 134–35). And why not? one is tempted to ask. Would an inevitable *ad infinitum* really make interpretation futile? It could be, conceivably, that the road leads always only from metaphor to metaphor, from outworn and no longer viable to fresh and newly appealing metaphor, since the ineffable "real" *can* perhaps be "said" only indirectly or not at all.

This would, then, also hold for philosophy, which is here to come to the aid of theology. That is not a very outlandish view. Hannah Arendt, e.g., held that the metaphors, as sensible representations of the invisible, as similes for what is beyond concept, were wholly ineradicable and in the highest instances were something like the dialect of eternity.[4] This referred to poetry, but in her posthumous work, *The Life of the Mind*, it was very definitely extended to philosophy. Its language, too, is metaphorical—"all philosophical terms are metaphors, frozen analogies, as it were"[5]—and especially so in all great metaphysics, which therefore always founders when taken literally. Whether universally true or not, the proposition is certainly true of Martin Heidegger, whose philosophical language is saturated with metaphorical picturesqueness and sometimes borders outright on the "mythological." But, of course, real myth is still something other than metaphorical language, and what Bultmann had to contend with was the massively substantive, not merely semantic, mythology of biblical eschatology with its stunning provocation to reason. In that quandary, to turn to philosophy for conceptual means of interpretation is as natural, and as risky, as it has always been for theology, which in this matter can look back on a long and varied history (beginning with Philo and the Church Fathers).

The *novum* in Bultmann's case is the determination to see the basic theme of the *interpretandum* to be "human existence," wherefore it must be a "philosophy of existence" that is to furnish the key for its interpretation. It is at this point that Bultmann himself speaks *expressis verbis* of philosophy and thus, on this one point at least, directly justifies my broader attribution of "philosophical aspects" to his work. This is what he says:

> If . . . the right questions are about the possibilities of understanding human existence, then we must . . . discover the appropriate representations [*Vorstellungen*] by which such an understanding must be expressed. To find these representations is the task of philosophy. . . . In other words, the question of the "right" philosophy poses itself ["right" is in quotation marks, for Bultmann knew, of course, that there is no such thing in a definitive sense]. "Our question is simply: which philosophy today offers the most appropriate representations for the understanding of human existence? (vol. 4, 169)

Bultmann's answer is well known: existential philosophy, and in particular Heidegger's *Being and Time*. Here was a case of "elective affinity," immersed in that circle of understanding which is peculiar to such relationships: the choice of the philosophical tool was determined by the view of the matter that was to be worked at, and the view of the matter by the philosophical standpoint which the tool represented. This circularity of reciprocal confirmation is the inevitable toll of our historicity—contemporaneity of spirit is an essential element in the cogency of what there was to choose from—and there is nothing wrong with that.

Of course, this still leaves the question of how "right" that philosophy is to which Bultmann entrusted himself with his hermeneutics; but that question would lead us too far afield. It hardly needs saying that Bultmann himself acknowledged historicity also in that he was conscious of the nondefinitive nature of every such temporal (= temporary) rightness and thus of the temporal character of his own interpretation as a way station on an endless road: to break out of this *ad infinitum* was far from his mind. A price had to be paid in any case, for a decision on method not only opens paths, it also closes others. The whole can never be had. What ultimately counts, here as always, is this: You will know them by their fruits; and what these are depends at least as much on the hand that wielded the tool as on the properties of the tool that was at its disposal. It is the Christian theologian's business (not mine) to judge the worth of the fruits for the concerns of the Christian ministry as also for the peace of mind of the minister plagued by the clamor of his modernity. By those criteria he will also judge the worth of the existential interpretation in general. To the outsider it behooves only to testify that, controversial as the method may be, its application in Bultmann's sincere, earnest, and discerning sensitivity has yielded insights which I for one would not like to miss in the understanding of these texts.

III

Beyond these matters, however, we must not forget that demythologizing, besides its function in the service of existential hermeneutics, has also what we called a "defensive," almost tactical component, concerned not as the other with *gaining* the true *content* of faith, but with *saving* its very *possibility*, which is threatened by modern thought: mythology must be sacrificed to the latter, having become untenable in its light. Seen from this angle, it is almost a lucky coincidence that the same encumbrance obstructs its right understanding of itself, so that the external duress happens to benefit the internal interest, and the seeming sacrifice turns out to be a blessing in disguise. We leave it open how far this is a case of making a virtue out of necessity. The necessity at any rate is unmistakable and has an historical and psychological priority, for the siege of religion by the modern mind dates back to the latter's very beginnings. Now, since this heteronomous side of demythologizing, its "defensive" component, implies on Bultmann's part a particular view of modern thought, of its right and its force, it represents the second "philosophical aspect" of his work, and on this, being a philosophical theme in its own right, the theologically uncommitted person also may have his say. Here then, no longer hampered by the outsider's restraints, I will go into some greater detail.

Undeniably, since the age of enlightenment, religion has been on the defensive, psychologically no less than intellectually. It is the de facto force of the historically nurtured habits of thought—the *faith* engendered by science almost more than the knowledge proved by it—which has brought religious faith into discord with itself. Bultmann often refers to this as a given fact whose uncontested rule speaks for itself. He simply states, "The mythological way of thinking has become alien to modern men" (vol. 3, 84); "Contemporary man presumes that the course of nature and history, as also his own inner life and his practical life, are nowhere breached by the action of supernatural forces" (vol. 4, 144). And again, "Nobody reckons with the direct intervention of transcendent powers" (vol. 4, 157); "For the man of today the mythological world view, the idea of the 'end,' of the savior and the salvation are past and done with" (vol. 4, 145). And what has led to this mental stance of modern man and legitimates its force? In the last analysis, it is modern *science*, most of all natural science plus the technology guided by it. Thus it is proven knowledge and by no means a mere whim or contrariness of modern man.

Nonetheless, the question is permitted whether Bultmann, totally conceding the modern axiom of immanence, has not given more to modern science than is its due. This seems to be the case, for instance, when he writes, "Modern science at any rate does not believe that the course of nature can be breached by supernatural forces" (vol. 4, 144)— and he means to say that it believes that this cannot occur. But on such a "can" or "cannot" science does not pronounce. Many scientists indeed have this belief about the world, and so do some philosophies, as that of Kant, where a breaching of the causal sequence would be counter to the a priori conditions of possible experience and therefore incapable of being experienced at all, or the philosophy of Spinoza, where it would be counter to the nature of divine necessity. But science merely says that for every occurrence one should seek a natural explanation until it is found, yet without endowing the laws of nature (= rules of connection), to which the explanation is to conform, with that kind of inviolability on principle (brooking no exceptions) which only logical and mathematical rules enjoy. In other words, science issues a methodological command, not a metaphysical proposition. To be sure, the overwhelming cumulative success in obeying that command stifles the thought of possible exceptions, but the *concept* of exceptions in no way contradicts the concept of rules of *fact*. Their apodictical exclusion is itself a faith or a metaphysics.

However, this objective logical consideration with its "fideistic" conclusion helps little. For Bultmann is, of course, right that *subjectively* this very faith, i.e., the science inspired *idea* of a natural law that brooks no exception, is the dominant faith of "modern man" *including* the theologian (though less, perhaps, lately the scientist himself). And he rightly calls it, against Karl Barth, "an imperative of truthfulness . . . to consider anything true which contradicts the truths actually presupposed in the understanding I have of the world—the understanding which is the guide for all my activity" (*Essays Philosophical and Theological*, 261). Thus, behind demythologizing there stands the imperative of intellectual honesty, so dear to Bultmann's incorruptible nature—nay, the imperative of the person's being in accord with himself, ultimately a *moral* imperative which even surpasses that of reason. For the rest, even he who takes a less rigid philosophical view of natural necessity must admit that the cause of religion would be in a bad way if it rested on the occasional breaching or disrupting of the world order. The real question seems to me whether an intervention by God in the course of things, of which religion must speak, can *only* be represented as a "breaching," "piercing," "disruption" of the causal chain, that is, as a crude miracle; and whether Bultmann with the choice of these violent expressions has not posed an unnecessarily crass alternative. Let us take a closer look at the matter.

The offensiveness of biblical mythology to modern man hangs on three points: the worldview, the miracle, and causal action by God in general. The worldview (or, world model) is the plainest case and actually admits of no dispute. Since Copernicus, we *know*—and this with ever-increasing certainty and range—that "up" does not go into heaven but into infinite space, and we therefore must discard the bodily ascension, since we do not want to picture Elijah, Jesus, and Mary as astronauts. Generally, concerning the space-time *shape* of the universe, modern science has in fact (whatever Karl Jaspers has contended against Bultmann to the contrary) produced a world image and has imposed it on thought with incontrovertible proofs to which even the most defiant faith must bow.

Of "miracles," secondly, we must distinguish between such that run counter to nature, and those that are only extraordinary events, where the miraculous resides not so much in themselves as in their just then and there, i.e., their coincidence with some humanly significant, critical, extreme situation. Only the first are strictly impossible, and to them belong, of course, in the first place those mentioned before which involve a total, discarded worldview and simply make no sense in the corrected one; and also those that imply a massive suspension of the laws of nature, like raising the dead. Most of the biblical miracles are not of that kind. The burning bush, the Egyptian plagues, smoking, quaking and thundering of Mount Sinai, collapse of the walls of Jericho in the Old Testament, the healing of the sick in the New Testament—all these are by themselves not physically impossible, but in part even well-known occurrences (like volcanism). Religiously they are not really important, rather only underlining accompaniments—exclamation marks, as it were—of the really important. Not the shaking of the mountain but what Moses listened to in solitary encounter on its summit was the important thing.

And here is an occasion to observe that in the question of miracles the Jew is in a less difficult position than the Christian. The nature miracles of the Bible (I mean, of the Old Testament) in their entirety do not touch upon the substance of his faith; he can accept or reject them without great consequences for the cause of faith, on the one hand, or for the modern concept of nature, on the other hand. The only two, as far as I can see, which he *must* sacrifice to science—the standing still of sun and moon (which got Galileo into such contretemps with the Church), and Elijah's ascension in the burning chariot—are as episodic in the unfolding of God's drama in history as the others: on them too, nothing much hangs. But on the corresponding ones in the New Testament—birth, resurrection and ascension of Jesus (as also his promised second coming in the clouds of heaven)—there hangs for the Christian, because of the unique theological status of Jesus, a great deal indeed: *these* miracles, by their connection with Christology, touch upon the core of his faith. The Jew has nothing to match the plight which *their* problematics inflict upon the believer. Here, Christianity has to pay a belated price for what once and for so long gave it a magnetic advantage in the souls over Judaism: the centrality of *mystery*, by virtue of the central idea of incarnation. Fortunately, it is not my job to judge how far the mystery of incarnation *can* be detached from its attestation by physical miracle (for instance, the resurrection, the empty tomb), and whether Bultmann succeeded in so detaching it at not too high a price. Wholly convincing to me is the present need for the heroic attempt, which no one has taken upon himself so unflinchingly as he. And quite apart from the particular Christian problem, I agree, theologically and philosophically, that the belief in God as such can do without visible, as it were spectacular, miracles. Let us then bypass this avoidable stumbling block (which Bultmann regards as the "false" to the detriment of the "genuine" one; vol. 4, 157).

IV

The real problem concerns the idea of *God's acting* in general, which religious faith cannot let go of on any account. Here Bultmann, too, saw *the* problem, and though it overlaps with that of miracles, it does not collapse into it. "Everything [so Bultmann says] gets focused into the question: is the talk of God's acting necessarily mythological talk?"

(vol. 4, 135). Bultmann treats this question in a special section entitled "The Significance of God as Agent" in his seminal essay "Jesus Christ and Mythology." Bultmann's difficulty is this: "I must . . . necessarily regard the events of the world as connected by cause and effect, not only as a scientific observer, but also in my daily life. If I do that, no room is left for God's acting" (vol. 4, 175). For, if "the divine causality is inserted in the chain of events that follow each other according to the law of causality," then what happens thereupon will be the result of a supernatural cause, thus a miracle in the offensive sense (vol. 4, 172–73), and that cannot be. So understood, demythologizing also "eliminates," together with the idea of miracle as a breaching of the causal context (vol. 4, 128), the idea of divine action. And yet we must speak of God's acting. What is the solution?

The error, according to Bultmann, consists in representing God's acting in terms of worldly actions or events, divine power in terms of natural power—precisely the error of mythology, "which by rupturing the continuity inserts supernatural events in the chain of natural events" (vol. 4, 175). In the broadest sense, it is the error of objectification and "mundification" (so to speak) in general. Contrary thereto, God's acting must be thought of as "a non-worldly and transcendent one, which does not take place *between* worldly actions or worldly events but happens *in* them" (vol. 4, 173). "*In* [the natural, worldly events that are visible to everyone] God's hidden acting occurs" (ibid.).

This, then, is Bultmann's resolution of the dilemma, which makes it possible to regard the same occurrence, happening to *me*, on the one hand, "as a link in the chain of the natural course of things," and on the other hand—namely, in faith—as a gift or punishment of God; likewise to regard "a thought or decision [in me] as a divine inspiration, without untying it from its connection with its psychological causes" (vol. 4, 173–74). Faith insists not on the direct identity of God's action with worldly events, but "on the paradoxical identity which only here and now can be believed in against the seeming non-identity" (vol. 4, 173). Put somewhat differently from Bultmann's own words, we have here something like a difference between seeing "from without" (objectifying) and understanding "from within."

What can we say philosophically to this solution? I find it most similar to Kant's position that distinguishes between *phenomenon* and *noumenon*, between appearance and thing-in-itself. In the realm of "appearance," all things follow one another according to a necessary rule; in the "thing-in-itself," that *which thus appears* can be a causality of freedom. Therefore, I cannot know indeed, but can believe that my action, which in terms of appearance (including psychological appearance) is *determined* throughout, is in truth, by origin and execution, the work of my *freedom*. Likewise does a world event, "behind" its apparent, *intramundane* causality, on principle admit of an—albeit unknowable—*divine* causality as *that which* comes to appearance in it. For behind all the immanence of appearance stands the transcendence of the "thing-in-itself" which is not subject to the rules of the former. What seen "from without," as it were, *must* appear as mere nature, *can*, seen "from within," stand forth as a deed of human freedom or, as the case may be, of divine initiative.

To this Kantian position I see a likeness in Bultmann's statements on God's acting as something that does not insert itself "between" worldly events, as one of them, but is hidden "in" them; and the comparison, as regards the religious implication of the phenomenon-noumenon distinction, finds support in Kant's famous dictum that he "found it necessary to deny knowledge so as to make room for faith"—it being understood that only the phenomenal is knowable and the noumenal is accessible to faith alone. I do not know whether Bultmann was conscious of such a similarity, and am not sure how far it really goes. But as far as it does go, Bultmann's position shares with the Kantian the latter's strengths and weaknesses. To the weaknesses for Bultmann's own theological concern (and for the cause of religion in general) belongs the circumstance that the indicated two-sidedness of things in general merely admits on principle God's action in all of them, but excludes his self-revelation in particular events. The hiddenness of transcendence, that is, its nonappearance, is as irrefrangible as the determinism of appearances.

I believe, however, that Bultmann shared with Kant an exaggerated conception of the tightness and rigidity of worldly causality. By this conception, it is so univocally determinative that any introduction of a nonphysical cause into the concatenation of nature is tantamount to the rending of a chain, and therefore to a case of the tabooed miracle. But we must remind ourselves that the "miracle" of nonphysical intervention in the physical world, with no rending of its connectedness, thus without any miraculous quality about it, happens incessantly and as the most familiar of things, namely, each time when we *act* from conscious choice— which means nothing else but to codetermine, from our inwardness, the external course of things, so that it now takes a different route from the one it would have taken without this transphysically originated contribution of ours, i.e., if left to itself.

This again implies the premise that, at the point of our intervention, a plurality of possibilities had been open, *each* of which equally well satisfied the requirements of the laws of nature. Otherwise, all our acting were only a deceptive illusion. But nobody, not even the physicist, lets the frown of physicalist determinism deter him from reckoning, at the moment of deliberation, with more than one possibility being open as the very premise of deliberating itself. Practically, the faith of his freedom always takes precedence over the faith in a theory that anyway overreaches itself. But to him who nevertheless feels intimidated by that frown and by the prestige of natural science supposed behind it, one can say by way of easing his theoretical conscience that natural science need not create the alleged dilemma at all, and only a metaphysics of physical science presumes to its imposition.

It is up to philosophy to *show* that the laws of nature are quite compatible with neutral threshold situations, zero points of indifference, as it were, from which as from a divide the further process could take several directions, even indefinitely many, *all* of them conforming to the constancy laws, if greatly differing in degrees of probability. Blind nature will nearly always select the most probable, but man can let the most improbable become actual. This is to say that philosophy must construct a model of nature by which causally equivalent alternatives are possible in it, so that human acting, availing itself of their latitude, is possible in concord with the laws of nature. The basic experience of acting charges theory with this task. I add that such a model *can* be constructed with the preservation of everything that science (not scientistic metaphysics) tells us about nature.[6]

The theologian, however, to return to him, must tell himself that what is conceded to human action cannot be denied to divine action. If *we* can daily perform the miracle (and in some sense it *is* a miracle), with the choice of our souls, with our wishing and willing, our insights and errors, our good or evil aims—nonphysical, mental factors all of them— to intervene in and give *our* turn to the course of the world, then that kind of miracle that leaves the natural order intact should be possible also to God, although He may reserve such intervention for rare occasions and ends. Bultmann gave himself the cue to this analogy without following it when he said, "I deny the worldly connection of events when I speak of myself; for in this connection of world events, my ego, my own 'existence,' is no more visible than the acting God" (vol. 4, 175). Indeed not! In our case, too, the origin in the ego is invisible. But what this invisible works in the visible, which without this interjection of mind by word and deed would continue differently, that is in the visible world as objective a fact as any can be—even if the possibility for it to have been otherwise and its origin in the freedom of the mind must remain forever unprovable. For we know what happens only after it has happened and the alternatives have been voided. But unconcerned about provability, among human beings neither the doer nor the recipient or witness of his deed doubts this origin in choice and this possibility for the done not to have been done. It would be different if such doing could be infallibly predicted. But it is of the essence of acting that it brings the unexpected, unanticipatable into the world, and the smug assertion that it *had* to go this way from the start always limps behind the surprise that it went the way it did.

The human side of the analogy here invoked extends from the small to the large, from our daily doings, whose impact on the world is mostly insignificant, to extraordinary deeds that give a new direction to *history*. I am not ignorant of the several doctrines of historical determinism; but he who says, with whatever exquisite or prestigious theory, that here "in the large" that foregone and in principle foreseeable necessity rules which "in the small" perhaps is loosened, shows only that he does not know what history is and how things come to pass in it. Here eminently, hindsight prophecy can have its vain triumphs—something very different from understanding what has happened in the past.

I ask permission to relate a personal reminiscence. When I stood in the Birth Chapel in Bethlehem, I was suddenly overwhelmed by the thought that at the time of this birth (whether it happened here or elsewhere), no knowledge and no imagination, and not even the most penetrating understanding of historical mechanisms which we may ever attain, could have foretold, nay remotely have entertained by wildest guessing, what over millennia would follow from it—as little as the birth of this individual itself could be foretold. From the secular point of view, outside the Christian explanation, the birth of this person, and that his life was not prematurely cut off by infant disease or infant murder, and whatever else had a positive or negative part in the factual sine qua non, were the most enormous of accidents which then decided subsequent world history. To be sure, with the figure once there in the fullness of its appearance, one can retrospectively, in conjunction with the conditions of the time and the mental climate of contemporary humankind, somehow "explain" its historic effect (as also conversely the influence of the time on the person) and thereby impart to the further course of things a semblance of "necessity." But precisely the meeting of the person with the conditions was the accident of accidents, and if it would have failed to happen, world history would have run otherwise. We do not know how, but we know that it would then again have exhibited the same relative necessity.[7] The laws of history, whatever they are, would have been satisfied in either case, although in an utterly different manner. But as it was, the thought, speech and visible life of this one individual, physically almost a null in the enormous mass and force field of mankind, gave the whole further sequence a direction which it would not have taken without him, and which only after him to some extent emerges again from sheer contingency. The law says only that if a stone drops into the water, wave rings will spread from the point of impact. Whether, when and where a stone will fall, the law knows nothing about.

To add, however, the ignominious example to the hallowed one: Who doubts that without Hitler the world history of our time would have gone differently and today's world map would look vastly different: no divided Germany, no standing of the Russian power in the heart of Europe, etc.? Without him there would not have been the "final solution," no Holocaust, therefore perhaps no State of Israel and with it the crisis of the Middle East, that new element in world politics. But who, on the other hand, would contend that a timely car accident or lucky assassination attempt or fatal illness would have been contrary to the laws of history or of causality or of nature, and that the then so differently ensuing historical process would have been less natural, less necessary, and less explainable than what actually happened? But as it was, things went, not as of necessity they had to go, but as once again a mind, acting through words, moved the world, this time to disaster.

Both these cases are examples of an "intervention" in the great march of events which world causality obviously permits. The second example also shows us the true reason, certainly the *theologically* relevant reason, why we are unwilling to attribute a constant world regiment to divine omnipotence: not out of deference to the laws of nature and history (of the latter we know next to nothing anyway), nor from the Marcionite motive that caring about every sparrow that falls from the roof would be beneath God, but because too horrible things happen in the world and in history that we could ascribe them to His intention and hold Him responsible for them. Different from the case of miracles, here the Jew is in greater difficulty than the Christian. To the Christian (of the stern variety), the world is anyway largely of the devil and always an object of suspicion (the human world in particular, because of original sin); but to the Jew, God is eminently the lord of history; and how after Auschwitz the believing Jew should explain to himself God's lordship, and how to rethink the traditional concept of God, that is his agonizing problem today.[8]

In any case, whether for this reason or for the Bultmannian reason of intellectual honesty and of respect for unalloyed immanence, the believer must suppose something like an abstinence of God vis-à-vis the world: as if, with the creation of the world, and then once again with that of man in consideration of his freedom, he had largely renounced the exercise of his omnipotence and wished to let creation be on the whole what it would make of itself. Thus, I agree with Bultmann's *result*, though for reasons different from his, that believers and unbelievers alike must acknowledge the autonomy of the natural world, i.e., its conforming always to its own laws (which fact indeed, and alone, makes atheism a viable option). Our conceding that inviolateness to created immanence in our thought would match, according to this theological view, the Creator's conceding the same to it in his will. It was said before that by itself that integrity of the natural order would well permit an occasional intervention by the transcendent God without the fireworks of miracles, as it does after all constantly permit the intervention of innerworldly human freedom. But already in the case of man, where one *sees* at least the *bodily* origin of action, the genuine intervention is notoriously disputable from the view of determinism, and in the case of the invisible God it would be totally unrecognizable, not merely unprovable as in the human case. Thus one should, perhaps, better not speak of this abstract possibility at all, if only to protect faith against misuse as an *asylum ignorantiae*, which already Spinoza has scourged. In this sense, somewhat diverging from that in Bultmann's mind, we can agree with him that "statements about God's acting as a cosmic occurrence are illegitimate" (vol. 4, 178), and that one should generally keep to the natural explanation.

V

And yet, *one* exception at least religion must admit as vital to itself and inalienable from its claims—one that has to do no longer with the general, abstract possibility but with a highly specific mode of divine intervention in the matters of this world: *revelation.* Here the believer can—and it seems to me, *must*—go beyond Bultmann's ascetic abstinence, to whose general maxim we have just assented. That he can, has been shown before; that he must, will be argued now.

If I understand Bultmann correctly, revelation, too, falls for him under the disjunction of divine action interpolated "between" worldly events, which he denies, and hidden "in" them, which he affirms, but which as little as anything else represents a "direct intervention of transcendent powers": rather by *me* only, when *I* encounter it, and with the paradoxical defiance of faith, *can* it be understood as *also* an act of God, even though, in itself, it is completely intelligible within the natural-psychological train of events. That means: also the word of God, also revelation, is hidden on principle. It is up to me, and to me alone, to *hear* God's word addressing me *out* of men's words, to discover *in* the natural the revelation of the supernatural, and to *understand* as divine inspiration what in me, and even in others, came forth in the way of psychologically well-explained thought. For the inner life too—on this, modern man relies—is "nowhere breached by the action of supernatural forces" (vol. 4, 144); nor is history: there too, no "singling out of particular, identifiable areas" as sacred history is permitted. All of nature and all of history are "profane" (vol. 4, 188), and under this verdict also falls the inner life of individuals, even that of the prophets. Thus, there only remains "the paradoxical identity of innerworldly event with the acting of the transcendent God" (vol. 4, 136), which only *I*, in the existential encounter, can experience *as such* "here and now" and must accredit with *my* faith even for the past speakers of the Word—authenticating it over their heads as it were, for they themselves were mundanely determined like everybody else. In other words, the revelation happens primarily with and on me, I am its ultimate, transmuting subject, for whom there is no telling *what* may at some time become revelation to him. Any "direct identity" of a worldly given with divine authorship is excluded.

So it seems on the one hand. But on the other hand, Bultmann also says—as he cannot avoid saying as the confessor of a religion founded on *one* revelation—that in the Bible we have "authorized words" (vol. 4, 168), that certain words, spoken at a certain time, possess *authority once for all.* And of God's heralds in the Bible—prophets, Jesus, apostles—he says, "What they proclaim are not their own thoughts . . . but the call of God, which they must proclaim, whether they will or not," and he quotes Amos: "'The lion roars, who is not afraid? Yahweh speaks, who does not become a prophet?'" (vol. 3, 123). What is here talked about if not an *irruption* of transcendence into immanence? Those who experienced and spoke thus were not discoverers of a hidden God, but hearers of a God *making himself* known and *willing,* through them, to make himself known to all the world. The initiative is his (unless we contend to know better than they), and that presupposes a *will* on the part of Him who reveals himself (therewith also a temporal aspect in himself!), and *power* to do so, that is, to act into the world, and this via the human soul. I repeat: "into" the world and by particular act, not simply "in" the world and by way of its ever-present fitness for a transcendent interpretation. In this case, therefore, we would be faced (if we believe) with a "between" after all. With the admission of this exception from the immanence rule, the religion of revelation stands or falls.

It is obvious that this idea of God's acting crosses Kant's dividing line, because it does not seclude that acting within the parallel transcendence of the "thing-in-itself," but lets it ingress into *appearance itself,* and into *public* perceptibility at that, not only a private one: and that, it seems to me, is what matters, for human action as well as for religion. Human acting cannot be content with the consciousness of an "intelligible," hidden freedom but must be able to see its effect, visible also to others, in the world of appearance, and to attribute it to itself; and religion cannot be content with the inwardness of the "word" in individual existence, but must have before its eyes its originally public appearance in the world as the self-revelation of divine will through human speech, and attribute it to this causality. Only on this ground can it base its own public-mundane existence, as God's people or Church. At least this holds for every religion of obedience, which must have a knowledge of God's *will*.

VI

Let us sum up. The position here argued makes its statements in two directions, that of religion and that of philosophy. On the side of religion, whose cause as a philosopher I adopt only hypothetically, it states that for certain events an exception must be made from the immanence-rule of all events; and on the side of philosophy (for which I speak categorically), it says that this kind of exception does not contravene any knowledge we have of the world, nor can it indeed be confirmed by any. Its admission has nothing of mythology about it—neither the admission of its possibility by philosophy nor that of its reality by religion. No demythologizing, therefore, needs to disavow this admission. No article of the right scientific faith, as distinct from science-superstition, is violated by it.

In actual fact, the deeply religious Bultmann has made the exception himself, inasmuch as he rested his whole life on the New Testament as *the* revelation, but he was unable to make room for it in theory, because he felt compelled to concede more to the "scientific worldview" than science itself demands. Here is where I wish to come to his aid with the means of philosophy. The plain fact, then, is this: Just as only an overrating of the determinism of nature leads to the belief that one must deny the possibility of causal freedom in our external acting (which Bultmann does *not* do), so it is an overrating of the (almost unknown and mainly postulated!) "laws" of the soul that believes them to block entry to transcendent causation of a direct kind into the context of our inner life—as Bultmann thinks they do: although he, and he in particular, emphatically does believe that the word of God comes to us in the words of men. But he means this in a paradoxical sense, in the sense of an "and yet!" of faith, whereas, if truth be told, only a direct inspiration of uniquely elect ones can give to the message that authority which revealed religion claims and faith in revelation needs. Only in contradiction to the inherent and asserted claim of the professed religion can faith deny that *direct* source. And we have shown that to do so is unnecessary.

Here, then, no defiance of faith is asked of the believer. The "and yet," to be sure, may still be demanded by the *content* of the word, which may indeed be paradoxical, as for instance the message of the cross; but the *fact* of a transcendent initiative in mortal minds—that fact as such the believer *can* accept without paradox and without conflict with the rest of his thought when he accepts the claim of a particular revelation. This acceptance itself, of course, remains a pure decision of faith. I can, of course, choose not to believe and to view the matter with Moses or Amos or Jesus as wholly natural, and will have no difficulty with it, rather the much easier stand. (For the uniform view of things, incomplete as its verification may remain, is theoretically preferable to the nonuniform one, especially when one component of the latter is entirely and on principle unverifiable.) The risk of error, however, is common to both decisions, though for the believing decision for many reasons far greater than for the nonbelieving one—let alone that the latter is spared the difficulty which the always particular decision of faith incurs from the rivalry of the manifold revelatory claims in the broad record of mankind. (Indeed, I consider this, given some respect for the integrity of human intuition and devotion, a much graver difficulty for the position of faith than the conflict with the scientific mode of thought: it is the difficulty of arrogance in the concept of the "true religion"—one's own—in contradistinction to all others.)

I come to the end. It may seem paradoxical that the philosopher should concede more to the possibility of faith, or accord less weight to its modern impediments, than the theologian, so overawed by the authority of science. It is less strange when one considers that the philosopher knows by profession about the *limits* of knowledge, because he constantly bumps against them, and therefore is perhaps more immune to the pressure of what is carried along with the mighty prestige of science but is itself a faith. In the essentials, religious faith is not made easier thereby. To paraphrase Bultmann: only a "false obstacle" has been removed, the true offense of faith remains undiminished. As far as *my* argument goes, even the most demanding Kierkegaardian can rest assured that also with the removal of the pseudo-obstacle, the cause of faith remains difficult enough. I have not been pleading that cause itself. Philosophizing, I have treated of possibilities not of realities. Those lie, as regards our theme, behind a veil of ignorance. Through Bultmann's work I have been led to such musings in the void of permanent ignorance—tentative tracings on its blank but forever beckoning, forever re-voiding page. It is a dialogue with him, from philosopher to theologian, from Jew to Christian, most of all from friend to friend. More than once I saw him in my mind raise his eyebrows skeptically, shake his head doubtfully, and I almost hear him say now: "But my friend, aren't you speculating here? Aren't you speaking of God in the objective mode, from outside as it were, when you consider that through man—through him at least—he might move the world in definite, nameable acts, thus interfering in the creation toward which he has otherwise imposed abstinence on himself?" Yes, I would reply, so be it, and would try to explain that at some point even here one must, for the sake of thought and of faith, dare to become objective . . .[9]

How dearly I would love to continue this dialogue, begun so long ago, with the living friend, though I can do it only with his remembered image. A man of moving purity has departed, a consummated life, always in accord with itself. Not he is to be deplored, but once again the world has been made poorer by losing one of those whose presence in its midst can fortify the ever-threatened faith that "it is worth the toil to be a man."

8

Matter, Mind, and Creation: Cosmological Evidence and Cosmogonic Speculation

Foreword

The essay presented here received its initial impetus from an "Outline on the Theme: Cosmos and the Second Main Principle," sent by a friend for my perusal. In this outline, as the first step toward a complete cosmology, an hypothesis was proposed for explaining the tendency of nature, beginning from structures of a lower order, to create a higher order such as we know. The hypothesis was that at the universe's moment of origin (the so-called "Big Bang") there had also arisen, apart from the total energy of the cosmos, the *information* that would lead to further developments.

From the "chaotic explosion" this information would lead, at first, beyond the immaterial forms of energy and the primordial particles progressively differentiated from them to protons, to hydrogen atoms, and from these to the formation of further ordered systems, such as the periodic table of elements, inorganic compounds, and the beautiful world of crystals. Eventually this information would yield unified *cycles*: in

A much abbreviated version of what is presented here can be found in *Scheidewege* 18 (1988), with the title "Mind, Nature, and Creation." It formed the third of the opening lectures held in May 1988 at the international congress "Mind and Nature," sponsored by the Stiftung Niedersachsen in Hannover. For its part the abovementioned "Outline" has since found its own equally independent realization. (See Max Himmelheber, "Die Trinität der Natur," *Scheidewege* 18 [1988]).

the universe the astronomical cycles, and here on Earth the atmospheric and life cycles, in particular. The "Big Bang" already contained, therefore, a "cosmogonic logos," an idea that makes room for the concept of a "cosmogonic eros" coined by Ludwig Klages.

It was my simple wish to oppose this concept of "information" and "logos" by way of a very brief letter, without going into the entire plan. But in sketching a counterproposal that seemed acceptable, I suddenly found myself drawn into my own cosmogonic speculations in which decades of thought about ontology and the philosophy of nature found expression. Instead of the intended letter there arose the present essay, and this mode of origin explains why it begins with the rejection of an hypothesis. From this starting point it takes its own path, parts of which I have already traveled at an earlier time, without further reference to the occasion that enticed me to this theme once again so late in life.

Since this essay is in many points a distillation of lines of thought presented more fully in my earlier writings, I have assumed permission to refer the reader to these works in footnotes wherever the density of the present text has had to forbid an appropriate justification.

The sequence of words in the title—matter, mind, creation—should indicate the course of this study. It begins with the quantitatively over-whelming aspect of the universe, its *material content* extended in space and time, as natural science describes it (secs. 1–2). It proceeds to that aspect which announces itself only in the small living part of the natural world, namely *subjectivity* (secs. 3–4), and advances to that which again stands out from the material world, but is still bound to it: the mystery of *mind*, as we know it only in humans, thus only in our own self-experience (sec. 5). At this point our investigation raises the question of the creative ground of these stages, i.e., the question of *God* (secs. 6–16).

In taking up the *evidence* of cosmology, therefore, we progress from the outer to the inner. This means that we progress historically, from the earlier to the later; quantitatively, from the most frequent to the rarest; structurally, from the simplest to the most complex; developmentally, from seeing and feeling to thinking. Then from that which is innermost, rarest, and latest we turn back to that which is first of all, which even pre-ceded matter. We must shift, therefore, from the cosmological evidence to cosmogonic *speculation*, which recommends itself to reason but cannot compel it. More we cannot expect from speculation about the beginning of all things.

In taking up the cosmological evidence, the factor of development is decisive. Accordingly, in regard to universal matter, which underlies everything and is everywhere the same, the question is: From what prin-ciple of progress can its development—that of the whole cosmos and then especially that of the Earth up to the most subtle forms of the organic world—be explained? The riddle here is the physically improbable, antientropic direction from disorder to order (only the opposite is probable), and from the lower to the higher. On this issue, we ask: Is the concept of "information" of some use? Can we employ, therefore, the idea of a program, inhering in the matter of the universe, arising along with it in the "Big Bang," that guides its becoming to higher orders of nature? Recalling the tradition of the Greeks, we could probably designate such prior, universal, and controlling "information" as the "cosmogonic logos."

1. Is There a Cosmogonic Logos?: Why We Cannot Assume any "Information" in Primordial Matter

"Information" requires for itself, as its physical substrate, a differentiated and stable system. For living things this would be the genome with its molecularly full articulation and constancy. (For the computer it would be the magnetically spelled-out programming or "software.") Information, therefore, is not only a cause, but already a result of organization. It is a deposit and expression of something previously attained, which is perpetuated through this information, but not surmounted by it. Now *neither* articulation *nor* stability have a place in the totally undifferentiated and dynamic "substance" (hypothetically speaking) of the "Big Bang" or in any "chaos" at all. For this reason the hypothesis of a cosmological "logos"—in general, every preestablished programming and systematic arrangement—dwelling already in developing matter right from the start, is eliminated as an explanatory model of development. Briefly put, information is something stored, and the "Big Bang" had no time for storing anything.

The concept of "information," i.e., of an already present "logos," breaks down not only from the genetic point of view, but also from the standpoint of logic. In whatever manner a permanent articulation might come about in the individual case, it can only repeat itself, maintain its level, and extend its place in the world. It cannot explain the step beyond itself; for that we have need of a transcending factor that is joined to it and leads to something new. What could that be?

I am inclined to answer that the new comes about more trivially and anarchically, on the one hand, and more mysteriously, on the other, than is suggested by the concept of information or logos, a concept so reasonable in itself, postulated by working back from the result, and ultimately deterministic. The "trivially and anarchically" apply to the physical side, the "mysteriously" to the mental side.

2. The Alternative to the Logos: Order out of Disorder through Natural Selection

We have at first, therefore, an aimless disorder in the emergence of natural order. The foundation of all order in nature, of any nature at all, lies in the laws of conservation. But these have come to govern because it is only self-conserving reality that conserves itself. This tautology explains the lawfulness of nature as it is given to us: nature itself is already a result of selection, a universal result which then posits rules for further, more specific, and local selections. This means that the laws of nature arose through the emergence—*also* in the midst of disorder—of stable, relatively long-lasting realities that behave always (or for a very long time) in the same way and thus "succeed."

Here we have the most primordial and fundamental instance of "the survival of the fittest." Order is more successful than disorder. That which has no laws and regularities, and obeys no laws of conservation, could have existed in some arbitrary multiplicity. But as something evanescent it disappears sooner or later and is outlasted by that which has such regularity; what follows laws constitutes nearly all that remains. The short-lived yields to the long-lived precisely on account of its short life—again the tautology—and finds almost no room for itself in the later expansion and solidification of what endures.

Thus there came about the formation and proliferation of protons and, as a result, the law of gravity and mechanics: from hydrogen atoms to the rise of the periodic table of elements and chemistry (including the beauty of crystals)—in brief, to the whole realm of matter. Likewise from the initial radiation there arose the quantum structure of electro-magnetic energy: in a word, the elementary particles, the four forces, etc. The laws of conservation and, along with them, strict causality as such and its cosmic predominance are products of development and selection. (I say "predominance"; of "sole dominance" we have no right to speak.) Having arisen from what is transient, they are themselves transient; they are not eternal, only very, very constant according to cosmic time. In essence their durability is relative, not absolute. Under their aegis arose also the widely prevailing cyclical movements of galaxies, suns, and planets. Their comparatively long-lived order sucked in more and more of the chaotic, and continues to do so.

But even this is not eternal. A "cycle" is not a principle of nature, but an achievement of nature, and it deteriorates. For example, the alternations of day and night, of winter and summer, of atmospheric renewal will come to an end, when finally, as a result of the braking effect of the tides on the Earth's rotation, the Earth will constantly have only one side turned toward the sun (which is already the case with the moon in regard to the Earth).[1] In the meantime, however, there is much time for development on the Earth (and in the cosmos).

How, then, does development come about? Why didn't the universe stop with the attainment of the elements, radiation, and the laws of causality? Why didn't it simply remain at this stage of most general order, with the macrocosmic and chemical formations that grew directly out of it? The answer to this question was given by Darwin. There was always enough "disorder" left over to occasion the formation of new characteristics (structural factors) by accidental, random events, and the momentary successes were subject to the process of selection with its criterion of survival by sheer numbers. *This* is the required "transcending factor" that leads to the new and then to the higher, and it does so without pre-information, without logos, without plan, even without striving, but only by means of the susceptibility of a given order, already coded for "information," to a surrounding disorder that forces itself upon it as additional information.[2]

The ascent, then, to the most complex and subtle life-forms (levels of organization) can be explained in this manner *if,* as Descartes asserted, those realities were only mechanical automata. But they are more than that. They contain something else, as we know first hand, for example, through our present inquiry into the nature of things. For there exists the dimension of the subjective—inwardness—which no material evidence by itself allows us to surmise, of whose actual presence no physical model offers the slightest hint. The physical cannot represent or clarify the subjective dimension with its concepts—indeed, it does not even seem to grant any room for the participation of inwardness, as undeniable as it is, in external occurrences.

Nor would the fullest objective description of the brain, down to its minutest structures and most delicate ways of functioning, provide any clue of the existence of consciousness, if we did not know about it through our own inner experience—precisely through consciousness itself. To include this inward dimension in our picture of the universe— as we are required to do since it comes to the fore *in the course* of natural events and appears *within* nature—we must once again, from the beginning, consider the question of cosmology, this time by looking into past accounts concerning Being.

3. The Riddle of Subjectivity

We come now to that which is beyond the physical, that which is nonmaterial and filled with mystery. Subjectivity or inwardness is an ontologically essential fact of Being. This is due not only to its own irreducible quality, which, if not included, would leave the ontological catalog incomplete. But, more to the point, it is because subjectivity's manifestation of such qualities as interest, purpose, goal, striving, longing (in short, "will" and "value") raises anew the whole question of teleology, and, along with it, the question of the causality of the world in general: issues that the physical data alone appeared to decide in favor of random causes.

The occurrence of subjectivity in the realm of living things, in organisms, is an empirical fact. The rise of the organic realm as a whole from the specifically chemical and morphological arrangements of matter is explainable through the external properties of matter itself, its "geometry," together with the "information" locked within it. What cannot be explained in this way, however, is the inner horizon (e.g., feeling) that opens up within it. This horizon was contained in none of the data from which the genesis of organic systems can be constructed. Nor can it be appended to this data retrospectively—as a supplement, so to speak— because it is of an entirely different dimension. It cannot be appended, for example, as the electromagnetic aspect of matter is added to mass, or as the "weak" and "strong" nuclear forces are added to gravity and radiation.

It is absolutely impossible to form a sum total from magnitudes of space on the one side and qualities of feeling on the other. Despite demonstrable relations between them, no common denominator permits "extension" and "consciousness" to be united in a homogeneous field theory. Yet they exist together, not only beside one another, but interacting with one another and interdependent on one another, and they exist in this fashion *in* "matter" and, at least as regards inwardness, inseparably from one another, for we have no experience of a mind without a body. How can thinking cope with something like this? What will a doctrine of Being look like that does justice to this riddle?

On this issue, age-old speculation, for as long as we can remember, has followed very different paths. Each approach can at best hope for a formulation that is somewhat more acceptable to the intellect than any other. The main divide lies between dualistic and monistic answers. The answers of dualism have long predominated in religion and metaphysics, and they were the powerful promoters and protectors of the self-discovery of the soul in its wholly separate status. Great gratitude is owed to its mighty heralds, from Plato and Zarathustra (to remain only with the Western tradition), along with St. Paul, the Orphics, the Gnostics, and Augustine, up to Pascal and Kierkegaard. Without their radical polarization of Being into body and soul, world and self, the external world and the invisible mind that turned our gaze inward—without this, the soul would remain quite shallow and ignorant of itself.

Yet the dualism of substances does not stand up to critical scrutiny. It founders on the key phenomenon of organic life, which testifies to the most intimate connection between both sides. Thus, for example, Descartes's hypostatizing separation of thinking and extended being is both logically and phenomenologically untenable. It is logically untenable because the ad hoc postulating of an independent thinking substance, which can never prove itself precisely in this characteristic, is an argument deus ex machina and, as Spinoza would say, a refuge for ignorance. It is phenomenologically untenable because not only the factual and causal imprisonment of soul in body, but even more the content of the life of the soul itself—perception, feeling, desire, pleasure and pain, and the reach of sensibility (in pictures and sounds) into the purest realms of thought—all of this is opposed to the notion that body and soul can be disentangled, and even makes *unimaginable* a consciousness "purified" of everything ("pure mind") and along with it any bodiless existence of the soul. An idea that cannot be imagined, however, is of no use at all as an hypothesis. When this falls away, there also falls with it the idea, held so dearly, of an individual immortal soul.

But equally untenable—to pass from dualism to monism—is the one-sided option of materialism, which turns the life of the soul and mind, "consciousness" as such, into a powerless accompanying phenomenon of physically determined processes within brains that arise from a purely physical genesis. This monistic "epiphenomenalism" suffers from self-contradictions that are even more lethal than the dualistic summoning of another world, and can be refuted on strictly philosophical grounds.[3]

Nevertheless, a monistic solution to our riddle is to be sought, since the voice of subjectivity in animals and human beings did emerge from the mute vortex of matter and continues to adhere to it. It is universal matter itself which, in becoming inward, finds its voice in subjectivity. Matter's most astounding accomplishment may not be denied it in any account of Being. What appears necessary, then, for a monistic solution is an ontological revision and replenishing of the concept of "matter" beyond the external qualities abstracted from it and measured by physics; and this means, therefore, a meta-physics of the material substance of the world. In statements that are just conjectures, proposed to stimulate further reflection, I will attempt to formulate what has imposed itself on me after many decades of pondering.

4. What Does the Fact of Subjectivity Contribute to the Evidence of Cosmology?

The very least that we must grant to matter that developed from the Big Bang, in regard to what ultimately emerged later on, is an original endowment with the *possibility* of eventual inwardness—not an endowment *with* inwardness, still long in coming, and not even an endowment *for* inwardness in the sense of being already prepared for it.[4] The mere potentiality for something is not yet a being-intended for something in such a way that the process of becoming is guided toward it. Our minimal conclusion from the fact of the emergence of the inner dimension in matter—whenever and wherever it occurred, and from its present and real existence within us—is just the nearly trivial result that this dimension was "possible," in accordance with the characteristics of matter as originally "created." But this already means that matter must have been more than what physicists ascribe to it in their speculation on the beginning of things and what can be derived from that for the development of the cosmos. Two questions arise on this issue: Who (or what) "endowed" matter in such a manner? and, What share did this "endowment" have in the course of cosmic events? What we are raising here is the question of an initial creative will and its further efficacy.

Let us proceed cautiously. It could well be that the first cause had nothing at all to do with something like a "will," neither with its initial presence nor again with its capacity to break forth later on. It could be that with the establishment of matter later possibilities occurred unintentionally, so to speak, or even unavoidably along with it, because without them matter was impossible. But it is an especially hard demand on thinking that what is emphatically nonindifferent, as subjectivity certainly is, should have arisen from what is entirely indifferent and neutral. Thus it is also hard to suppose that this arising itself was an entirely neutral contingency whose occurrence involved no favoring preferment of any kind.

It is more reasonable to assume such a preferment in the womb of matter, i.e., to interpret the witness of subjective life, which is will through and through, as not being utterly alien to that which brought it forth, namely matter. Therefore, although there should be no plan in it—this we have already rejected with good reason—we might ascribe to it a tendency, something like a yearning, which the chance opportunities of the world seize upon and then drive forward. To this extent a "cosmogonic eros" would come closer to the truth than a "cosmogonic logos," whose immanence in primordial matter we had to reject. But even then most of the story is left to chance—for example, to the enormously improbable and hence unlikely fortuity of a planet with the Earth's particularly favorable conditions for life occurring anywhere at all in the world process.[5] But when, by way of exception, it does occur, then the readiness is there, and subjectivity receives its opportunity.

The exploitation of this opportunity for life shows that more than a neutral accident is at work. Life is its own purpose, i.e., an end actively willing itself and pursuing itself. Purposiveness as such, by means of its eager "yes" to itself, is infinitely superior to that which is indifferent, and can easily be seen for its part as the purpose—the secretly longed-for goal—of the entire undertaking of the universe which otherwise seems so empty. This means that right from the beginning matter is subjectivity in its latent form, even if aeons, plus exceptional luck, are required for the actualizing of this potential. Only this much about "teleology" can be gleaned from the evidence of life alone.

The principle of our argument so far can be stated thus: since finality—striving for a goal—occurs in a certain natural being, i.e., a living being, in a manifestly subjective way and becomes effective there in an objectively causal manner, it cannot be entirely foreign to nature, which brought forth precisely this kind of being. Finality must itself be "natural"—in keeping with, conditioned by, and autonomously produced by nature. If follows from this that final causes, but also values and value distinctions, must be included in the (not utterly neutral) concept of the cause of the universe, and that they occur there as a potentiality for them and at the same time as a tolerant openness for their intervention into the determining system of efficient causes.[6] This much the report from the vital realm conveys to thinking, which here can still stand entirely within the immanent, for no one has yet deemed it necessary to bring in some kind of transcendence for interpreting life on its prehuman levels (what Aristotle would call the realm of the "vegetative" and "animal soul").

The inner dimension as such, from the dimmest feeling to the clearest perception and the keenest pleasure and pain, should be considered as an accomplishment proper to the material substance of the world, even if it remains dependent on particular external conditions. Whether and to what extent this teleological potency also played a role in the creation of those external conditions, i.e., of organic and especially cerebral evolution, or whether it can only wait for its heteronomous entrance, cannot be known. But conjectures are permitted. A "yearning" for it *could* be causally *active*, and increasingly work toward its own fulfillment—from the first chances presented by matter and then exponentially with the accumulation of these chances. This is what I believe, as I already indicated when I admitted the concept of an eros. But we do not know this, and in any event we are not able to make causal use of a general assumption of this kind in any individual scientific explanation (which is always after the fact in evolutionary affairs). But the phenomenological testimony of life speaks its own ontological word: one that is independent of science, but essential for the doctrine of cosmic being. And this is still a voice of immanence concerning itself.

5. The Transcending Freedom of the Mind

But this reflection on the nature of things and this arriving at conclusions (correct or not) is all being done by us. Thus, by means of thought itself, the human element is added to the vital evidence, and *with this*, certainly, an horizon of transcendence unfolds. It becomes apparent in three *freedoms* of thinking that go beyond everything ascribable to matter (including the dimension of inwardness), and thus beyond all of "nature."

(1) The freedom of thinking for *determining itself* through its choice of object: the mind (so long as the vital needs of the moment do not have the first word) can reflect on whatever it wants, seriously, playfully, even frivolously. (2) The freedom to *transform* the sensuously given into self-created inner images (preferably for the inner eye and ear): the *imagination's* freedom to invent in the service of cognitive or aesthetic interest, of veneration or anxiety, of love or repugnance, of utility or even for the pure enjoyment of inventing stories, and the like. (3) The freedom, finally, carried by the symbolic wings of language, *to transcend* everything that can ever be said and the dimension of the sayable as such: to pass from existence to essence, from the sensible to the supersensible, from the finite to the infinite, from the temporal to the eternal, from the conditioned to the unconditioned. The ability to grasp the *idea* of the infinite, the eternal, and the absolute, as even the youthful are able to do, indicates the transcending freedom of the mind, which an eros of its own urges on. Only through the medium of language, which represents things perceived, does it still remain bound to the world of the senses.

All three freedoms are unique prerogatives of the mind, designating that dimension of the human being that is beyond the animal.[7] The first freedom liberates us from attachment to the pressing theme of the moment, i.e., from the *situation* determined by the external world and one's own body. The second freedom liberates us from attachment to the given character of things and the preprogrammed behavioral response to it. The third freedom liberates us from attachment to the being of worldly existents in general. Now since the second freedom, the freedom of the imagination, contains within itself also the power of images to *move* us, as a transformation of what is beheld within into acts of bodily movement guided by it (making, dancing, singing, speaking, writing), so all of these freedoms include also the freedom of self-posited goals for behavior, and thus the realm of practical reason. In the case of the third, transcending freedom, however, this means that the human being can replace the loosened connection to present things and their demands with a freely chosen attachment to an imagined unconditioned and *its* demands. He can posit transcendent goals for his *conduct* and actually does so in such things as faith, devotion to an absolute ideal . . . or even a delusory construct of his fallible understanding of values, of a misguided eros.

In the understanding of values, where knowledge passes over into an *acknowledgment* of a *claim* upon me of what is known—an acknowledgment that underlies the attachment of the will, mentioned before, to an imagined unconditioned—in a passing over, therefore, from the "is" to the "ought," from the beheld quality to the heard command of value, there is added to all of the other freedoms the *moral* freedom of human beings. Of all of them it is the most transcendent and precarious, for it is also the freedom of self-refusal, of chosen deafness, yes, of an opting-against, all the way up to radical evil, which can still, as we have learned, dress up in the guise of the highest good. The knowledge *of* good and evil, the power of discriminating between them, is also the capacity *for* good and evil. It is apparent that the "eros" at work in the *motivation* behind every choice among goods still offers no guarantee as a *guide* for glimpsing and pursuing its true object—even and especially when it has become in great measure a matter of *seeing*, as in human beings. Yet here, where the deepest abyss of the perversion of insight and will yawn open, is also the place where the highest pinnacle of holiness of will and consecration of life to the commanding good towers up to heaven and casts its celestial brilliance over our earthly throng—the transfiguration of the temporal by a moment of eternity.

To grasp moral freedom, the locus of this possibility, in its complete sense, we must append one more aspect to intellectual freedom, an aspect in which the three freedoms of thinking collaborate: its capacity to turn back upon itself, to make itself and its subject, the "self," into its own theme; in other words, the freedom of *reflection*. We have good reason to award this freedom to human beings alone: to the mind, therefore, and not to the feeling, desiring, and sensibly perceiving soul. It is not as if freedom in *every* form is limited to human beings alone. A principle of freedom and actual modes of this freedom are already known in the being of metabolizing things as such, i.e., in all living things.[8] This suggests that also the dimension of subjectivity, which appears bound to organisms as the condition of their existence, goes far beyond its cerebral and neural foundation, and extends in degrees of clarity and obscurity through the entire realm of life. In human beings, however, all of this is surpassed once again in a qualitative leap, and the freedom of reflection is an eminent mode of this, so to speak, "immanent transcendence." What is "sighted" in reflection is something absolutely invisible, i.e., the subject of subjectivity itself, the "self" of nonphenomenal freedom (what Kant called a "noumenon"). It is forever a riddle to itself, ungraspable, unfathomable, and yet always present as the complementary pole of all values, which, in no way "merely subjective," are still essential *for* a responding subject.

Now—to come to the ethical—the genuine miracle of reflection occurs. The miracle is that this evaluating self for its part is also turned into an object of evaluation, i.e., it becomes subject to the judgment of conscience. Concern for the good of an object—for a non-I (either persons or conditions) outside in the world—calls forth a feeling of responsibility, but also contains in itself concern for the good within, for one's own potential and obligation for goodness. This is not what is willed *primarily*, which must always be the well-being of what faces us in the world. But it is something co-willed either hiddenly or openly, and only this self-inclusion of the subject elevates the merely moral aspect of worldly behavior to the more exacting level of personal ethics. The first kind of willing, that directed to another, can without question be fulfilled successfully in this or that given case.

But reflexive co-willing, the concern of oneself about the "how" of one's own being, must always remain unsatisfied, even plagued with doubt. This is so because and insofar as this self-concern stands under the norms of the third freedom listed above: the freedom to cross over to the infinite, the eternal, and the unconditioned. And it is also true *because* freedom for good is at the same time freedom for evil, which, masquerading in a thousand different ways, lies hidden *in* all willing of the good. The subordination of the self to transcendent criteria turns care itself into something infinite and unconditioned. By concerning itself in the light of eternity *with this* and no longer only with the temporal and conditioned good of the finite, changing object, this freedom exposes itself to the cunning of a self emancipated to itself: to the irremovable ambiguity of all free will, which always indulges that which is impure (the height of earthly vanity, for example), or at least can never entirely shed the suspicion of tainted motives. Reflection as such, which, in its concern for and examination of the self involves at the same time a mirroring of the self, contains this ambiguity within it essentially.[9] Thus, we come to the awesome discoveries of those daring, contrite explorers into the depths of the soul, who burn with love for the highest good and suffer the torments of self-searching, to which the confessions of world literature bear such moving testimony.

6. What Does the Datum of Mind Contribute to the Evidence of Cosmology?: Arguments from Western Metaphysics

We have strayed from cosmology into the definition of being human. Our question now becomes: What does this definition have to contribute to our actual theme, cosmology—and perhaps even to the theme of cosmogony, i.e., the question of creation? Does the anthropological situation tell us something about the first causes of all things? Does the presence of human beings tell us anything about the distant "In the beginning . . ."?

Here, first of all, we must remember what the spokesmen of both pure interiority, the idealistic philosophers, and pure exteriority, the materialistic physicists, so easily forgot. We must recall the apparent "paradox," not a real one at all, that the presence of the subjective is itself an *objective fact* in the world (only solipsism can deny it), and that consequently even the anthropic evidence belongs in cosmology. As facts of the universe, human beings must be analyzed and evaluated cosmologically. A philosophical anthropology, therefore, is an integral part of every ontology deserving of the name, or, let us say it directly, of every teaching of nature as it really is, not as it has been expurgated for the purposes of natural science.

From early on, according to the captivating proposition that like is known by like, something divine has been seen in certain powers and experiences of the mind, those covered under the attribute "transcendent." As Plato and Aristotle argued (and Pythagoras before them), the mind that is able to behold, or even touch, the unchangeable, the eternal, the divine, must be originally related to it in kind. And the mind participates in the being of what is known to the degree that it knows it. Thus, the soul—admittedly, not the entire soul, but its highest cognitive part, reason—soars beyond all of nature, which is immersed in coming-to-be and passing-away. Reason itself is "eternal" and "divine." Similar in form to the Greeks, though very different in content, is the Bible's account in Genesis (through the mouth of the serpent) of man's resemblance to God. It places the godlike character of human beings, and thus the quality of "image and likeness" designated as the intention of the Creator Himself, in man's knowledge of "good and evil."

In both cases, the Hellenic and the Hebraic, the conclusion of resemblance is arrived at by proceeding from the intentional object to the intending thought itself and its subject, the soul or mind. From the fact of our thinking about what is true or what commands beyond time there follows a corresponding dimension beyond time in our essence. Logically we are not able to make this conclusion our own, but this much remains to be considered. When the timeless truth of his theorem dawned on Pythagoras, moving him profoundly, when the prophets of Israel first perceived the unconditioned character of the ethical demand as the word of God, and when at similar moments in other cultures the same thing occurred, there opened up an horizon of transcendence in immanence: an horizon which, going beyond what has directly been said within it, has something to say about the character of the being *in* which the opening occurs—and this being is as much that of perceiving as it is that of what is perceived.

The above conclusion, moreover, can also be reversed in the following way: instead of moving from what is thought to thinking, we proceed rather from thinking to its object. And so it happened—at first in Anselm's ontological argument for the existence of God, which proves from the *concept* of the most perfect of all beings, from its being thought, therefore, the necessary *existence* of such a being. Since Kant, the logical untenability of this proof can be considered as demonstrated. But even from this "proof" a meaning remains preserved—an indicative, even if not logically compelling meaning for the question about the nature of a being who can bring such a concept to consciousness.

Descartes followed this direction in the *causal* turn that he gave to the ontological argument. In accordance with the principle that the cause must contain in itself at least as much "reality" as is contained in the effect, the finite and imperfect mind of human beings cannot have produced from itself the idea of an infinite and perfect being, which they nonetheless find in themselves. Therefore, its presence in consciousness is to be explained only through a commensurable cause outside of consciousness, precisely the infinite being itself, whose existence is thereby proven. The argument of resemblance in favor of the knowing subject is replaced, therefore, by the argument of sufficient reason in favor of the known object. But this proof for the existence of God also fails to stand up to logical examination, for the intentional object (*realitas objectiva*) of an idea and the existential content (*realitas formalis*) of an entity—in general, consciousness and thing—can enter into no quantitative comparison at all. No common denominator of measurability, as it joins together all quantities of the external world, befits the causal communication between the external and the internal, as unavoidable as such communication is. Yet something remains even from this failed attempt: the connection of the inner evidence of transcendence with the question of the first *causes*. It is here that we make our proposal.

7. The Speculative Character of the Following Reflections

The existence of inwardness in the universe, and along with it the anthropic evidence of reason, freedom, and transcendence, are, so we have said, cosmic data. As such they belong together among the generically indispensable elements of a cosmology. Their testimony says: the universe is of the kind that such things are possible in it, perhaps even necessarily flow out of it. Does this also teach us something about its first causes, about creation? With this question we make the decisive transition from the cosmological evidence to *cosmogonic speculation*. The speculative character, I believe, is irremovable. Everything I have to say from now on is a groping attempt and in all probability a mistaken one. But ventured it must be from time to time, for the enormous question to which the human mind here aspires leaves it no peace.

In this attempt knowledge passes over unavoidably into faith. It strives to be rational faith and not the faith demanded by revelation, although the voices of the great religions also belong in the testimony to which we must listen. It renounces the capacity for proof, which is prohibited here. Yet the present approach to the question of all questions still sets out by appropriating whatever was of hidden validity in the old and constantly failed attempts at a demonstrable *theologia naturalis*. Strains from the cosmological, teleological, and ontological proofs for the existence of God, no longer clearly separated from one another, will not escape the trained ear. It should be enough for me if I have joined to the oft-repeated failure one more failure still, but perhaps in its own way an instructive one. Let us venture our own attempt, therefore, in the unending series.

There has repeatedly occurred in our exposition an argument of the following form: Since life, having inwardness, interests, and purposive willing, has come forth from the material substance of the universe, such qualities cannot be entirely foreign to this substance in its essence; if something cannot be foreign to its essence (at this point the argument becomes cosmogonic), then it also cannot be foreign to its beginning; thus in the matter under formation in the "Big Bang" there must have already been present the possibility of subjectivity—the inner dimension in latency, which awaited its external opportunity in the cosmos for manifestation. Further speculations concerning this "waiting" as a "yearning" that collaborates in the development of the physical conditions for its own fulfillment, a secret teleology, therefore, in the colossal predominance of mechanical contingency in the cosmic prehistory of life, or even a cosmogonic speculation concerning a factor of a "willing," directed to this end, already in the first origin itself—speculations of this kind, so we discovered, do not step beyond the limits of an immanent philosophy of nature. No "seeing" intelligence at the beginning, no eternal providence concerning what ultimately comes to fruition, need be assumed. Unconscious tendency suffices for the evidence of life. Even panpsychism, to which this evidence offers some support, is not yet theology. In a word, the testimony of life, immeasurably meaningful for ontology, is still a voice of immanence concerning itself.

8. The Question Concerning the First Cause of Mind: Can It Have Been Less Than Mind?

Is this also valid for the testimony of the mind, for the anthropic evidence, therefore, which is still a part, even if a minute part, of the cosmic evidence? We can see in this question traces of Descartes's idea of an equality of rank between the cause and its effect, detached from the logical nonsense of its quantitative version. From the qualitative standpoint we may ask: Can something that is less than mind be the cause of mind? We mean here the "first" cause, the cause at the basis of all things. As regards secondary causes, it is undeniable that mind can proceed from what is not mind and actually does so, as we see every day before our eyes, so to speak, in human ontogenesis (and, beyond that, as we postulate for phylogenesis). In the embryo there is fashioned the brain, the future physical carrier of the mind, under the exclusive physico-chemical direction of the genome, a pure ordering of material in germ, which contains in complete ignorance the "information" for the process of becoming and, just as ignorantly, does its work. It comes about entirely without mind in the process.[10]

Of course, no one considers this deposit of information and programming, preexisting in matter, to be the first cause. But when one asks "Who or what laid down the code with this information?" one comes to the again purely physical and totally ignorant transmission of material patterns along the hereditary line. One goes further back to the gradual, blind construction (steered only by the selecting process of survival) of the phylogenetic pattern itself through chance mutations from patterns more impoverished in information and further removed from mind in ontogenetic result. One moves beyond the innumerable interim results of the genetic toss of the dice, from the eukaryotes to the prokaryotes, down to the first occurrences of self-replicating molecules, the first minimum of information, and from there down into inorganic, universal, and so-called neutral nature, to an initial zero of information. Thus, the regress of temporal causes does not lead closer and closer to mind, but further and further away from it.

Yet it is our own mind that has followed the causal path backwards and, obedient to its will to truth, arrived at this strange insight. And it is mind, too, that knows it is indebted to this universal matter—to that tiny bit of matter organized so exactly in the brain—allowing mind to exist and to think. Thus to that which is alien to mind it must still grant, besides all the properties that physics teaches the mind about it, the endowment with the possibility of mind, the *enabling* of mind, however tied it might be to particular conditions.

I speak of mind—and this is more than life and subjectivity. For if we now assert, with a metaphor that might be permitted, that matter from the very beginning is mind asleep, so we must immediately add that the really first cause, the creative cause, of mind asleep can only be mind awake. From potential mind we must infer actual mind. This is otherwise than with living things and subjectivity as such, which, in accordance with the gradual nature of their occurrence, can indeed begin in a sleeping, unconscious manner and yet require no consciousness in the first cause, in the act of their physical birth. So the anthropic evidence, then, as part of the cosmic evidence—the self-experience of the mind, therefore, and especially its reaching out by thinking into the transcendent—lead us now to the postulate of a mental, thinking, transcendent, supertemporal being at the origin of things. It is conceived as a first cause, if there was only one of them, or as a co-cause, if there was more than one.

I know that this is no proof and compels no one to agreement, but it seems to me the most illuminating of the conjectures permitted to reason at this point, and for the sake of making progress I ask the reader to go along with it and just try it out awhile as an hypothesis. For if it be accepted, there result at least specific questions which can be clearly discussed in the daylight of rational argument. My discussion will be mainly a careful weighing of the various great answers from the history of thought—it would be foolish to ignore them—augmented by a suggestion of my own that seeks to do justice to a knowledge later and more bitterly acquired. I hope that my colleagues in analytic philosophy will pardon me for this straying into metaphysics, which has been prohibited since Kant and especially despised by the analytic school.

9. The Objection of Anthropomorphism

Since we are calling upon the anthropic testimony, our first concern must be the old objection of "anthropomorphism" and the related reproach of human vanity. Are we not creating for ourselves a divinity according to our own image (though not the bodily one) when we speak of divine thinking, willing, and judging? But from what, then, should we extrapolate? From bulls and owls, snakes and monkeys? All that has been done, as we know. But here we have the God of Israel who acknowledges His similarity to human beings in saying that He wanted to create them in His own image—surely, a superior conception. Obviously we must proceed from the highest thing that appears in being to fashion for ourselves a concept of the divine, and our mind *is* the highest thing known to us in the universe. No suspicion of partiality toward ourselves can change the situation. Should He lack what we have? An anthropomorphism in thinking about God is as legitimate as it is irremovable. Of course, it must know about its inadequacy, as Thomas Aquinas urged with his concepts of the *analogia entis* and the *modo eminentiae*.

Concerning the reproach of vanity, of anthropocentric arrogance, the phrase, "the crown of creation," which in truth is somewhat boastful, could well justify it. Only by understanding itself as an enormous burden, as a command to imitate the divine likeness, can this dignity prove itself. And here we find shame much sooner than pride of place when we look at the human spectacle, for betrayal of this likeness overwhelmingly outweighs faithfulness to it. We must be grateful for the rare confirmations that repeatedly shine forth, and sometimes in our darkest hours. For without them we would have to despair before the procession of those things in world history that refute this image, before this mixture of cruelty and stupidity; I daresay, we would have to despair of the very meaning of the human adventure. The example of the just ones saves us; indeed, by itself it rescues us time and time again. But the human race, God knows, has no reason for self-boasting. So much for the theme of anthropomorphism, a question for theology.

10. Mere Compatibility of Material Substance and Mind: The Dualism of Descartes and Its Breakdown before the Phenomenon of Evolution

The cosmological question is: How are we to understand the endowment of primordial matter with the possibility of mind? The minimal sense of this question is that matter *allows* the appearance and then also the operation of mind in its midst—that matter gives way to mind in good time, or when things have reached a certain point in the material world. This much can be established from the pure *fact* of that appearance in accordance with the almost tautological inference that what became actual must have been possible. Translated into the language of creation, this means that the mental cause or co-cause at the beginning created a universal matter with such properties and laws that it left room for the co-presence of mind. This would be the property, in itself only negative, of nonhindering, of sheer compatibility. (This view is not self-evident, as the longheld doctrine of a complete materialistic determinism betrays.) In this case the Creator-mind must have become causally active once again—if and when the space it had carefully saved for this possibility opened up for actual occupation somewhere, as it did in fact here on Earth. The cause of this opening could be the material substance of the universe itself, but the cause of filling it through finite minds could only be mind operating from without.

Such a course of events would harmonize well with the Cartesian dualism of two substances alien to one another: matter, which is mere extension, and mind, which is nothing but thinking. If human beings had appeared in the world suddenly and in a finished state, at whatever time, then such a unique and overpowering intervention of the creator, by which he completed his original creation at the right moment, could provide an explanation of the heterogeneously new. The "right moment" would have been the presence of the human body-machine that came into being by chance from mechanical causes. But we did not arise suddenly. The evidence of evolution teaches us that human beings came to their consciousness through a long prehistory of advances of the animal soul toward mind. Likewise, the present evidence of the thinking mind itself teaches us that it is not to be separated from those things that belong to the sensible soul—perception, feeling, desire, pleasure, pain—all of which are bound to the body. But if the coming-to-be of humans, and thereby of mind, extends through biological eras and stages, even then, in accordance with our minimal hypothesis, divine intervention would have to have done it. Consequently, according to what is shown by both evolution and introspection, this would have involved continual, not a one-time, intervention—in a word, divine governance of the world.

Descartes had absolutely no place for this. He was concerned solely with the founding of an exact science of nature based on the laws of the *res extensa* and their necessity, and he knew well what he was doing when he declared animals to be automata without feeling, denying them, therefore, any soul at all. The science of nature, inherently materialistic, can reconcile itself with the unique miracle of the incarnation of mind in man as the single exception to the rules of nature. But science cannot put up with this miracle, repeated over and over again in the history of Being, as a principle of explanation. Still, Descartes attained nothing with his last-ditch dualistic blow, meant to save the situation. The impudent fiction of animals as automata is dashed to pieces at the slightest acquaintance with the animal realm, and the fiction of the abrupt epiphany of mind in human beings is shattered by the facts of evolution paving its way.

For the hypothesis, then, of a material substance merely compatible with mind—the minimal assumption of creation—there remains, for explaining the fact of mind, only the alternative already mentioned: the supplementary assumption of a divine governance of the world, a *providentia generalis et specialis* always intervening anew in the course of the world. And this assumption we must reject, not only because it is of no use methodologically as a principle of explanation—indeed, it destroys the very idea of explanation—but also because too much in our knowledge of nature and history—too much theoretically and morally—runs directly counter to it. We will have more to say about this later. The first cause, therefore, instead of placing the destiny of mind under his continual guardianship, must have given to the primordial matter released into time *more* than neutral compatibility with mind, mere toleration of its coexistence. A relation of outer and inner, more intimate than the former dualism permits, must in any case be assumed.

11. Total Congruence of Matter and Mind: The Psychophysical Parallelism of Spinoza and Its Breakdown before the Cosmic Rarity of Mind

This path was pursued by Spinoza, the great rectifier of Descartes, with his psychophysical parallelism, and in so doing he went right to the other extreme. All Being, in its essence and at every moment, is both together: extension and thought, matter and mind, nature and its own idea. Both of these are only two sides of the same coin—the eternal, absolute substance—that expresses itself in both of them equally. To each "outer" there corresponds an "inner" belonging to it; these together (in addition to the attributes unknown to us) are the ways in which the infinite deity exists from all eternity. That this takes place in a series of states is due to the fact that the divine plenitude, as infinite, cannot present itself in finite modes all at once, but each such modal state of the whole in every "now" represents the divine perfection, each state being equal in this perfection to the other, whether it comes before or follows after.

But even this imposing conception does not withstand the judgment of our experience. For here there is no beginning and end, no success and failure, no better and worse, and, all the more so, no good and evil. What appears to be such appears so only from the standpoint of the particular. The whole, the psychophysical universe, is always in the state of perfection. Chance has no place here, and freedom is an illusion. Mind is just as determined as bodily nature, whose exact equivalent it is at every moment. In both of them reigns this one and the same necessity of the divine nature, which cannot give preference to any of its attributes. So also time is not a field for actual decisions, but only an irresistible and endless development, without alternatives, of that eternal necessity, its ultimately timeless self-presentation. Even the becoming of mind, except in the individual case, is out of the question in this universe. It was always already there—that means from all eternity—with the external matter of the world, extended in space, as its equiprimordial complement—the eternal self-thinking thought of the infinite substance.

On this point alone—the eternity of the universe and of the mind currently in it—Spinoza's entire vision proves unavailing for the knowledge attained since his time. All of its other unacceptable aspects, against which our intuition puts up resistance, can thus be allowed here to go unchallenged. Nevertheless, of these we can mention the theological objection that a purely immanent pantheism and panpsychism—one, therefore, without a transcendent criterion of the good—can be just as much a pandemonism, indeed a pandiabolism.

Here it will suffice to mention a more modest but well-rounded objection. The battle between the notions of eternity and the beginning of the world in time, fought for so long in the Middle Ages between Aristotelians and believers in creation, appears meanwhile to have been settled. On better empirical grounds than Kant in the antinomies of pure reason could credit to human experience, the battle seems to have been decided in favor of a beginning in time—in other words, in favor of that faith from which Spinoza had so strenuously dissociated himself. It must be added that the same modern knowledge of nature disproves the biblical belief in a multiplicity of finished and separate species created at the same time, just as it refutes the Aristotelian belief in such a multiplicity existing forever. And this adds to our cosmological objection a second, equally weighty element. More certainly than the "Big Bang," we know about the later, precarious, cosmically isolated becoming of mind out of the slow, tortuous becoming of life, which for its part is already a local exception in an enormous spatiotemporal universe of matter and emptiness, without life and without mind. We must bring into the question of cosmogony, then, both of these cosmological discoveries: the beginning of the world, and the late appearance and rarity of mind in the universe.

12. Reformulating the Question of Cosmogony in Accordance with the Corrected Evidence of Cosmology

We must take our starting point, therefore, from the creation (or "origin," as the case may be) of a primordial matter which is still without mind, but endowed with the possibility of mind. This "possibility," so we said, must not be a mere giving-way or an empty compatibility, which would require a further, ongoing intervention of the otherworldly, mind-bestowing cause. Furthermore, if we adhere to the intuitive thesis that the first creative cause of mind must itself be mind—a mind, however, which refrains from any later intervention in the course of the world—then our question now reads: In what manner has this cause entrusted the issue of mind to the initial, mind-less material of the universe?

Now in this original mind, I suppose, there could have been present a cosmogonic "logos"—a plan that requires a planner, a program that requires a programmer. But right at the start of this investigation we discovered that the original cause could not have embodied such a logos in primordial matter as information, since chaos lacks the stability and articulation necessary to be a bearer of such information. A cosmogonic eros, blindly working in this direction, was the most that we could grant as the original endowment of matter for the positive possibility of mind (a possibility that is more than just permissive). Everything else had to be left to the inner dynamism of matter. But apart from the mechanical causality, neutral to any goal, that has been and can be discovered by natural science, what could this dynamism be such that the plan of the world logos, in its own planless way, still came to realization? Let us consider that the whole process began from that which is totally other than mind, from its extreme opposite pole, so to speak.

13. The Beginning of the World as Self-Alienation of the Primordial Mind: What Is True and Untrue in the Dialectic of Hegel

At this point, let us recall the one doctrine that likewise had the world process begin with the extreme self-alienation of mind, and gains precisely from this antithesis the principle of movement for the further process: the principle of becoming by which the mind wins itself back again in the world. This is Hegel's universal dialectic, which progresses necessarily, powerfully, and with the unerring cunning of reason, through thesis, antithesis, and synthesis, repeated over and over again, and which ultimately reaches its pinnacle in the realm of reason and human freedom, having come home to itself. The first step in this alleged process, the founding, primordial act of the world drama, is precisely the one to which we see ourselves more and more compelled in our own cosmogonic speculation: the extreme self-divesting of the Creator-mind at the beginning of all things. The continuation of this, however, in Hegel's majestic account of all becoming, step by dialectical step toward us and through us to completion—in general, the whole edifying idea of an intelligible lawfulness of *one* total process that is assured of success right from the start—this doctrine we must deny, being, as we are, more sober onlookers of the large and small theaters of the world, of nature and history. The counterevidence is too overwhelming.

The most external piece of this evidence, the sheer magnitudes involved, has already been sufficiently discussed. Hegel knew too little of the enormity of the universe in space and time and consequently of the minuteness of the human place in it, which he saw in almost pre-Copernican dimensions. The statement that frightened Pascal, but was still vague and abstract at its time—"The infinity of those spaces that know me not"—has only now, through the tremendous swell of measurable distances and masses, become concrete for us, and thus all the more overwhelming, accompanied as it is by a similar increase in the measurable past—the earthly past before human beings, and the cosmic past before life. The final, latest, local, and infinitesimal appearance of mind in the universe—in us (the only appearance we know of)—is to be compared more to a lost flicker in universal night. And if mind was the goal of this gigantic spectacle, one is tempted rather to speak of the great expenditure that was lamentably squandered, given the quantitative disproportion (so far as we know) to what was achieved. To put it more kindly, one might speak of a stroke of luck in the coming together of conditions, a game of chance, rather than something like the majestic march of reason through the world. The latter is simply out of the question.

If this objection, however, appears to someone as too superficial and quantitative (although here is a case where Hegel's formula of the transformation of quantity into quality could be rightfully invoked), he should kindly take for the highest qualitative witness *our very selves*, the balance sheet of human history, on this question of the triumphal procession of mind through the world. Is the world spirit imperturbably close at hand in us, or has it even already arrived, having come to the definitive form of its truth and perfected its original determination with wise necessity? Are we its chosen executors, willingly or unwillingly, knowingly or unknowingly, yet always infallible? I must beg your pardon! The disgrace of Auschwitz is not to be charged to some all-powerful providence or to some dialectically wise necessity, as if it were an antithesis demanding a synthesis or a step on the road to salvation. *We* human beings have inflicted this on the deity, we who have failed in the administering of his things. It remains on our account, and it is we who must again wash away the disgrace from our own disfigured faces, indeed, from the very countenance of God. Don't talk to me here about the cunning of reason.

14. The Weakness of Every Metaphysics of Success: Misunderstanding the Divine Risk in Creation

There is simply nothing, therefore, to this unique, brilliant alternative to Aristotelian teleology, i.e., Hegel's dialectic; still less, of course, to his minor successors, such as Teilhard de Chardin's doctrine of the increasing spiritualization of the universe in the direction of a pan-mental omega point. The common substantial objection (not the formal epistemological objection) against all these fictions of speculative reason is that they tell us self-guaranteed success stories of Being, stories that cannot go amiss. Every great metaphysical system known to me from the history of thought seems to be just such a history of success: the apotheosis of what is.

The term "apotheosis" applies to Spinoza's *deus sive natura* with its static and permanent perfection, to the universal logos of the Stoics, or to the cosmos of Aristotle, eternally and teleologically moved by the unmoved mover. In the sense of an eschatological and perfecting dynamism it applies to Hegel, who, precisely with this dynamic aspect, this option for becoming, proves himself nevertheless to be a modern among the metaphysicians, similar to the other thinkers of the modern age, such as Leibniz and Whitehead. The evidence of both cosmology and anthropology, which we may not ignore, flies in the face of all these high-minded and optimistic constructions. A metaphysics, therefore, that resists the temptation of "Behold, it is good!" and yet does not disregard the witness of life and of mind for the nature of Being, must leave room for the blind, the planless, the accidental, the incalculable, the extremely precarious in the adventure of the world—in a word, for the enormous *gamble* that the first ground, if mind was present then, wagered with creation. Here began years ago my own attempt at cosmogony, which, not accidentally, was connected with the name "Auschwitz," for that was for me also a theological event.[11] My speculation is no less a fiction than all that I had to reject, but perhaps still a fiction that does a little more justice to the evidence of the universe as we now can and must see it. About this I would like to say a few words.

15. Alternative Speculation of Cosmogony: God's Renunciation of Power in Favor of Cosmic Autonomy and Its Chances

As our first proposition we say that the self-divesting of mind at the beginning was more serious than the cheerful prophet of reason was willing to admit. He abandoned Himself and his destiny entirely to the outwardly exploding universe and thus to the pure chances of the *possibilities* contained in it under the conditions of space and time. Why He did this remains unknowable. We are allowed to speculate that it happened because *only* in the endless play of the finite, in the inexhaustibility of chance, in the surprises of the unplanned, *and* in the distress caused by mortality, can mind experience itself in the variety of its possibilities. For this the deity had to renounce His own power. Be that as it may, from then on things proceeded only in an immanent manner, with no further intervention of transcendence. Creation had no power at all to bring forth antitheses out of itself, but had to tread its long path through space and time, bound to the gradual, cumulative transformations permitted by the self-developing and consolidating law of nature, external chance, and its own inner endowment.

In this view, secondly, the overwhelming argument from quantity against the importance of mind (thus of ourselves)—the argument from a comparison in size between the enormity of a dead universe and the tininess of life and of mind in it—is turned around into an explanation. Only a universe colossal in space and time, in accordance with the rule of mere probabilities and with no intervention of divine power, offered any chance at all for mind's coming to pass at any time or place whatsoever. And if this and the self-testing of mind in a finite world were the intention of the Creator, then he had to create precisely an immense universe and leave finitude in it to its own career.

Thirdly, since mind can arise only from the living organism and can exist only as borne by it, so we must now correct our earlier assertion. We stated that feeling in the animal soul is to be regarded as entirely immanent in matter, while the thinking of the mind is to be explained only by recourse to transcendence, with mind as its first creative cause. Yet they cannot be quite so heterogeneous. The dimmest feeling and clearest thinking have one thing in common, subjectivity, and so the very appearance of inwardness as such and its entire animal development should be seen as paving the way for mind. Therefore, the creative source, if it willed mind, also had to will life. And this it says in the beautiful attribute ascribed to God that we Jews so often recite in prayer: *rozeh bachajim*, "he who wills life": not only "the living God," but "the God who wills life," both for its own sake and, by means of the soul, as a cradle for the mind. Thus to a certain degree we might speak of the sacredness of life, although life can be a wasteland, as can mind.

And with this we come, fourthly, to ourselves, the only bearers of mind known to us, i.e., beings capable of reflective knowing and, as a result, of acting from free will in the world—an acting that in the light of our knowledge is becoming more and more powerful. And here our cosmogonic hypothesis, forced upon us by the cosmological evidence, yields a certain fact. It arises from the combination of mind's character of being willed in the stream of becoming, on the one hand, and of the renunciation of power by the primordial mind precisely for the sake of the unanticipated selfhood of finite minds, on the other. From all this, the fact follows that the destiny of the divine adventure is placed in our unsteady hands in this earthly corner of the universe, and that the responsibility for it rests on our shoulders. So the deity, I imagine, must become anxious about His own cause. There is no doubt that we have the power in our hands to thwart the purpose of creation—and this precisely in its apparent triumph in us—and that we are perhaps energetic in doing so.

Why are we not permitted to do this? Why may we not, like the animals, do *everything* that we are able to do, including self-annihilation? Because Being tells us so? But as we know from the teaching of all modern logic and philosophy, Being tells us nothing whatsoever about this: from an "is" there follows no "ought." It all depends, however, on "what is." We must see it and hear it. What we see encompasses the testimony of life and of mind—witnesses against the doctrine of a nature devoid of values and goals. What we hear is the call of the good that we have seen, its indwelling claim on human existence. Our *ability* to see it and to hear it turns us into those who are called by its command of acknowledgment and thus into subjects of a duty toward it.

This duty, which exists constantly, becomes acute and concrete with the growth of human power through technology, which endangers the entire habitat of life here on Earth. This belongs to the most current evidence, to the "is" that we can see and hear. It tells us that we must now protect from ourselves the divine cause in the world that has become threatened by us, that we must come to the aid of the deity who has become powerless for Himself regarding us. It is the duty of power that knows, a cosmic duty, for it is a cosmic experiment, which we can wreck along with ourselves and spoil within ourselves.

16. That We Must Help God: The Testimony of Etty Hillesum

By the events of Auschwitz and from the rather safe harbor of not having been there, wherefrom one can easily speculate, I was impelled to the view, which every doctrine of faith would probably find heretical, that it is not God who can help us, but we who must help God. This view became more valid with the confession of an actual witness, sealed with her own life, of whom I learned much later. These words of a confessor are found in the preserved diaries of Etty Hillesum, a young Jewish woman from the

Netherlands, who in 1942 voluntarily reported to the camp at Westerbork in order to be of help there and to take part in the destiny of her people. In 1943 she was sent to the gas chamber in Auschwitz.

> I will go to any place on this earth where God sends me, and I am ready in every situation and until I die to bear witness . . . that it is not God's fault that everything has turned out this way, but our fault.

> . . . and if God does not continue to help me, then I must help God. . . . I will always endeavor to help God as well as I can.

> I will help you, O God, that you do not forsake me, but right from the start I can vouch for nothing. Only this one thing becomes more and more clear to me: that you cannot help us, but that we must help you, and in so doing we ultimately help ourselves. That is the only thing that matters: to save in us, O God, a piece of yourself. Yes, my God, even you in these circumstances seem powerless to change very much. . . . I demand no account from you; you will later call us to account. And with almost every heartbeat it becomes clearer to me that you cannot help us, but that we must help you and defend up to the last your dwelling within us.[12]

I cannot close with this kind of statement. A philosophical discourse, which this essay (in spite of its confessional content) still strives to be, should not end with the emotional overpowering of its readers, and as for myself the words just cited are overwhelming. Permit me, then, to touch upon two further questions that are able to be treated soberly and even— a rarer privilege—to be answered in a rationally comprehensible way. The first is whether such conjectures as I have introduced here and have proposed to my presumed readers are philosophically permitted. The second is how important is the question, moving so many minds today, whether there is other intelligent life in the universe besides ourselves.

17. Is Philosophy Allowed to be Speculative?

As to the first point, I am aware that in the preceding remarks I have persistently sinned against two powerful interdicts of contemporary phi- losophizing, which, over the rather long history of modern thought, have almost attained the status of articles of faith. These are, first of all, that one should steer clear of the unprovable, and secondly, as a special case of the first, that there is no way leading from the "is" to the "ought," from fact to value. To put it briefly, there is the prohibition against metaphysics, and the dogma of the sheer subjectivity of values, hence also of obligation and ethics. The near unanimity on these issues should not startle us. It reflects the succumbing of philosophy to the success of natural science, which it would like to imitate.

The materialistic science of nature actually owes its success to the fact that it wants to be precisely this—materialistic—and nothing else. It owes its success, therefore, to the definition of its object, which presents an expurgated edition of the ontological evidence, *ad usum Delphini,* for the use of the natural scientist: the elimination of ends, sense qualities, and subjectivity; the reduction to what is quantitatively measurable in space and time. Ontologically this is a fiction; methodologically, as the yield of knowledge shows, it is of the greatest use. The philosophy that followed the example of Descartes answered with a similar and, so to speak, complementary expurgation of *its* object: the truncated ego of pure consciousness, of subjective idealism, especially the transcendental kind in which the German philosophers excelled. Admittedly, Husserl's pure consciousness knows how to give an account of a "lifeworld," but only as a datum "for" consciousness, constituting itself in consciousness or even constructed by it. Consciousness itself is not part of the "lifeworld," not dependently interwoven with it, and so even the body occurs only as an object of lived experience, only as a phenomenon, not *in reality.*

Such artificial expurgations perform their service and justify themselves by the results from the disciplines that they make possible on the one or the other side of the division. But when they become hardened, each in its own standpoint, when method is identified with subject matter and part with whole, then the beneficiaries fall victim to these guiding fictions. From critics we now get dogmatists; antimetaphysicians become involuntary metaphysicians. The natural sciences are not to be blamed for this and should remain at their enterprise. It is only that physicists should beware of making their physics into a metaphysics, i.e., to pass off the reality known by them for the whole of reality. The physicists that I have gotten to know I have found remarkably free from this temptation, but among their admiring onlookers, as naive as they are philosophical, it is widespread. In any case, it is the task of *philosophy* to reflect on this whole. But, intimidated by the exact sciences and (along with Descartes) elevating "certainty" to the hallmark of knowing, it has renounced this noble but inexact calling and has entrenched itself as a special science in its own half of the totality. This is shown by the gross overestimation of epistemological, logical, and semantic themes, going all the way to the comic situation of leaving philosophy alone—as if what mattered primarily was *how* human beings understand and not *what* there is to be understood. In regard to this "what," the division of labor cannot be the last word. Ultimately the parts still belong together and must be brought together under *one* formula for understanding the world.

"Pure nature," "pure consciousness," materialism, idealism, and even dualism were useful fictions; under their protection important insights were attained and will be attained in the future. But there comes a time when we have to perform our first long-distance swim and risk the plunge into deep water. It is certainly no safe bet that we can do it. But that the "ultimate questions" encountered there, which cannot hope for a *demonstrable* answer, are therefore *meaningless* (as one is likely to hear), is not to be taken seriously. They lurk behind every effort of thinking, and even the declared agnostic answers them with his own, hidden metaphysics.

Of course, every attempt to get a grip on the riddle on the universe must end in disrepute. But this must ever be risked anew, each time as a different and unique venture, and mitigated by the consolation that at least in doing so one finds oneself in good company, even in the best company of all: that of the *philosophia perennis*. My own attempt, undertaken with far weaker powers, to find my way back to this company, can be seen as presumptuous of me. Yet there is one grain of humility that must be allowed my endeavor, for I simply cannot believe that all those great thinkers, from Plato to Spinoza, Leibniz, Hegel, and so forth, were blind and foolish, and that only we today, thanks to the Vienna Circle, have become clever and wise. They dared to ask speculative questions concerning the whole; for that they do not deserve criticism, but eternal thanks. Our criticism must test how their answers stand fast before our later ontological evidence. But we must go to school with them and through them in order to learn how to ask questions and to be instructed by their victories and defeats. This much we may say to the question whether or not what I have attempted here is in any way permitted.

18. How Important Is It to Know Whether There Is Intelligent Life Anywhere Else in the Universe?

It is much easier to answer the second question, in itself more innocent than the first: Is it important to know whether there is intelligent life anywhere else in the universe? Our natural curiosity finds the factual question uncommonly interesting; in particular, a verified affirmative answer to it would not be without significance for our own feeling about the universe. A knowledge of beings like ourselves "out there," for example, would enlarge for us the anthropic portion of the cosmological evidence and, therefore, would also strengthen the cosmogonic speculation based upon it. A negative answer is, by its very nature, not verifiable, because to do this we would have to examine all the heavenly bodies in the universe. A negative answer can become part of the conversation only in the form of information that has remained wanting: as a not-knowing, therefore, in regard to the question of the relevance of our knowledge about this issue. The "no" that we now recognize for our solar system says nothing for the universe.

On this point one could well repeat the words of Christian Morgenstern: "There was time enough and numbers, too." In other words, from the sheer magnitudes of the homogeneous universe—the numbers of galaxies, suns, spans of time—we can be tempted to deduce, in accordance with statistical probabilities, the likely occurrence of another manner of intelligent life, even contemporaneous with us in the course of cosmic chance. (The astronomer, Carl Sagan, for example, comes to very high numerical estimates for the existence of developed civilizations in our galactic system alone.) But, as a mathematician of some authority once informed me, this would be totally inadmissible, given our ignorance of the number of unknowns in our calculating of conditions, and it would remain a matter of subjective credibility according to one's personal need or temperament. That this occurrence is possible implies nothing more than that it is not impossible. The one thing that we *know* is that *we* are here, though not for a very long time, measured by the history of life on Earth (not to mention the universe). What existential, rather than theoretical, difference, would it make to know more—to learn of the existence of life somewhere else that is mentally similar to our own? My answer is: no difference at all.

Certainly, it would make no practical difference. Where a sole back and forth of signals ("address and answer") would at least require decades even in the neighborhood of our own galaxy, but much more likely would have to calculated in centuries and millenia, a real communication, a *conversation,* is impossible. Not only would the speakers be long dead, but their communication or question would be long out of date. Furthermore, a contact by signals would be possible only with civilizations at least as technically far advanced as our own, and we have developed this way only after millennia of high human cultures brought about through chance historical events in the West—a further burden on the scale of probabilities. In any case, earthly concerns will have gone forward between the sending and receiving of any possible communication, and the later generation, to which the answer arrives, will place it in the archive of cosmic miscellany.

Would it remove a feeling of cosmic loneliness? I cannot debate with someone who asserts that he feels this way, but I find it difficult to believe him. Four (or soon five) billion members of the family of homo sapiens living together on this globe offer plenty of protection against feelings of being alone in the world, and the species is not a subject that can have feelings. In any case, the "feeling" just mentioned is a very abstract one, produced by the recondite theory of cosmic expanse, and no less abstract would be the knowledge, from a deciphered code, about any other instance of our own kind in that expanse, with whom, as I have said, we are still not able to come in contact. Communication we have only among ourselves, and if one calls that "loneliness," so it stands.

But does the discovery in the universe of other intelligence, presumably also endowed with feeling, change the consciousness so movingly depicted by Bertrand Russell in a partly lamenting, partly heroizing way—the awareness that we have, with our striving, choosing, and judging, of standing face to face with an indifferent universe, alien to values and hostile to life? Not at all! The one who could ignore, in the portrait of an uninterested universe, that it has nevertheless from itself produced us, beings moved by interests and discovering values, can do this just as well also for other islands of feeling and willing in this same universe of nonfeeling, and so on. The latter, then, share with us the destiny of cosmic isolation of interest and of heroically defiant existence on the basis of value fictions arbitrarily invented by themselves. Only the one who reads the anthropic evidence in a different way and draws from it a cosmological conclusion can be confirmed in this through further examples. Whoever cannot conclude this from one example, also cannot perceive in other examples any reason for doing so, but only find further isolated cases of the same nihilistic situation.

To come now to my main and concluding point: Would the news of other intelligent life in the universe make a moral difference? Would it change something in our responsibility? Can we perhaps console ourselves that if we botch our great opportunity here, it will be continued somewhere else in better hands? That it might not rest solely on our shoulders? May we risk yet something more, therefore, with our portion of it? Absolutely no! We alone are responsible for the destiny of mind here where we rule, the exclusive preserve of our power, just as those hypothetical intelligences, if there are any, are responsible in theirs. No one can take away anything from the others' responsibility, and no one can help the others to fulfill their responsibility—neither they us, nor we them. In this sense we are alone. This we do know: that with us and in us, in this part of the universe and at this moment of our fateful power, the cause of God trembles in the balance. What does it matter to us whether somewhere else it prospers or is endangered, is rescued or squandered? That *our* signal going out somewhere or other in the universe may not be a death notice—with this we have enough on our hands. Let us concern ourselves with our Earth. Whatever might exist out there, here is where our destiny is decided—and, along with our destiny, that share of the wager of creation which lies in our hands can either be preserved or betrayed. Let us care about it *as if* we were, in fact, unique in the universe.

Translated by Paul Schuchman and Lawrence Vogel

Epilogue
The Outcry of Mute Things

T
he gratification, the gratitude, the joy and pride, with which I accept the honor of the Premio Nonino for 1993 are fused with a very special emotion apart from all these; and of this I wish to speak first before I turn to the more impersonal subject proper to my talk.

When, last December, the news of the jury's decision reached me in my American home, the pleasure of the surprise was for a moment dimmed by the warning voice of my recent vow of no more transatlantic travel in my ninetieth year or any still to come. Just for one moment. Then my eye fell on the bracketed name "Udine" behind "Percoto" in the donor's address—and with the force of invincible conviction, against all counsel of prudence, I knew that *there* I *must* go! For, by the accident of history, that name denotes a milestone in my life and enshrines one of its most unforgettable memories.

It was in Udine, in the early summer of 1945, that World War II ended for me—five years of soldiering against Hitler in the Mediterranean theater. Here, after the German surrender, my formation, the Jewish Brigade Group in the British Eighth Army, came to rest on its long trek north from Taranto on. We were all volunteers from the Jewish population of Palestine (then under British Mandate), many hailing from German-speaking countries in Europe that had fallen under Nazi domination. We had insisted on a visible identity as a Jewish fighting force and indeed were easily recognized by insignias like the Star of David on our uniforms. So it happened again and again on our slow progress up the length of Italy that Jewish survivors emerging from their hiding places—mostly women—greeted us and told us their stories. From them we got our first idea of

This talk, published here for the first time, was delivered on 30 January 1993, on the occasion of receiving the Premio Nonino, honoring *The Imperative of Responsibility* as the best book translated into Italian during 1992. Hans Jonas died six days later on 5 February 1993, at the age of eighty-nine, upon returning from Italy to his home in New Rochelle, New York.

the true extent of the Holocaust horror, but also heard moving tales of courageous pity and humanity among Italian people, to which they owed their survival—a much-needed antidote against the growing outrage of our hearts. The most moving of these tales was told to me personally here in Udine, and I bring it back to its place of origin on this visit nearly half a century later, so that light in the darkness be not forgotten.

One morning some of us strolled on the bustling marketplace, when two elderly ladies accosted us. As it turned out, they were fluent in German, and it fell to me in particular to listen to their story. They were sisters from Trieste, of an apparently well-to-do Austrian-Jewish family, Italian citizens since 1919, one widowed, the other unmarried, who had quietly lived together in their native city right into the first years of the war. Then, one day, word reached them that the rounding-up of Jews for deportation had started in Trieste. Hastily, they packed two suitcases, took their cash and jewels, hurried to the railway station, and bought tickets to seek refuge in a place where nobody knew them. As they approached the gate to their platform, they froze in their steps, for beside the ticket-taker stood one of the dreaded Fascist security guard, checking identity papers. Immobilized and near despair, they noticed a railway official inside the gates making furtive signs to them, and following his pantomimic directions, they got through an unguarded gate and could board their train. Udine qualified for a try; nobody knew them and they knew nobody. They found an unfurnished attic room for rent, took it, and had that much of a shelter to begin with. A few days later, a van stopped in front of the house, two beds were unloaded, lugged up the stairs to their door, and delivered with the oral message that his Eminence the Archbishop had heard of their situation and wished to make them more comfortable in their new abode.

Over the long months thereafter, the two women, nonregistered strangers with no ration cards, sold piece after piece of their jewelry to buy food on the costly black market. One day they heard of a woman dealer in another part of town who had lard to sell. Their reserves were dwindling, but the opportunity was too rare to let pass. Quickly another jewel was sold and they were in time to buy a precious kilogram—at an exorbitant price, of course. Late at night that same day, there was a knock at their door. Fearfully they opened it—and there stood the hard-boiled black-market operator who said, "Forgive me, please. I didn't know who you were when I sold you that lard this morning. I was told later and have come to apologize. From you I will take no money." He thrust an envelope stuffed with their banknotes into their hands, turned, and fled down the stairs. Having finished that story, the narrator added, "And now, perhaps, you understand why the two of us will not emigrate to Palestine"—as we of the Jewish Brigade urged of all survivors we met—"but wish to live and to die among the Italian people."

For my own part, I have carried this story through my life like a sacred trust. It rectified forever a love I had conceived for the people of Italy in earlier, happier days. I have told it many times and each time had to fight being overcome by emotion. Forgive me if I have not completely succeeded on this occasion either. At any rate, I am as grateful for this late opportunity to render honor where honor is due as I am for the Nonino Prize itself. Incidentally, you will not have missed the lovely irony in the reassuring phrase, "Nobody knows us here." Many, it seems, knew of them without their knowing it, and it is to the lasting glory of Udine that this did not imperil but, on the contrary, protected them.

From here it is easy to pass to the topic which Mrs. Nonino wished me to talk about: *racism.* In recalling, as I did, some lonely lights, I have also re-called the night in which they shone: Europe's darkest night of genocide in the name of race. To condemn the unspeakable crime is not to deny the reality of race itself. Mankind does exist in the shape of racial diversity, and humans would have to be angels to keep tensions and antagonisms—unilateral or mutual—out of this field of interaction. Otherness as such is an easy target for caricature or unflattering stereotyping, and in a majority/minority setting this inevitably works to the detriment of the weaker part. Some psychological vagaries of unreflective racism will always be with us. Perhaps I disappoint my listeners with voicing my conviction that as long as there is racial diversity—and, mind you, I hope there always will be, as its loss would impoverish the spectrum of humanity—there will be racial tensions, too: chronic or acute problems of coexistence. The vitality of this murky complex, with its potential for murderous hatred, has shown itself curiously impervious to the progress of rationality in the general conduct of our affairs. To the bitter disappointment of one of the sanguine expectations of the European Enlightenment, the deep-seated propensity has endured. The difference still open to us lies in what we do about its ever ready presence—about it, against it, for it. It is an ever repeated test of how civilized, in the moral sense of the word, we are as persons and as groups—a test indeed of the maturity of our humanness—how well or badly we behave in dealing with those tensions that will not go away. To my already professed belief—even paradoxical wish—that we will never be spared the test, I now add my anti-utopian disbelief that we shall ever pass it with flying colors. Yet we surely can do better, and most surely must do better, than we have in the past.

By "we" I mean preeminently us of the most developed, vaunted, Euro-American, white civilization. Tolerance, one of the prides of progress, but always at the mercy of the majority that granted it, has proved a slender safeguard of the defenseless "other" when "race" was involved. Of the almost intractable legacy of black slavery in contemporary America I will here not speak. The record on the European continent, the cradle of Western modernity and its world leadership, is somber enough. After a deceptive century of improving humaneness and tolerance, we had this century's hellish revelation of the bottomless pit of racist counterhumanity in one of the heartlands of our celebrated culture. The reality of race alone is insufficient to explain it. A mythology, nay demonology, of race was conjured up—from what dark recesses of the collective mind remains itself a dark mystery—and was enabled to put the means of advanced technology, the fruits of reason, to the service of its perverse, insane purpose. I need not say another word about this blot on humankind; nor have I anything new to say about the lesson we must draw from this experience, which more than any ever before called into question man's title to the image of God: namely, to marshal all the forces of moral education and unbending political watchfulness against this scarcely ever dormant beast lurking in our fallible condition.

This, I am afraid, is not very helpful and surely as unoriginal as can be. But perhaps I do have to add a word about one aspect of the race question which only the post-Hitler era, the second half of our soon expiring century, has brought to light and which is not usually mentioned among the arguments against racism. This is the fact that race questions become anachronistic, irrelevant, almost farcical before the all-encompassing challenge which an endangered global environment flings in the face of all mankind. In the grip of this challenge, mankind for the first time truly becomes one, whether knowing it yet or not: one in despoiling their earthly home; one in going to share the fate of its ruin; one in being the only possible saviors of both, Earth and themselves. A new solidarity of the whole of humanity is beginning to dawn on us. A common guilt binds us, a common interest unites us, a common fate awaits us, a common responsibility calls us. In the blinding light of this newly opening horizon, racial conflicts pale and their clamor should fall silent. I know, it will not fall silent, but from now on we can hush it with the novel appeal to that awesome commonality never apparent before.

Let me close with this symbolic appraisal of the altered "human condition." It was once religion which told us that we all are sinners, because of original sin. It is now the ecology of our planet which pronounces us all to be sinners because of the excessive exploits of human inventiveness. It was once religion which threatened us with a last judgment at the end of days. It is now our tortured planet which predicts the arrival of such a day without any heavenly intervention. The latest revelation—from no Mount

Sinai, from no Mount of the Sermon, from no Bo (tree of Buddha)—is the outcry of mute things themselves that we must heed by curbing our powers over creation, lest we perish together on a wasteland of what was creation.

Notes

Editor's Introduction

1. For Jonas's moving account of this moment in his life, see "Is Faith Still Possible?: Memories of Rudolf Bultmann and Reflections on the Philosophical Aspects of His Work," chapter 7 in this volume.

2. For Jonas's own story of how he came to study Gnosticism and complete his work on it, see "A Retrospective View," chapter 6 in *On Faith, Reason and Responsibility: Six Essays* (Claremont: Institute for Antiquity and Christianity, 1981).

3. All quotations from the books of Hans Jonas are footnoted in brackets within the text of my introduction. His books are designated as follows:

PL = *The Phenomenon of Life: Toward a Philosophical Biology* (New York: Delta, 1966).

IR = *The Imperative of Responsibility: In Search of an Ethics for the Technological Age* (Chicago: University of Chicago Press, 1984).

PE = *Philosophical Essays: From Ancient Creed to Technological Man* (Chicago: University of Chicago Press, 1980).

4. Jonas, "Gnosticism and Modern Nihilism," *Social Research* 19 (1952). A revised version of this essay appears in both *The Gnostic Religion* (Boston: Beacon Press, 1958) and *The Phenomenon of Life* (New York: Delta, 1966).

5. Jonas, "Heidegger's Resoluteness and Resolve: An Interview," in *Martin Heidegger and National Socialism*, ed. Günther Neske and Emil Kettering (New York: Paragon House, 1990), 200.

6. Martin Heidegger, *Being and Time*, trans. John Macquarrie and Edward Robinson (New York: Harper and Row, 1962), *SZ*, 179. All references to the text will be from this translation. Page numbers will correspond to the standard German edition of *Sein und Zeit* (Tübingen: Neomarius Verlag, 8th ed., 1957) and will be preceded by *SZ*.

7. Jonas, "Gnosticism," in *The Encyclopedia of Philosophy*, vol. 3 (Macmillan: New York, 1967), 341.

8. Jonas, "Heidegger's Resoluteness and Resolve," 201.

9. Karl Löwith, "Nature, History and Existentialism," in *Nature, History and Existentialism*, trans. Arnold Levinson (Evanston: Northwestern University Press, 1965), 28, 37.

10. For a good anthology of writings along the ecological spectrum, see *Environmental Ethics: Divergence and Convergence*, ed. Susan J. Armstrong and Richard G. Botzler (New York: McGraw Hill, 1993).

11. See Aldo Leopold, "The Land Ethic," in *A Sand County Almanac: Sketches Here and There* (New York: Oxford University Press, 1949).

12. From Jonas's 1968 essay, "Contemporary Problems in Ethics from a Jewish Perspective."

13. See Richard Rubenstein, *After Auschwitz: Radical Theology and Contemporary Judaism* (Indianapolis: Bobbs-Merrill, 1966), esp. 46.

14. This survey owes a deep debt to Steven J. Katz, "Jewish Faith after the Holocaust," in *Post-Holocaust Dialogues: Critical Studies in Modern Jewish Thought* (New York: New York University Press, 1983).

15. See Ignaz Maybaum, *The Face of God after Auschwitz* (Amsterdam: Polak and Van Gennep, 1965).

16. See Emil Fackenheim, *God's Presence in History: Jewish Affirmations and Philosophical Reflections* (New York: New York University Press, 1970).

17. See Rabbi Jack Bemporad, "Toward a New Jewish Theology," *American Judaism* (Winter 1964–65), 42.

18. See Henry Slonimsky's paper, "The Philosophy Implicit in Midrash," summarized in Rabbi Bemporad's "What Can We Jews Affirm About God after the Holocaust?" a talk delivered at the 51st General Assembly of the Union of American Hebrew Congregations in Los Angeles, 1970.

19. See Eliezer Berkovitz, *Faith after the Holocaust* (New York: Ktav, 1973).

20. For an account of Jacobs's objection, see Karen Armstrong, *A History of God* (New York: Ballantine, 1993).

21. See Leon Kass, "Appreciating *The Phenomenon of Life*," Hastings Center Report, Special Issue, 1995.

22. See Stephen Jay Gould's credo in *Living Philosophies*, ed. Clifton Fadiman (New York: Doubleday, 1990).

23. Garrett Hardin, Review of *The Imperative of Responsibility*, Hastings Center Report (December 1984).

Chapter 1

1. For a more thorough treatment of this theme see Jonas, *The Phenomenon of Life* (Chicago: University of Chicago Press, 1982), 33–37.—ED.

2. In connection with these remarks on the philosophical aspects of the theory of evolution, especially Darwinism, I would call the reader's attention to the chapter "Philosophical Aspects of Darwinism," in my book *The Phenomenon of Life*, 38–58.

3. For a more detailed treatment of this thought-experiment, see "Is God A Mathematician? (The Meaning of Metabolism)," in *The Phenomenon of Life*, 64–92.—ED.

4. For further elaboration of the differences between machines and organisms, see "Cybernetics and Purpose: A Critique," in *The Phenomenon of Life*, 108–127.—ED.

5. For development of the claim that individuality is exhibited only by organisms and, in some measure, by all organisms, see Jonas, "Biological Foundations of Individuality," in *Philosophical Essays: From Ancient Creed to Technological Man* (Chicago: University of Chicago Press, 1980). For the roots of this idea in the thought of Spinoza, see "Spinoza and the Theory of Organism," also in *Philosophical Essays.*—ED.

6. For a fuller exploration of what distinguishes animal from plant life, see "To Move and To Feel: On the Animal Soul," in *The Phenomenon of Life*, 99–107. —ED.

Chapter 2

1. See the previous essay, "Evolution and Freedom: On the Continuity among Life-Forms," for an account of the mediate nature of all organic existence. —ED.

2. Cf. Jonas, "The Nobility of Sight: A Study in the Phenomenology of the Senses," *The Phenomenon of Life* (Chicago: University of Chicago Press, 1982), 135–52.—ED.

3. The phenomenology of "image" is discussed more fully in Jonas, "Image-Making and the Freedom of Man," in *The Phenomenon of Life*, 157–75.—ED.

4. See the previous essay, "Evolution and Freedom," for the history of this growth.—ED.

Chapter 4

1. Jonas takes up the is/ought question in greater detail in his book, *The Imperative of Responsibility: In Search of an Ethics for the Technological Age* (Chicago: University of Chicago Press, 1984). See esp. 44–50, 79–90.—ED.

2. For a full-scale discussion of how the Western ethical tradition leaves us ill-equipped to cope with the scope of our responsibilities today, see Jonas, "Technology and Responsibility: Reflections on the New Tasks of Ethics," and "Contemporary Problems in Ethics from a Jewish Perspective," in *Philosophical Essays: From Ancient Creed to Technological Man* (Chicago: University of Chicago Press, 1980). Jonas builds on these pieces in "The Altered Nature of Human Action," chapter 1 of *The Imperative of Responsibility.*—ED.

3. See, e.g., Jonas, *Technik, Medizin und Ethik* (Frankfurt: Insel, 1985), 64–66. [Also see "On Principles and Method," chapter 2 of *The Imperative of Responsibility.*]—ED.

Chapter 5

1. This essay has been the subject of penetrating discussion in the article "Death, Dying, and Immortality" by Philip Merlan, and in the counterthesis "The Dialectic of Death and Immortality" by Maurice Natanson, in the *Pacific Philosophy Forum* 3, no. 1 (1964), 3–45 and 70–79, respectively. To these public voices must be added extensive comment in numerous private communications. Among the latter were the searching comments by Rudolf Bultmann which have been included, together with my reply, as an Appendix in the German publication of the essay in Hans Jonas, *Zwischen Nichts und Ewigkeit* (Göttingen: Vandenhoeck and Ruprecht, 1963), 63–72. The virtually unchanged reprinting of the essay here does not mean that I have closed my mind to the important issues raised, but merely that I have neither succeeded yet, with their help, to advance beyond its admittedly tentative position, nor felt constrained, under their pressure, to retreat from it.

2. This concept of immortality is found throughout Greek letters, from Homer to Plato, who marks the philosophic overcoming of the ideal but gives it eloquent expression in the words of Diotima:

> Think only of the ambition of men, and you will wonder at the senselessness of their ways, unless you consider how they are stirred by the love of an immortality of fame. They are ready to run all risks far greater than they would have run for their children, and to spend money and undergo any sort of toil, and even to die, for the sake of leaving behind them a name which shall be eternal. Do you imagine that Alcestis would have died to save Admetus, or Achilles to avenge Patroclus, or your own Codrus in order to preserve the kingdom for his sons, if they had not imagined that the memory of their virtues, which still survives among us, would be immortal? Nay, I am persuaded that all men do all things, and the better they are the more they do them, in hope of the glorious fame of immortal virtue; for they desire the immortal. (*Symposium*, 208c–d; trans. B. Jowett)

Perhaps the loftiest statement of the ideal occurs in Pericles's Funeral Oration on the Athenian dead in the first year of the Peloponnesian war:

> They received, each for his own memory, praise that will never die, and with it the grandest of all sepulchres, not that in which their mortal bones are laid, but a home in the minds of men, where their glory remains fresh to stir to speech or action as the occasion comes by. For the whole earth is the sepulchre of famous men, and their story is not graven only in stone over their native earth, but lives far away, without visible symbol, woven into the stuff of other men's lives. (Thucydides, II 43; trans. A. Zimmern, *The Greek Commonwealth*, 207)

Not long ago, I encountered the ancient sentiment unalloyed in (of all places) television when one of our astronauts-in-training, asked what had made him volunteer for the task, answered, "Frankly, the chance of immortality; for this, I would willingly give my life." Given with engaging simplicity, there was no doubting the candor of the reply. Events in the meantime may have caused some reflections on how much, besides the merits of dedication and ability, also opportunity and luck—and not only our own, but that of unknown others—rule over this kind of immortality.

3. In discussing why honor cannot be "the good": it rests in those who bestow it rather than in him who receives it, whereas the good must be one's inalienable own; further, we seek it, i.e., the reputation of being good, as a confirmation of our being good, therefore from people who have good judgment, and adequate knowledge of us, and who accord honor to virtue which on this admission stands as the primary good: *Nichomachean Ethics* 1095b22–30.

4. Ginza, left, 31 (end): M. Lidzbarski (trans.), Ginzā. *Der Schatz oder Das Grosse Bach der Mandäer* (Göttingen, 1925), 559, 29–32. In an Avestic source, this image addresses the Soul thus: "I am, O youth of good thoughts, good words, good deeds, good conscience, none other than thine own personal conscience. . . . Thou hast loved me . . . in this sublimity, goodness, beauty . . . in which I now appear unto thee (Hadokht Nask 2.9ff.).

5. "The Hymn of the Pearl" (or "Hymn of the Soul") is a gnostic poem included in the apocryphal Acts of the Apostle Thomas: on text and interpretation, cf. Hans Jonas, *The Gnostic Religion* (Boston: Beacon Press, 1958), chapter 5, 112–29; for bibliography, cf. ibid., 296.

6. Or: "the Last Statue"—the Coptic uses of Greek word *andrias*.

7. Kephalaia V. 29, 1–67; XVI. 54, 14–24: *Manichäischce Handschriften der Staatlichen Museen Berlin*, vol. 1: *Kephalaia, 1. Hälfte* (Stuttgart, 1940).

8. Genesis 6:6–7.

9. Sanhedrin 97b; Sukkah 45b.

10. Deuteronomy 30:14.

Chapter 6

1. Hans Jonas, "Immortality and the Modern Temper," the 1961 Ingersoll Lecture at Harvard University, first printed in *Harvard Theological Review* 55 (1962), 1–20; now in Hans Jonas, *The Phenomenon of Life* (Chicago: University of Chicago Press, 1982), 262–81. [Included as chapter 5 herein.]

2. The same principle has been argued, with slightly different reasoning, by Rabbi Jack Bemporad, "Toward a New Jewish Theology," *American Judaism* (Winter 1964–65), 9ff.

3. An occasional miracle, i.e., extramundane intervention in the closed causality of the physical realm, is not incompatible with the general validity of laws of nature (rare exceptions do not void empirical rules) and might even, by all appearances, perfectly conform to them. On this question, see Hans Jonas, *Philosophical Essays* (Chicago: University of Chicago Press, 1980), 66–67, and, more extensively, my Rudolf Bultmann Memorial address of 1976 at Marburg University, "Is Faith Still Possible?: Memories of Rudolf Bultmann and Reflections on the

Philosophical Aspects of His Work," *Harvard Theological Review* 75, no. 1 (January 1982), 1–25, esp. 9–15; see also 17–18 of this address for a statement of the religious objection against thinking of God as "Lord of History."

4. For more about this inalienable postulate of revealed religion—the possibility of revelation itself, i.e., of God's speaking to human *minds* even if debarred from intervening in physical *things*—see Jonas, "Is Faith Still Possible?" [chapter 7 in this volume].

5. Originated by Isaac Luria (1534–72).

6. Genesis 6:6–7.

7. Sanhedrin 97b; Sukkah 45b.

8. The idea that it is we who help God rather than God helping us I have since found movingly expressed by one of the Auschwitz victims themselves, a young Dutch Jewess, who validated it by acting unto death. It is found in *An Interrupted Life: The Diaries of Etty Hillesum, 1941–43* (New York: Pantheon Books, 1984). When the deportations in Holland began in 1942, she came forward and volunteered for the Westerbork concentration camp, there to help in the hospital and to share in the fate of her people. In September 1943 she was shipped, in one of the usual mass transports, to Auschwitz and "died" there on 30 November 1943. Her diaries have survived but were only recently published. I quote from Neal Ascherson ("In Hell," *New York Review of Books* 31, no. 13 [19 July 1984], 8–12, esp. 9):

> She does not exactly "find God," but rather constructs one for herself. The theme of the diaries becomes increasingly religious, and many of the entries are prayers. Her God is someone to whom she makes promises, but of whom she expects and asks nothing. "I shall try to help you, God, to stop my strength ebbing away, though I cannot vouch for it in advance. But one thing is becoming increasingly clear to me: that You cannot help us, that we must help You help ourselves. . . . Alas, there does not seem to be much You Yourself can do about our circumstances, about our lives. Neither do I hold You responsible. You cannot help us, but we must help You and defend Your dwelling-place in us to the last.

Reading this was to me a shattering confirmation, by a true witness, of my so much later and sheltered musings—and a consoling correction of my sweeping statement that we had no martyrs there.

9. "Und was nur am Lob des Hochsten stammelt,/ Ist in Kreis' um Kreise dort versammelt" (Goethe, "Vermächtnis altpersischen Glaubens").

Chapter 7

1. *Forschungen zur Religion und Literatur des Alten und Neuen Testaments.*

2. All quotations in what follows are from Bultmann's collected essays published under the title *Glauben und Verstehen* [*Faith and Understanding*] (Tübingen:

NOTES

Mohr, 1933–65). Only the first two of these have been translated into English: *Faith and Understanding* (New York: Harper and Row, 1969), and *Essays Philosophical and Theological* (New York: Macmillan, 1955). Since all but one of my quotations are from later volumes, with this one exception the translations are mine and the references are to the German text. Volume and page numbers are indicated after each quotation without naming the individual essay.

3. The connection of the two purposes is expressed, e.g., thus: demythologizing "removes a false stumbling block and brings into focus instead the true one, namely, the message of the cross" (vol. 4, 157).

4. See Erich Heller, "Hannah Arendt und die Literatur," *Merkur* 30 (1976), 10, 999f.; and for what follows, Hans Jonas, "Acting, Knowing, Thinking: Gleanings from Hannah Arendt's Philosophical Work," *Social Research* 44, no. 1 (1977), 40. Also, see my statement, with special reference to Bultmann, toward the end of the essay "Heidegger and Theology," in *The Phenomenon of Life* (Chicago: University of Chicago Press, 1982), 260–61.

5. See Hannah Arendt, *The Life of the Mind*, vol. 1: *Thinking* (New York: Harcourt Brace Jovanovich, 1978), 104.

6. For my attempt at constructing such a model as part of a reappraisal of the psychophysical problem, see Hans Jonas, *Macht oder Ohnmacht der Subjektivität?* (Frankfurt: Insel, 1981). A first and shorter version of the argument was presented in "On the Power or Impotence of Subjectivity," in *Philosophical Dimensions of the Neuro-Medical Sciences*, ed. H. T. Engelhardt and S. F. Spicker (Dordrecht: Reidel, 1976), 143–61. [Also in the Appendix to *The Imperative of Responsibility*.]

7. It will be noticed that what we said about threshold conditions in *nature* opening into causally equivalent alternatives of succession, applies also—more palpably even—to *history*, which can be said to be a constant sequence of "threshold situations," where every moment is potentially a "zero point," a watershed for divergent continuations. To be sure, there are great differences of degree, of states more settled or more fluid, with option alternatives of smaller or larger amplitudes, and "small" is probably the rule. But sometimes, it seems, moments of exceptional pregnancy occur, in whose critical mix large issues are poised and wait as it were for the mover to come along and actualize the momentous possibility (or one of a prominent pair of alternatives) that lies ready to be "triggered." It is still a possibility only, and what will really happen is unpredictable. Even the "possibility" as such, though sometimes discerned by actor or contemporary witness, is more often known in retrospect only after having become reality.

8. Examples are found in the philosophical work of Emil Fackenheim and in the literary work of Elie Wiesel. A modest contribution on my part is "The Concept of God after Auschwitz," in *Out of the Whirlwind*, ed. A. H. Friedlander (New York: Union of American Hebrew Congregations, 1968), 465–76. [For the revised version, see chapter 6 herein.]

9. This turn of the dialogue is not wholly imaginary but once was actually taken in a correspondence between us over my Ingersoll Lecture, "Immortality and the Modern Temper," of 1961 (chapter 5 in this volume). Part of the epistolary exchange is appended to its German version in *Zwischen Nichts und Ewigkeit*

(Göttingen: Vandenhoeck and Ruprecht, 1963); for Bultmann's side, see 67, for mine, 71. Obviously, my resorting, in that lecture, to a symbolic myth— a liberty taken from the paradigm of Plato—was as such already at odds with Bultmann's rigorous demythologizing, and the divergence was later articulated by me in the ending of "Heidegger and Theology." Still later, I ventured to draw some conclusions from this hypothetical "myth" in terms of a rational "theology," thus going one step further on the road of "objective" doctrine which Bultmann shunned from deepest instinct. See "The Concept of God after Auschwitz" [chapter 6 in this volume].

Chapter 8

1. All dynamic equilibria are temporary. For example, the radius and period of the Earth's revolution—the kinetic equilibrium, functioning at the present time, between its moment of inertia and the attraction of the sun—could be changed through variables. Such variables include an increase in the mass of the Earth by means of an ongoing collision with meteors or the resistance of interplanetary material, a loss of mass in the sun through radiation in relation to the Earth's increase by meteors, and the expanding of outer space with a corresponding weakening of gravitation. I do not know how the entire calculation looks. My list is supposed to illustrate only the general thesis that equilibria in nature are not absolutely stable, but have the validity of *rebus sic stantibus*. Accordingly, the phenomenon of the "cycle," as consoling as it is in its longevity and constant renewal in the life cycles, is still rather passing and transient in the long view of nature, exposed as it is to degeneration. Cyclical motion is indebted to the early evolutionary victory of uniform causality over primordial chaos, and must now let the same causality constantly gnaw away at it. We should not let ourselves be frightened by this cosmic transiency. In the interval that has been attained and is for us long-lived—the interval of large, widely stretched articulations—lie chances for precisely that which constitutes the meaning of the whole, extravagant adventure of the universe, both for us and, I daresay, also for a divine spectator.

2. Here we can insert the comment that, with the appearance of self-replicating DNA sequences, the chemical preparation for life has been con-cluded, and that henceforth "information science" will itself be the principle for the development of life. From now on, therefore, the concept of information is, in fact, appropriate. But even here the *growth* of information (modification and enrichment of given information, precisely development, therefore) takes place without the involvement of present information *in its behalf*. The growth comes from the accident of disorder penetrating in, whose resulting "characters" are incorporated as a new element of meaning in the genetic text and are either preserved or not in somatic testing.

3. See Hans Jonas, *Macht oder Ohnmacht der Subjektivität?* (Frankfurt: Insel, 1981).

4. In *Process and Reality*, Alfred North Whitehead already postulates this for *every* "actual entity," hence for the elementary particle. The extension of inwardness into the realm of the pre-organic and the simplest realities of all—its congruence, therefore, with materiality in general—seems to me to be overbold and not covered by any datum of our experience, which allows us to discover or suspect traces of subjectivity only in high-level formations of organisms.

5. The prospect for life as we know it lies between the freezing point and boiling point of water, thus in the narrow band between 273 and 373 degrees Kelvin from the millions of degrees on the temperature spectrum in which cosmic matter exists. So that life can come to the development of higher species, this limitation must hold constant through billions of years. This is the case for the Earth and its oceans, thanks to its precise distance from the sun. Even a one-percent increase in the average of this distance would lead to the total freezing of water; a reduction of about five percent, to the total boiling of water. The probability of a repetition of this special case in other of the planetary systems of the universe, which are surely numerous, cannot at all be calculated.

6. Since the dissolution of classical determinism by quantum theory, this "openness," i.e., the causal giving-way for such purposive spontaneous inter-ventions, is no longer a prohibitive problem theoretically. See my *Macht Oder Ohnmacht der Subjecktivität*, esp. 89–116.

7. See Hans Jonas, "Tool, Image and Grave: On What Is Beyond the Animal in Man" [chapter 2 in this volume].

8. See Hans Jonas, *The Phenomenon of Life* (Chicago: University of Chicago Press, 1982) [and "Evolution and Freedom," chapter 1 in this volume].

9. See Hans Jonas, *Augustin und das paulinische Freiheitsproblem* (Göttingen: Vandenhoeck and Ruprecht, 1965), specifically Appendix 3, "Philosophische Reflexion über Paulus, Romerbrief Kap. 7," 93–105.

10. Still only the future, *potential* bearer of a mind is created in this fashion, not the mind itself. This arises first, and only, from the communication of the newborn—at the beginning entirely receptive, then visibly reciprocal—with already existing mental subjects, the adults surrounding it and communicating their thoughts to it. Without an environment that is linguistic and that addresses it, the young human animal, even in its bodily survival and growth, would not become a human being at all. That language is something learned from those already speaking it implies that mind, too, is something to be learned from a preexisting mind. Only in commerce with this does the new mind have its origin. The new mind makes use of the genetically prepared instrumentality of the brain, and only by this progressive use is the growth of the physical instrumentality itself also completed. Without that it would either atrophy or, as the case may be, just not ripen for use at all. With birth, therefore, the coming out into the world, there begins a new kind of ontogenesis consisting of mental information, superimposed on the fetal (still continuing) physical ontogenesis. And only a preceding mind from the outside can provide this and thus bring the potentiality, which arose out of the inner, blind "information" of the genome, to realization. It remains true, therefore, in every ontogenesis that actual mind in each case

already presupposes actual mind for its becoming. (I owe this remark to my friend Heinrich Popitz.) Our present argument points to a similar presupposition for the original equipping of matter on the whole with the general possibility of bringing it to a potentiality formed in such a way for the mind.

11. See Hans Jonas, "Immortality and the Modern Temper" [chapter 5 in this volume], and "The Concept of God after Auschwitz: A Jewish Voice" [chapter 6 herein].

12. From *An Interrupted Life: The Diaries of Etty Hillesum, 1941–43* (New York: Pantheon Books, 1984). Almost forty years had to pass before these notes, left in private hands before her deportation, found their first Dutch publication.

Bibliography

I. Books by Jonas published in English

The Gnostic Religion: The Message of the Alien God and the Beginnings of Christianity. Boston: Beacon Press, 1958. Enlarged edition, 1963.

The Phenomenon of Life: Toward a Philosophical Biology. New York: Harper and Row, 1963. New edition, New York: Dell, 1966. Second new edition, Chicago: University of Chicago Press, 1982.

Philosophical Essays: From Ancient Creed to Technological Man. Englewood Cliffs: Prentice-Hall, 1974. New edition, Chicago: University of Chicago Press, 1980.

On Faith, Reason and Responsibility: Six Essays. San Francisco: Harper and Row, 1978. New edition, Claremont Graduate School: Institute for Antiquity and Christianity, 1981.

The Imperative of Responsibility: In Search of an Ethics for the Technological Age. Translated by Hans Jonas with the collaboration of David Herr. Chicago: University of Chicago Press, 1984.

II. Books by Jonas published in German

Der Begriff der Gnosis: Inaugural-Dissertation zur Erlangung der Doktorwürde der Hohen Philosophischen Fakultät der Philipps-Universität zu Marburg. Göttingen: Huber and Company, 1930.

Augustin und das paulinische Freiheitsproblem: Ein Philosophischer Beitrag zur Genesis der christlich-abendländischen Freiheitsidee. Göttingen: Vandenhoeck and Ruprecht, 1930. Revised as *Augustin und das paulinische Freiheitsproblem: Eine philosophische Studie zum pelagianischen Streit.* Introduced by James M. Robinson. Göttingen: Vandenhoeck and Ruprecht, 1965.

Gnosis und spätantiker Geist, Part 1: *Die mythologische Gnosis.* With an introduction, "Zur Geschischte und Methodologie der Forschung." Göttingen: Vandenhoeck and Ruprecht, 1934. Part 2: *Von der Mythologie zur mystischen Philosophie.* Göttingen: Vandenhoeck and Ruprecht, 1954. The revised translation comprises *The Gnostic Religion.* Boston: Beacon Press, 1958, 1963.

Zwischen Nichts und Ewigkeit: Zur Lehre vom Menschen. Kleine Vandenhoeck-Reihe 165. Göttingen: Vandenhoeck and Ruprecht, 1963. Second edition, 1987. Includes the German version of "Immortality and the Modern Temper," chapter 5 in this volume.

Organismus und Freiheit: Ansätze zu einer philosophischen Biologie. Translated into German by Hans Jonas and K. Dockhorn from the English original, *The Phenomenon of Life: Toward a Philosophical Biology.* Göttingen: Vandenhoeck and Ruprecht, 1973.

Wandel und Bestand: Vom Grunde der Verstehbarkeit des Geschichtlichen. Frankfurt: Vittorio Klostermann, 1970. Simultaneously appears in *Durchblicke: Martin Heidegger zum 80. Geburtstag.* Edited by Vittorio Klostermann. Frankfurt: Vittorio Klostermann, 1970. The English translation, "Change and Permanence: On the Possibility of Understanding History," comprises essay 12 of *Philosophical Essays.*

Das Prinzip Verantwortung: Versuch einer Ethik für die technologische Zivilisation. Frankfurt: Insel, 1979. New edition as a Suhrkamp Taschenbuch, 1984. Published in English as *The Imperative of Responsibility.*

Macht oder Ohnmacht der Subjectivität?: Das Leib-Seele-Problem im Vorfeld des Prinzips Verantwortung. Frankfurt: Insel, 1981. New edition as a Suhrkamp Taschenbuch, 1984. Published in English as an Appendix to *The Imperative of Responsibility.*

Technik, Medizin und Ethik: Zur Praxis des Princips Verantwortung. Frankfurt: Insel, 1985. Second edition, 1987.

Wissenschaft als persönliches Erlebnis. Göttingen: Vandenhoeck and Ruprecht, 1987.

Der Gottesbegriff nach Auschwitz: Eine jüdische Stimme. Frankfurt: Suhrkamp, 1987. The English version, "The Concept of God after Auschwitz: A Jewish Voice," appears as chapter 6 in this volume.

Materie, Geist und Schöpfung: Kosmologischer Befund und kosmogonische Vermutung. Frankfurt: Suhrkamp, 1988. The English translation, "Matter, Mind, and Creation," appears herein as chapter 8.

Hans Jonas, Erkenntnis und Verantwortung: Gespräch mit Ingo Hermann in der Reihe "Zeugen des Jahrhunderts." Edited by Ingo Hermann. Göttingen: Lamuv, 1991.

Philosophische Untersuchungen und metaphysische Vermutungen. Frankfurt: Insel, 1992. Six of the ten essays appear in translation in this volume.

Dem bösen Ende näher: Gespräche über das Verhältnis des Menschen zur Natur. Edited by Wolfgang Schneider. Frankfurt: Suhrkamp, 1993.

Philosophie: Rückschau und Vorschau am Ende des Jahrhunderts. Frankfurt: Suhrkamp, 1993. The English translation appears in this volume as the Prologue, "Philosophy at the End of the Century: Retrospect and Prospect."

III. Articles by Jonas available in English since 1978

(For a comprehensive bibliography of Jonas's articles in both German and English prior to 1978, see *Organism, Medicine and Metaphysics: Essays in Honor of Hans*

Jonas on his 75th Birthday, ed. Stuart Spicker [Boston: Reidel, 1978]. The English versions of Jonas's most significant articles before 1978 are collected in the anthologies *Philosophical Essays* and *Faith, Reason and Responsibility*.)

"Acting, Knowing, Thinking: Gleanings from Hannah Arendt's Philosophical Work." *Social Research* 44 (1977), 25–43.

"The Right to Die." *Hastings Center Report* 8 (August 1978), 31–36.

"Toward a Philosophy of Technology." *Hastings Center Report* 9 (February 1979), 34–43.

"The Heuristics of Fear." In *Ethics in an Age of Pervasive Technology*. Edited by Melvin Kranzberg. Boulder: Westview Press, 1980. 213–21.

"Response to James N. Gustafson." In *Knowing and Valuing: The Search for Common Roots*. Edited by H. T. Englehart and Daniel Callahan. Hastings-on-Hudson: Hastings Center, 1980. 203–217.

"Parallelism and Complementarity: The Psycho-Physical Problem in Spinoza and in the Succession of Niels Bohr." In *The Philosophy of Baruch Spinoza*. Edited by Richard Kennington. Washington, D.C.: Catholic University Press, 1980. 121–30.

"Reflections on Technology, Progress and Utopia." *Social Research* 48 (1981), 411–55.

"Technology as a Subject for Ethics." *Social Research* 49 (1982), 891–98.

"Straddling the Boundaries of Theory and Practice." In *Recombinant DNA: Science, Ethics and Politics*. Edited by J. Richards. New York: Academic Press, 1983.

"Ontological Grounding of a Political Ethics: On the Metaphysics of Commitment to the Future of Man." *Graduate Faculty Philosophical Journal* 10 (1984). Already appeared as parts of *The Imperative of Responsibility*.

"Is Faith Still Possible?: Memories of Rudolf Bultmann and Reflections on the Philosophical Aspects of His Work." *Harvard Theological Review* 75 (1985), 1–23. Included as chapter 7 in this volume.

"Ethics and Biogenetic Art." *Social Research* 52 (1985), 491–504.

"The Concept of God After Auschwitz: A Jewish Voice." *The Journal of Religion* (1987), 1–13. Included as chapter 6 in this volume.

"The Burden and Blessing of Mortality." *Hastings Center Report* 22 (January 1992), 34–40. Included as chapter 3 in this volume.

"Philosophy at the End of the Century: A Survey of Its Past and Future." *Social Research* 61, no. 4 (1994): 812–32. The amended translation is included herein as the prologue.

"Not Compassion Alone: On Euthanasia and Ethics." *Hastings Center Report* 25 (Special Issue on the Legacy of Hans Jonas, 1995), 44–50.

Index of Names